Also Available from TOKYOPOP®:

CHOBITS 1-2 (of 5+)
In the future, boys will be boys and girls will be…robots? The newest hit series from CLAMP!

COWBOY BEBOP 1-2 (of 3)
All-new adventures of interstellar bounty hunting, based on the hit anime seen on Cartoon Network.

GTO 1-3 (of 24)
Biker gang member Onizuka is going back to school…as a teacher!

INITIAL D 1-2 (of 23+)
Delivery boy Takumi has a gift for driving, but can he compete in the high-stakes world of street racing?

ISLAND 1-5 (of 7)
When a young woman uncovers a web of demonic intrigue, a serial killer may be her only chance for survival.

LOVE HINA 1-3 (of 14)
Can Keitaro handle living in a dorm with five cute girls…and still make it through school?

PARASYTE 1-10 (of 10+)
They're faster, stronger, and smarter than us. We are their food, and they are hungry.

RAGNAROK 1-2 (of 10+)
In the final battle between gods and men, only a small band of heroes stands between total annihilation.

REAL BOUT HIGH SCHOOL 1-2 (of 5+)
At Daimon High, teachers don't break up fights…they grade them.

SKULL MAN 1-2 (of 7+)
They took his family. They took his face. They took his soul. Now, he's going to take his revenge.

PRIEST

BY

MIN-WOO HYUNG

English Adaptation - Robert Coyner and Jake Forbes
Editor - Jake Forbes
Cover Artist - Raymond Swanland
Graphic Designer - Anna Kernbaum
Retouch & Lettering - Monalisa J. de Asis

Production Manager - Joaquin Reyes
Art Director - Matt Alford
VP Production - Ron Klamert
Publisher - Stuart Levy

email: editor@TOKYOPOP.com
Come visit us online at www.TOKYOPOP.com

A  book

TOKYOPOP® is an imprint of Mixx Entertainment, Inc.
5900 Wilshire Blvd., Ste. 2000, Los Angeles, CA 90036

ISBN: 1-59182-008-1

First TOKYOPOP Printing: July 2002

10 9 8 7 6 5 4 3 2 1

Manufactured in the USA.

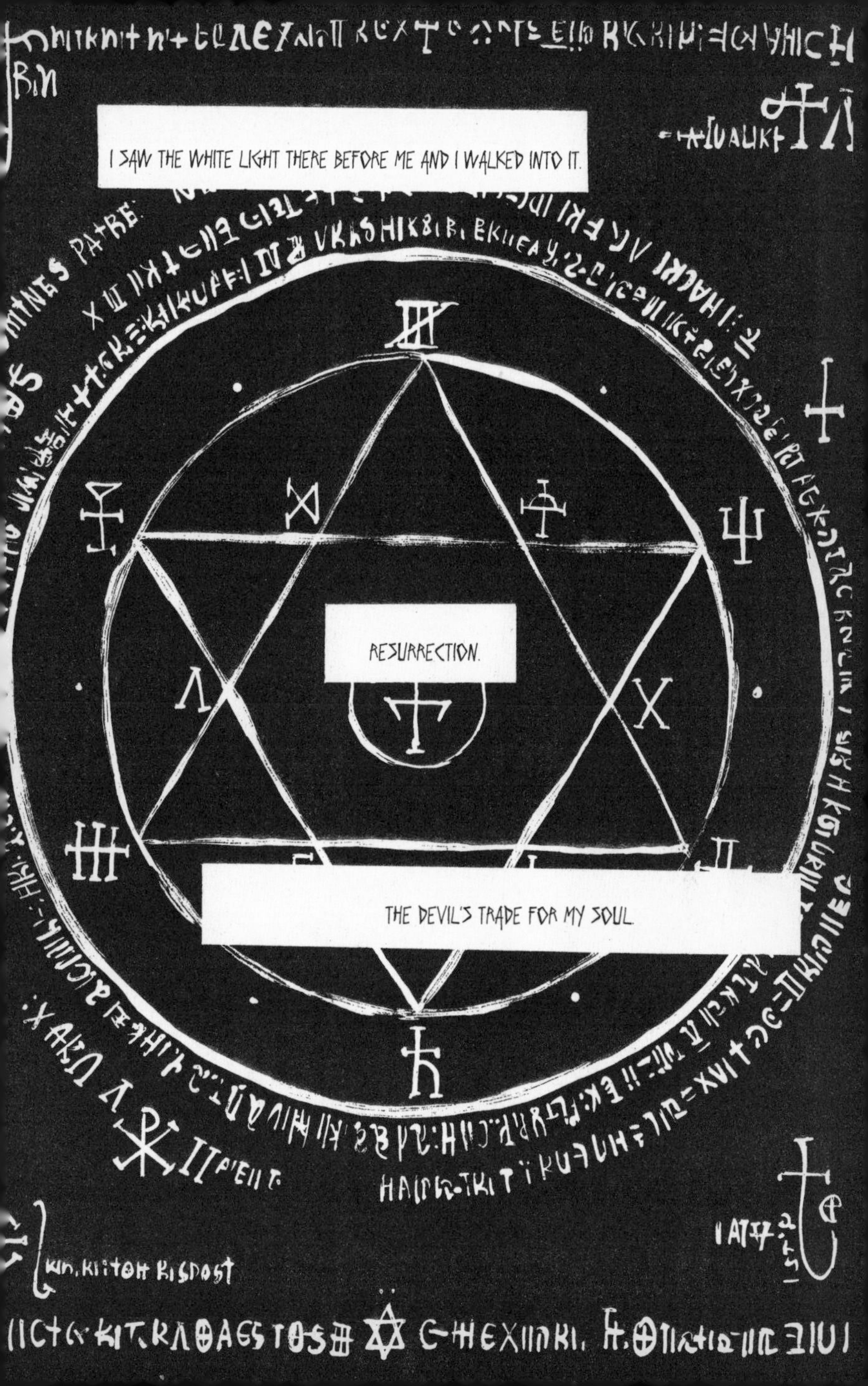
I SAW THE WHITE LIGHT THERE BEFORE ME AND I WALKED INTO IT.
RESURRECTION.
THE DEVIL'S TRADE FOR MY SOUL.

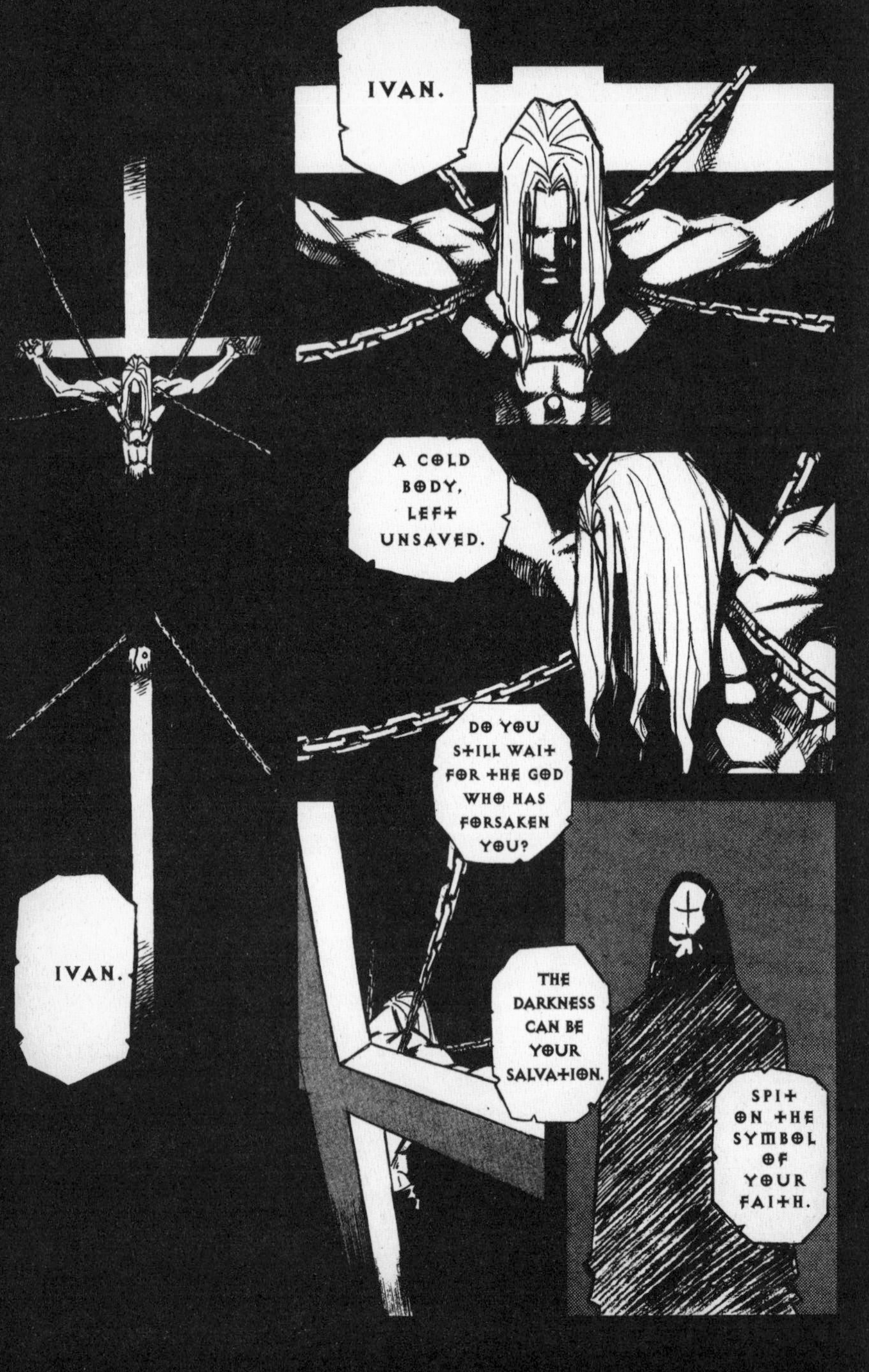
IVAN.
IVAN.
A COLD BODY, LEFT UNSAVED.
DO YOU STILL WAIT FOR THE GOD WHO HAS FORSAKEN YOU?
THE DARKNESS CAN BE YOUR SALVATION.
SPIT ON THE SYMBOL OF YOUR FAITH.

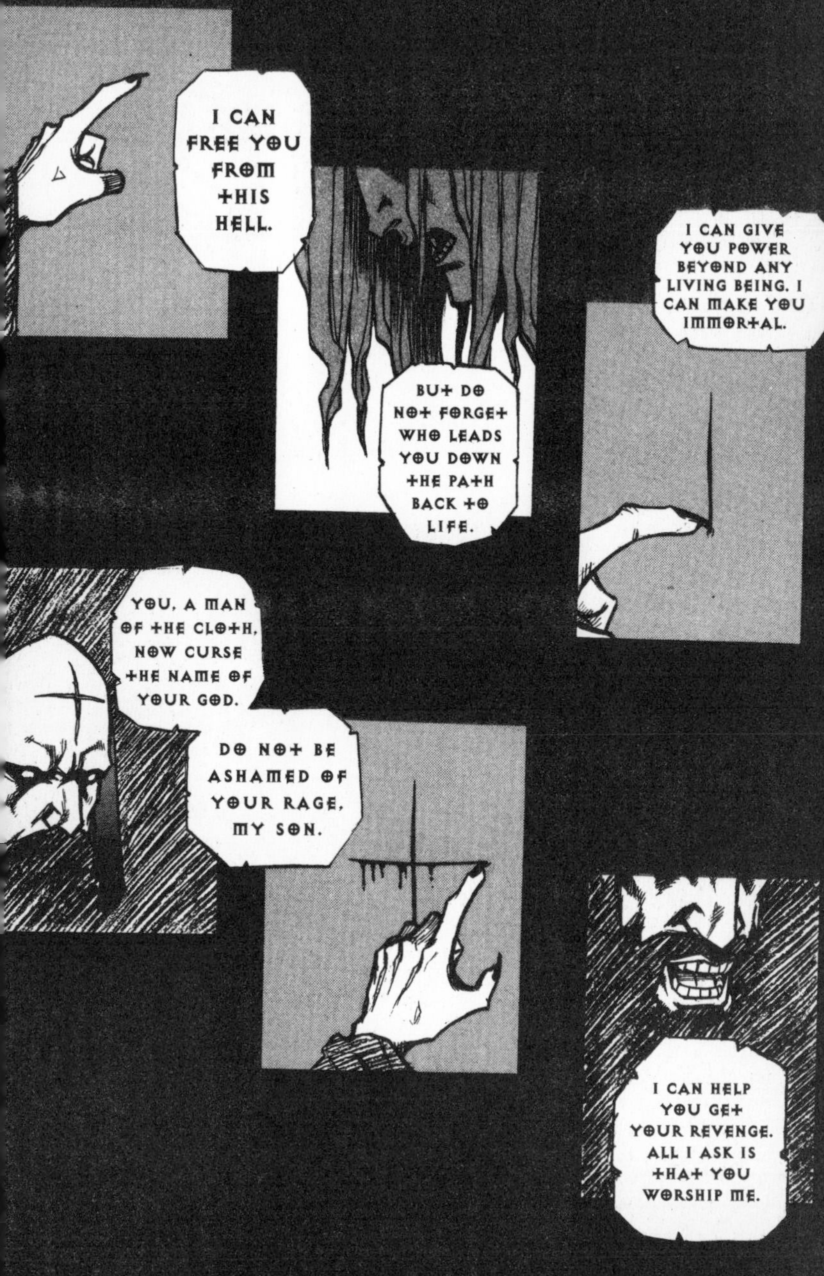
I CAN FREE YOU FROM THIS HELL.
BUT DO NOT FORGET WHO LEADS YOU DOWN THE PATH BACK TO LIFE.
I CAN GIVE YOU POWER BEYOND ANY LIVING BEING. I CAN MAKE YOU IMMORTAL.
YOU, A MAN OF THE CLOTH, NOW CURSE THE NAME OF YOUR GOD.
DO NOT BE ASHAMED OF YOUR RAGE, MY SON.
I CAN HELP YOU GET YOUR REVENGE. ALL I ASK IS THAT YOU WORSHIP ME.

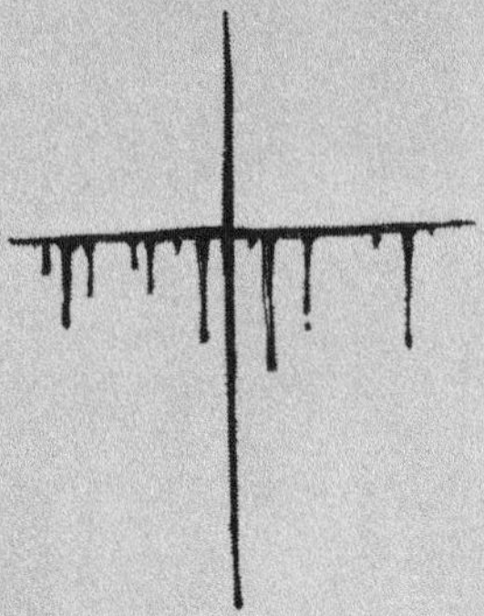

I THOUGHT THIS WAS A FINAL NIGHTMARE BEFORE THE END.
A LAST VISION OF LIFE WITHOUT GENA BEFORE I WOULD JOIN
HER FOR ETERNITY IN THE AFTERLIFE. I WRAPPED MYSELF IN
MY ARMS AS IF THEY WERE HERS AND WAITED FOR THE END.

BUT AS I AWOKE TO THE DA
AT ONCE THAT MY NIGHTMA
TAINTED BY HIS BLOOD.
FOREVER REMOVED FROM

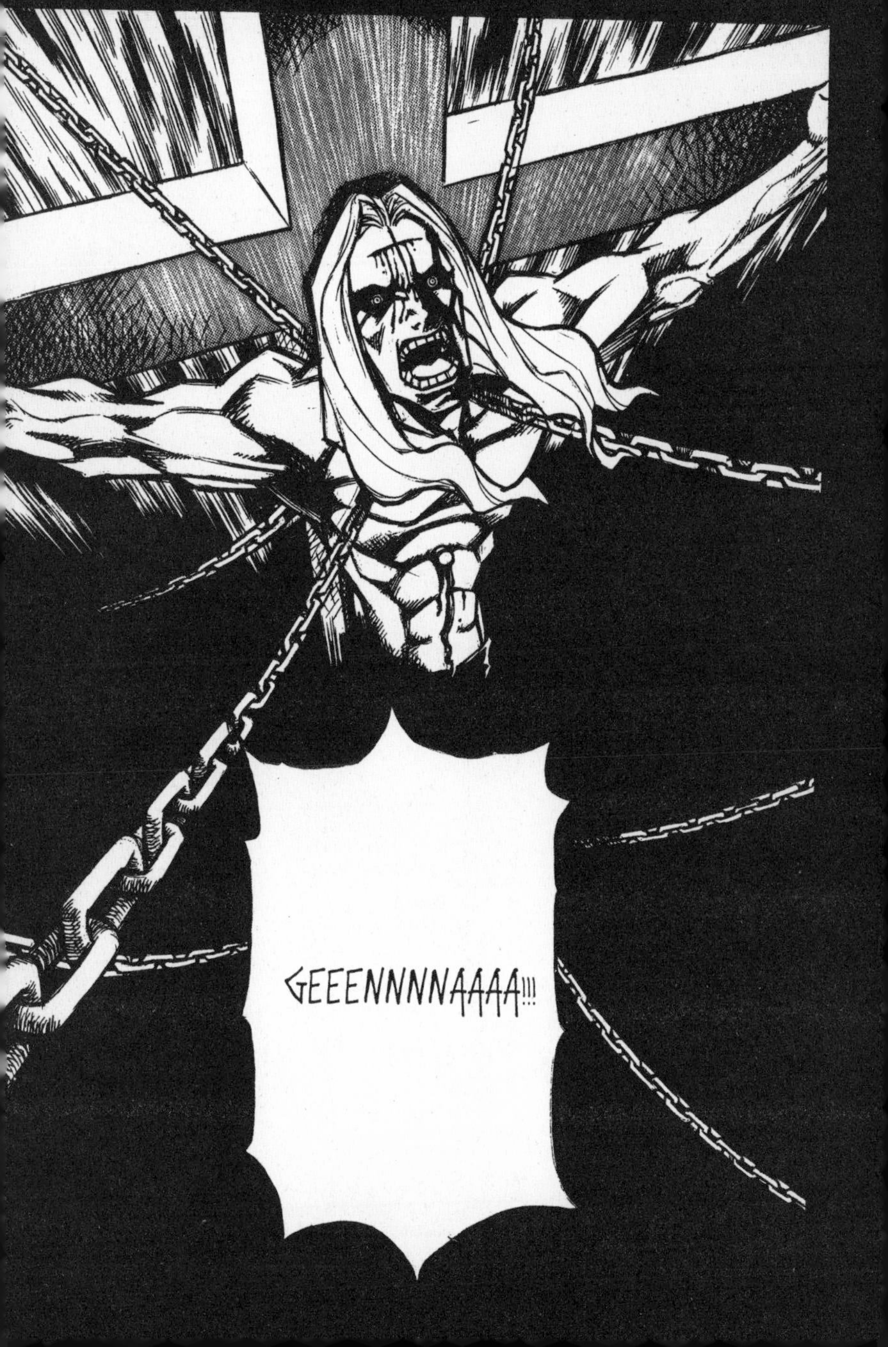
GEEENNNNAAAA!!!

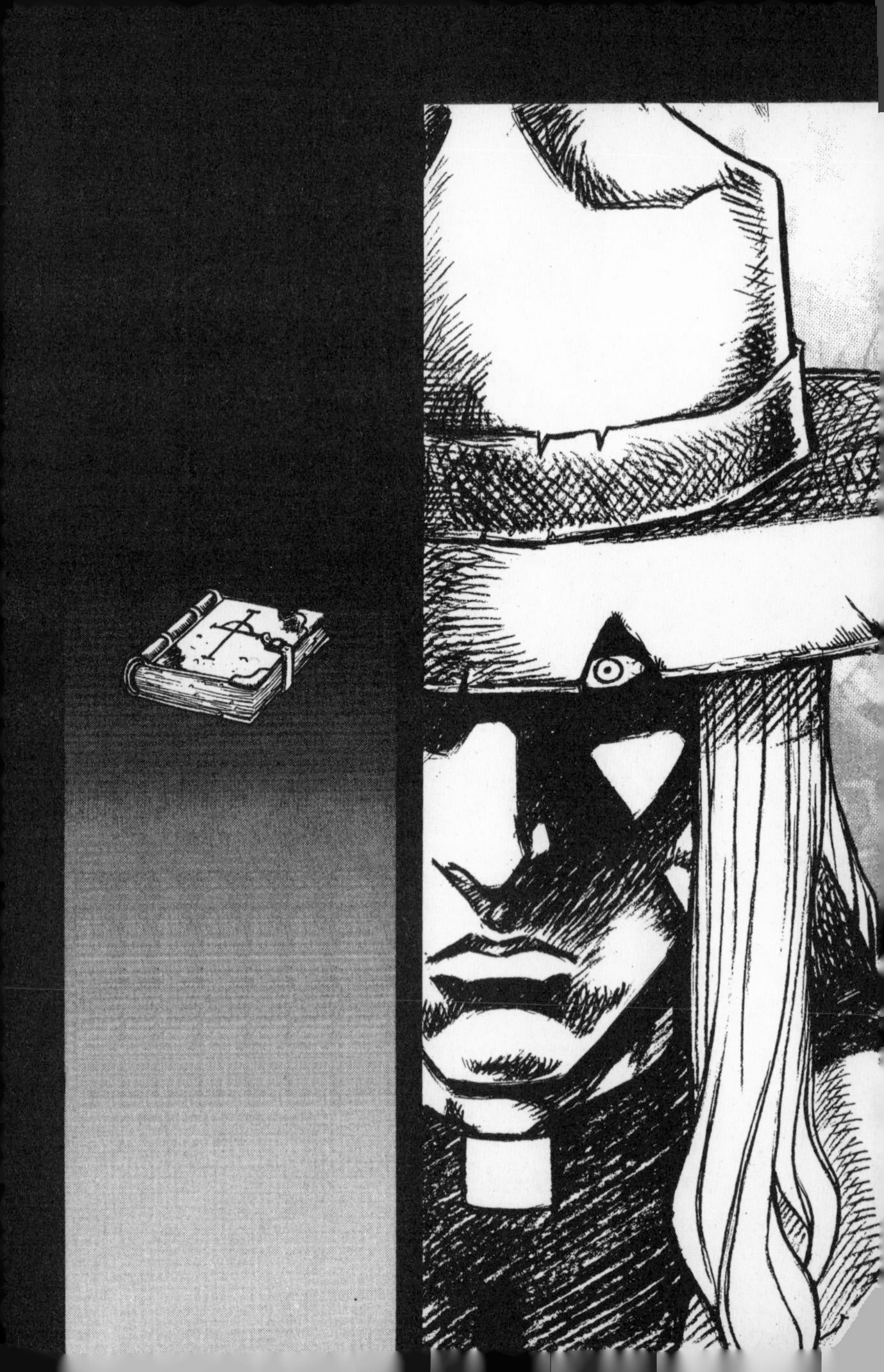

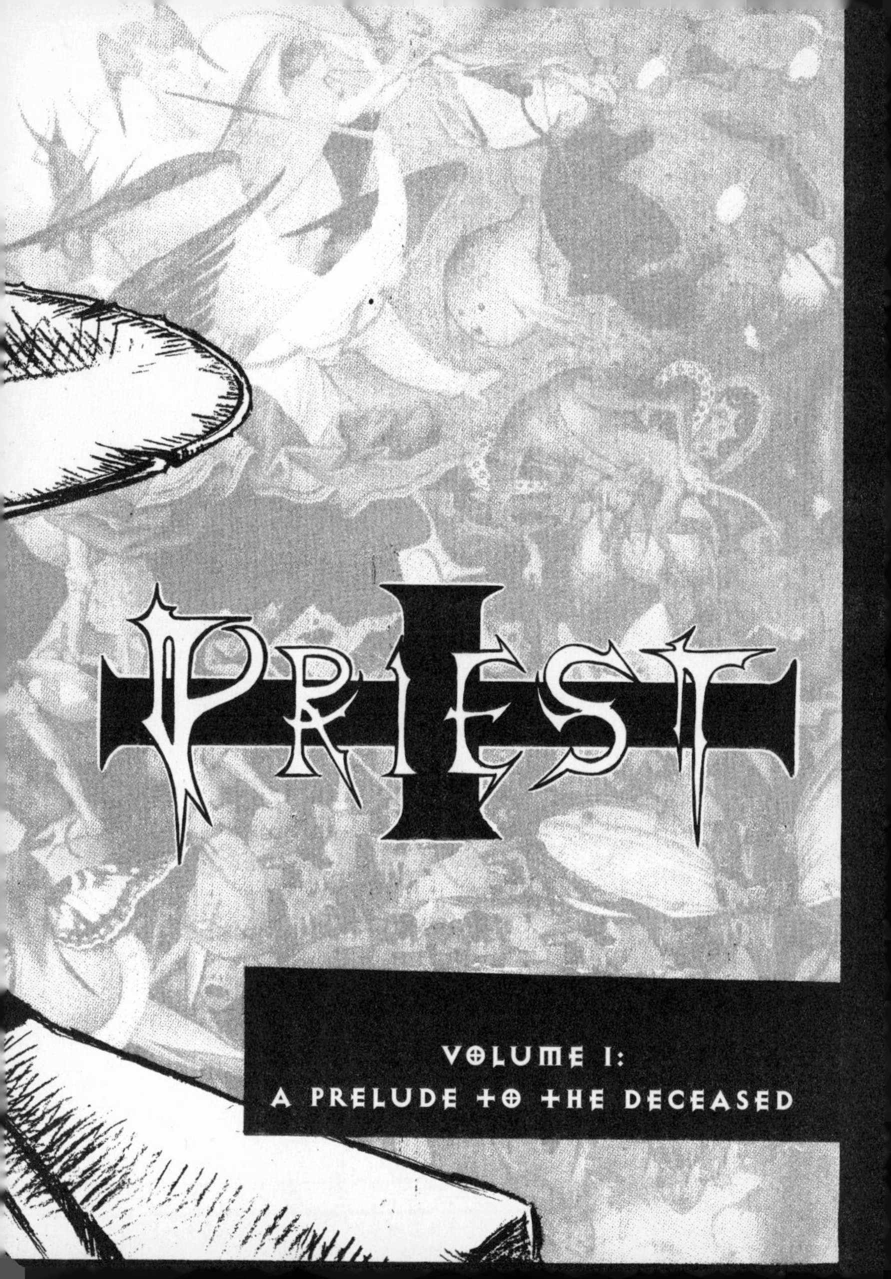
PRIEST
VOLUME I:
A PRELUDE TO THE DECEASED

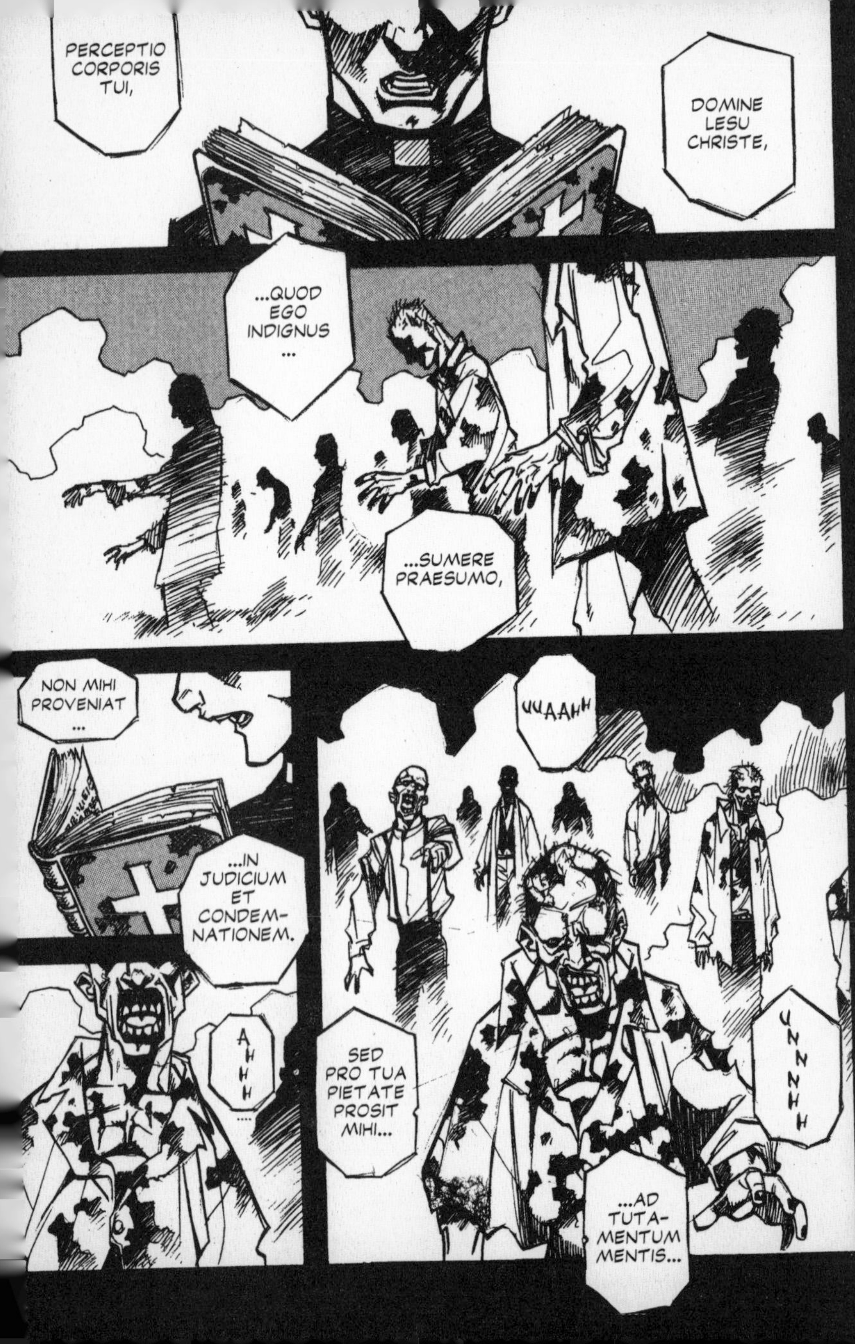

PERCEPTIO CORPORIS TUI,
DOMINE LESU CHRISTE,
...QUOD EGO INDIGNUS ...
...SUMERE PRAESUMO,
NON MIHI PROVENIAT ...
...IN JUDICIUM ET CONDEM-NATIONEM.
AHHH ...
UUAAHH
SED PRO TUA PIETATE PROSIT MIHI...
UNNHHH
...AD TUTA-MENTUM MENTIS...

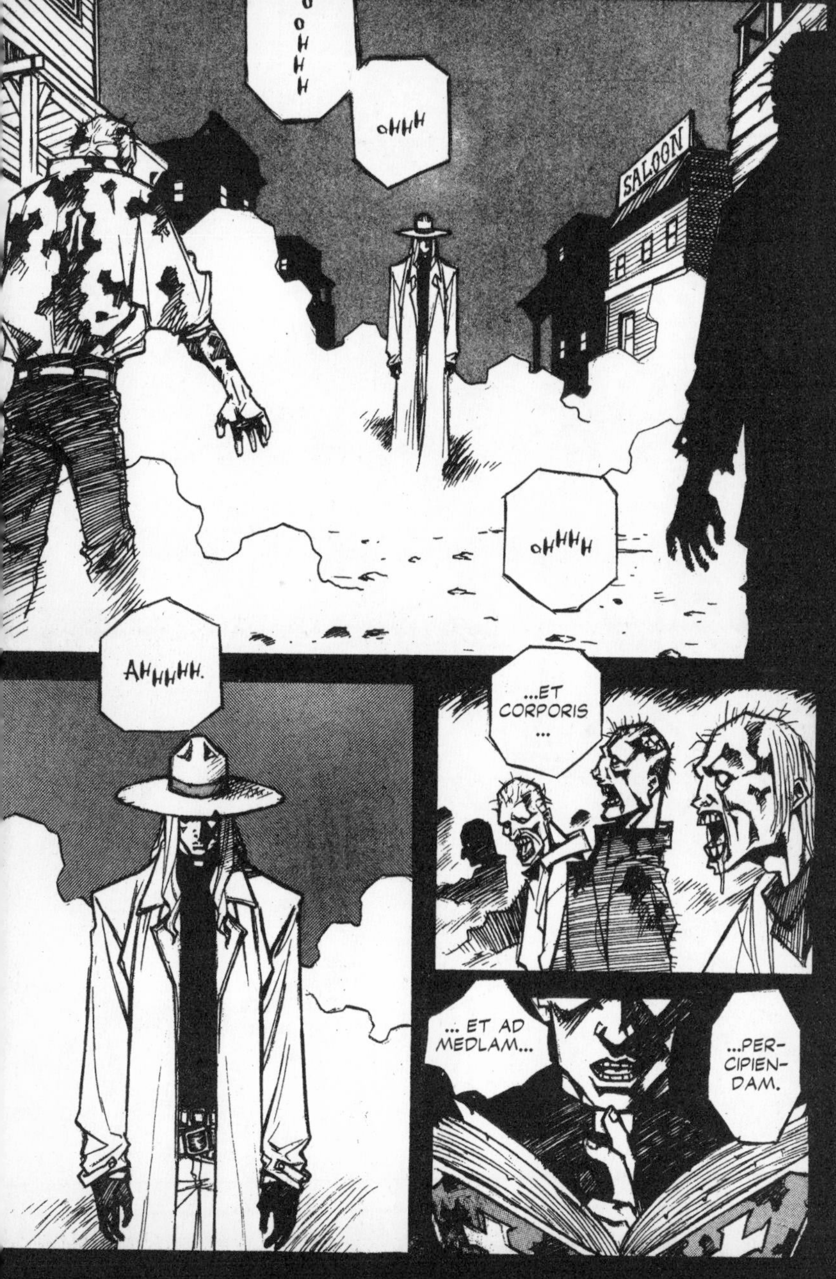
OOHHHH
OHHH
OHHHH
AHHHHH.
...ET CORPORIS ...
... ET AD MEDLAM...
...PER-CIPIEN-DAM.

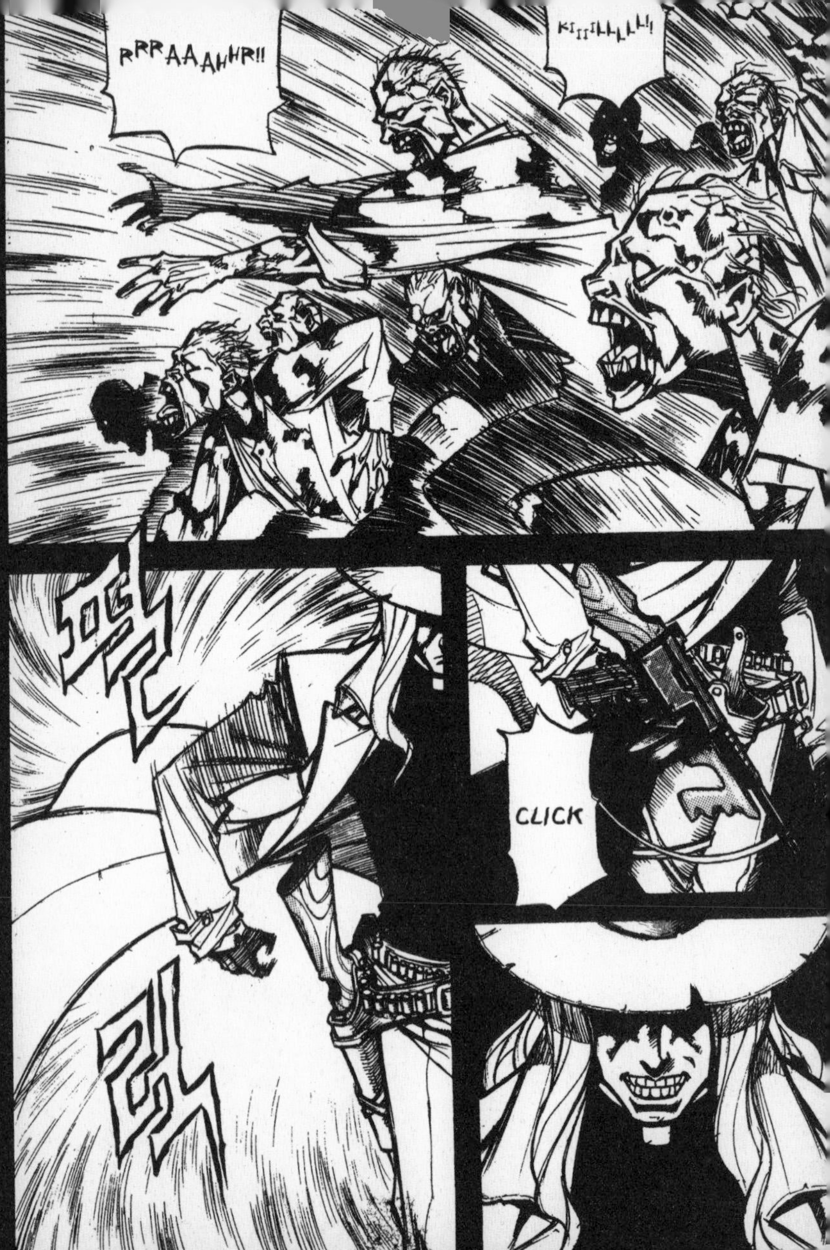
RRRAAAHHR!!
KIIIILLLLL!!
CLICK

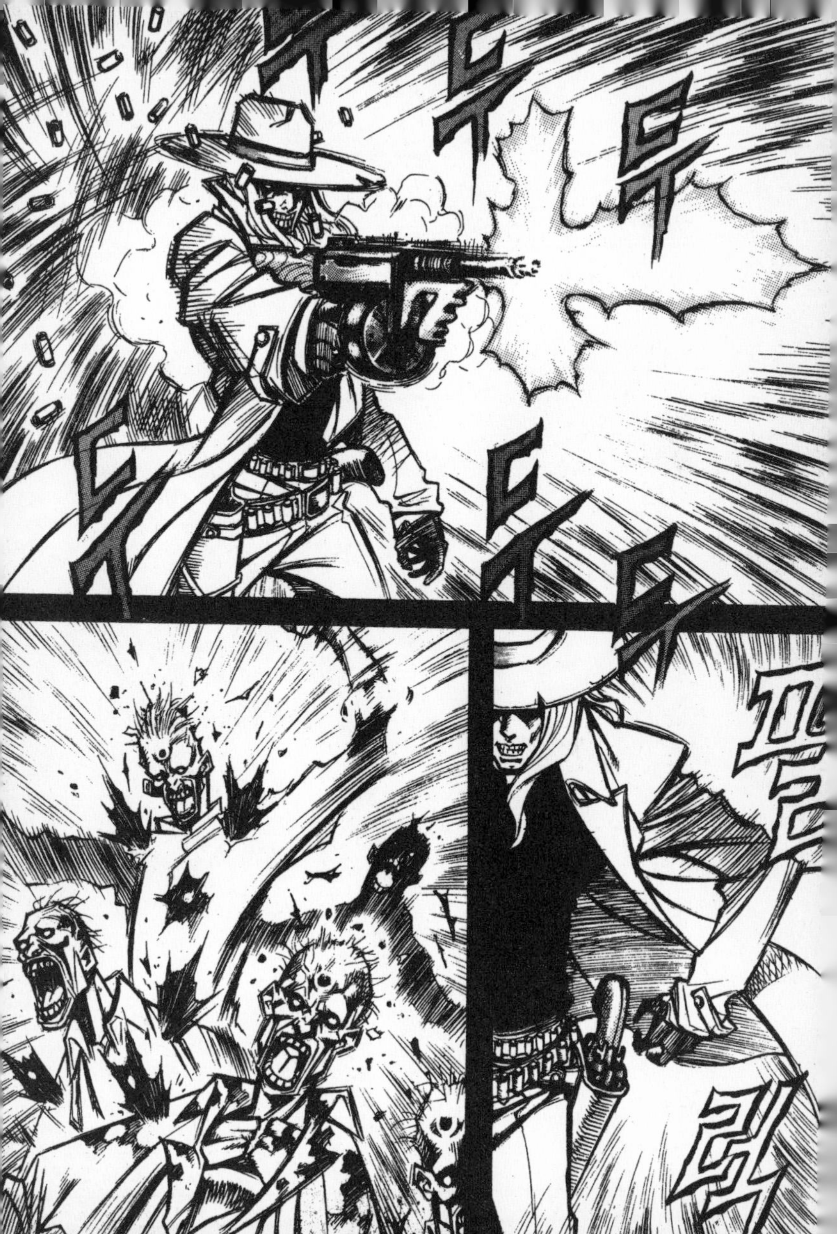

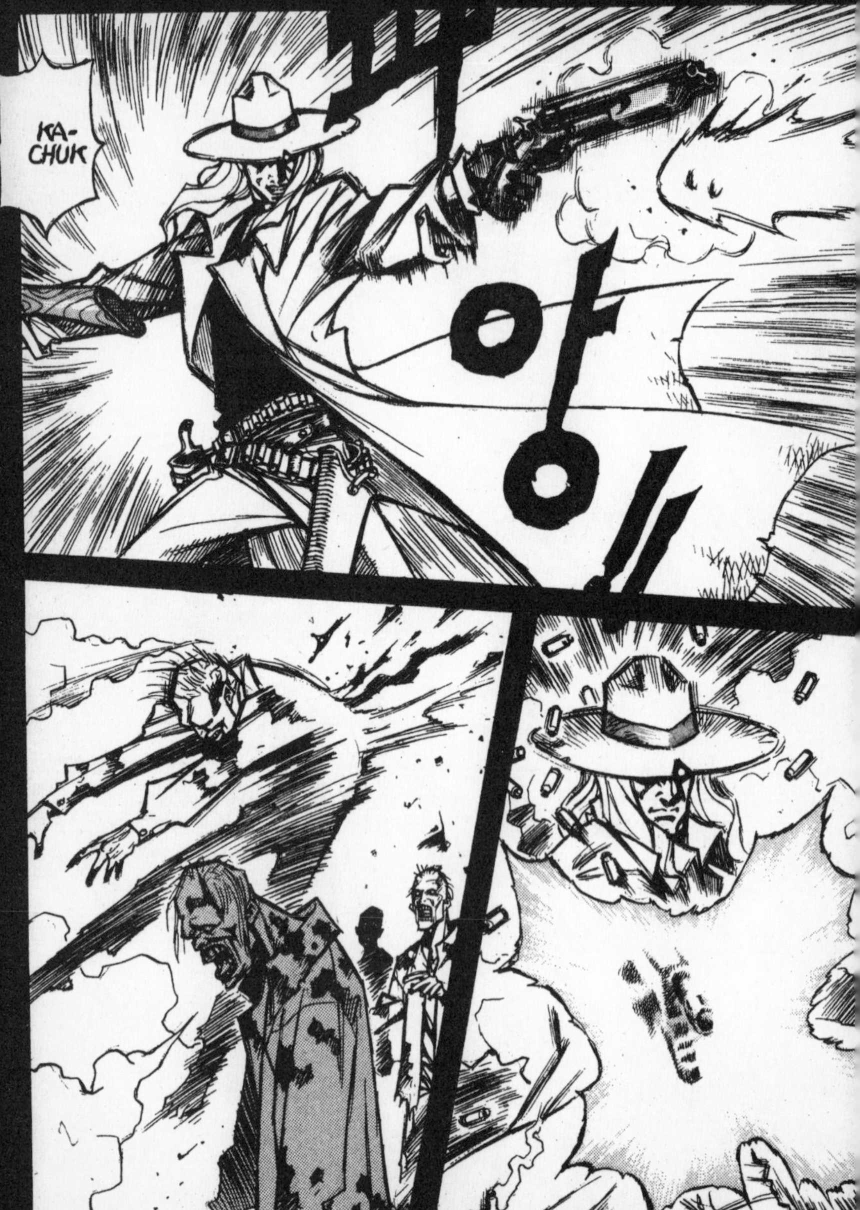
KA-
CHUK

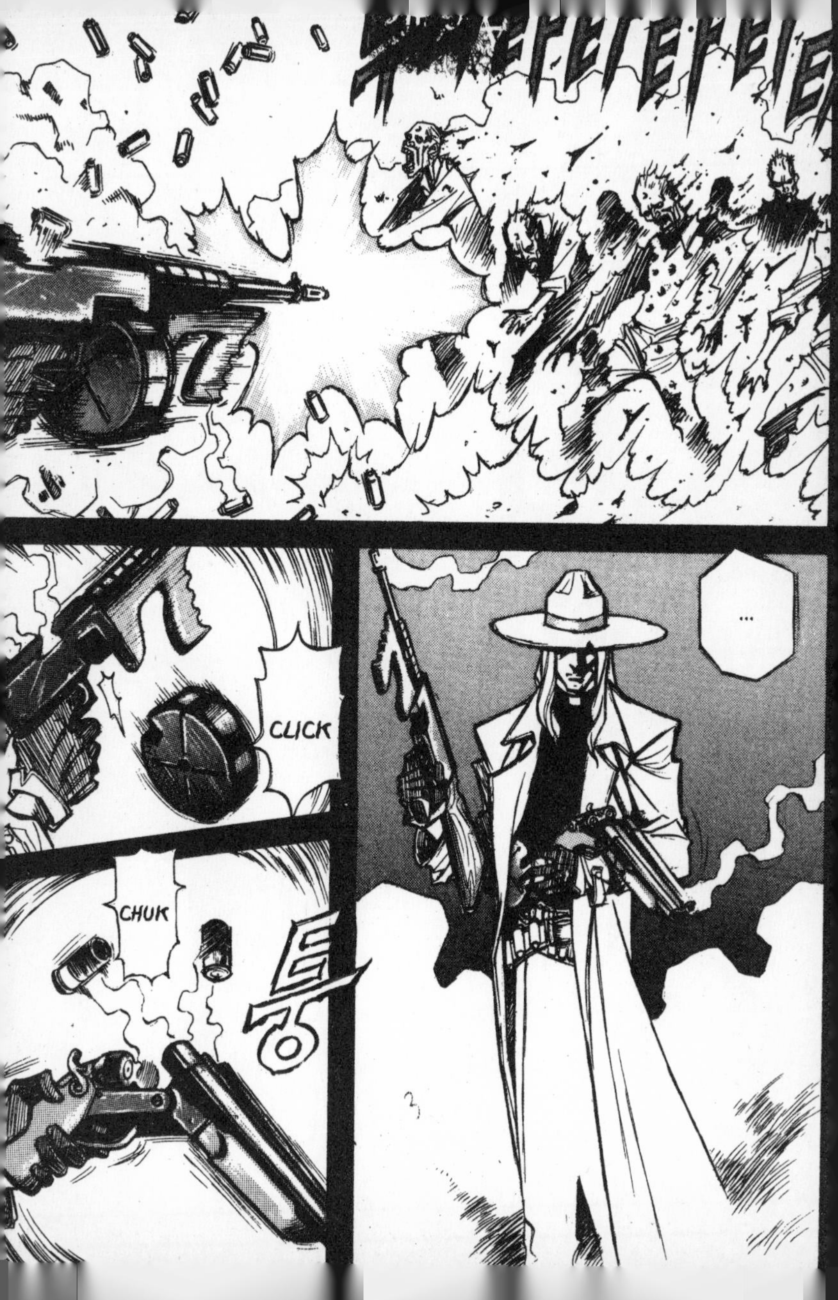
CLICK
CHUK
...

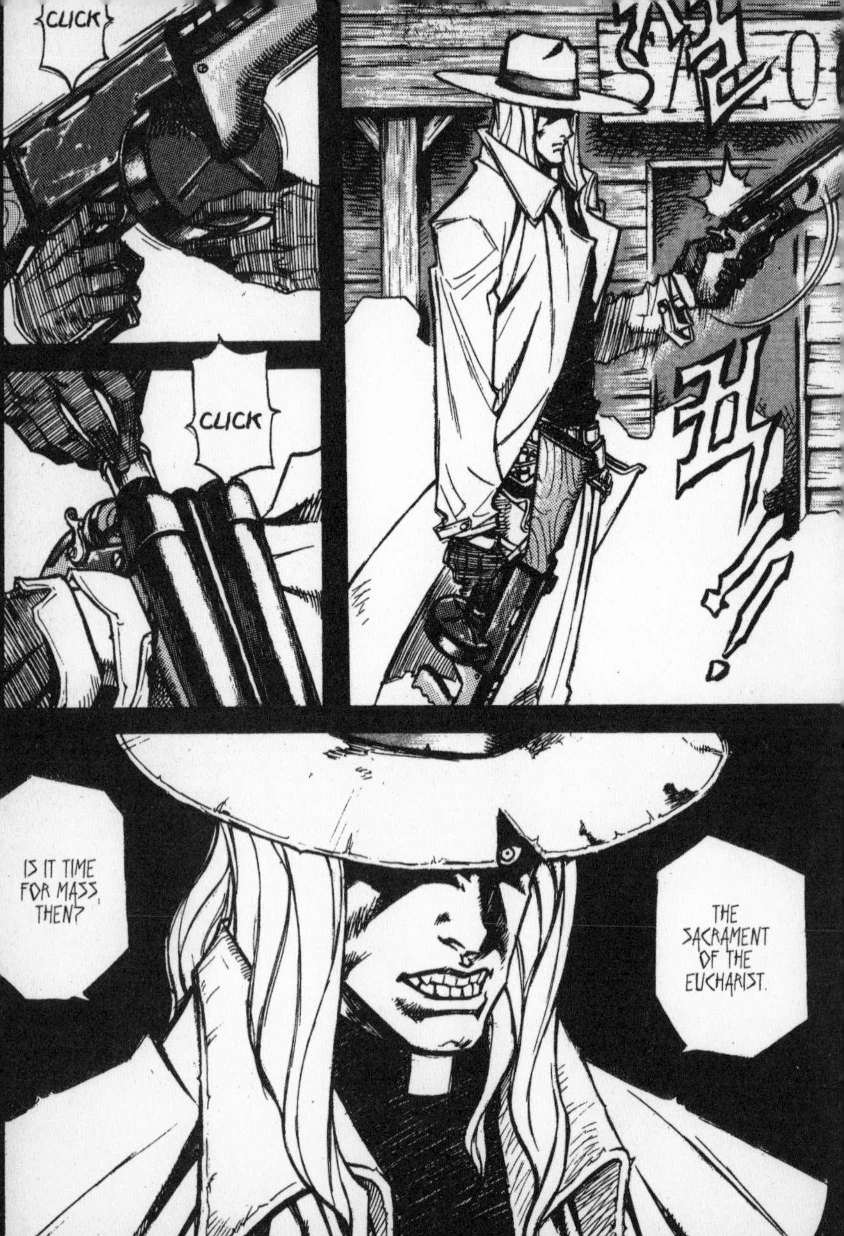
CLICK
CLICK
IS IT TIME FOR MASS, THEN?
THE SACRAMENT OF THE EUCHARIST.

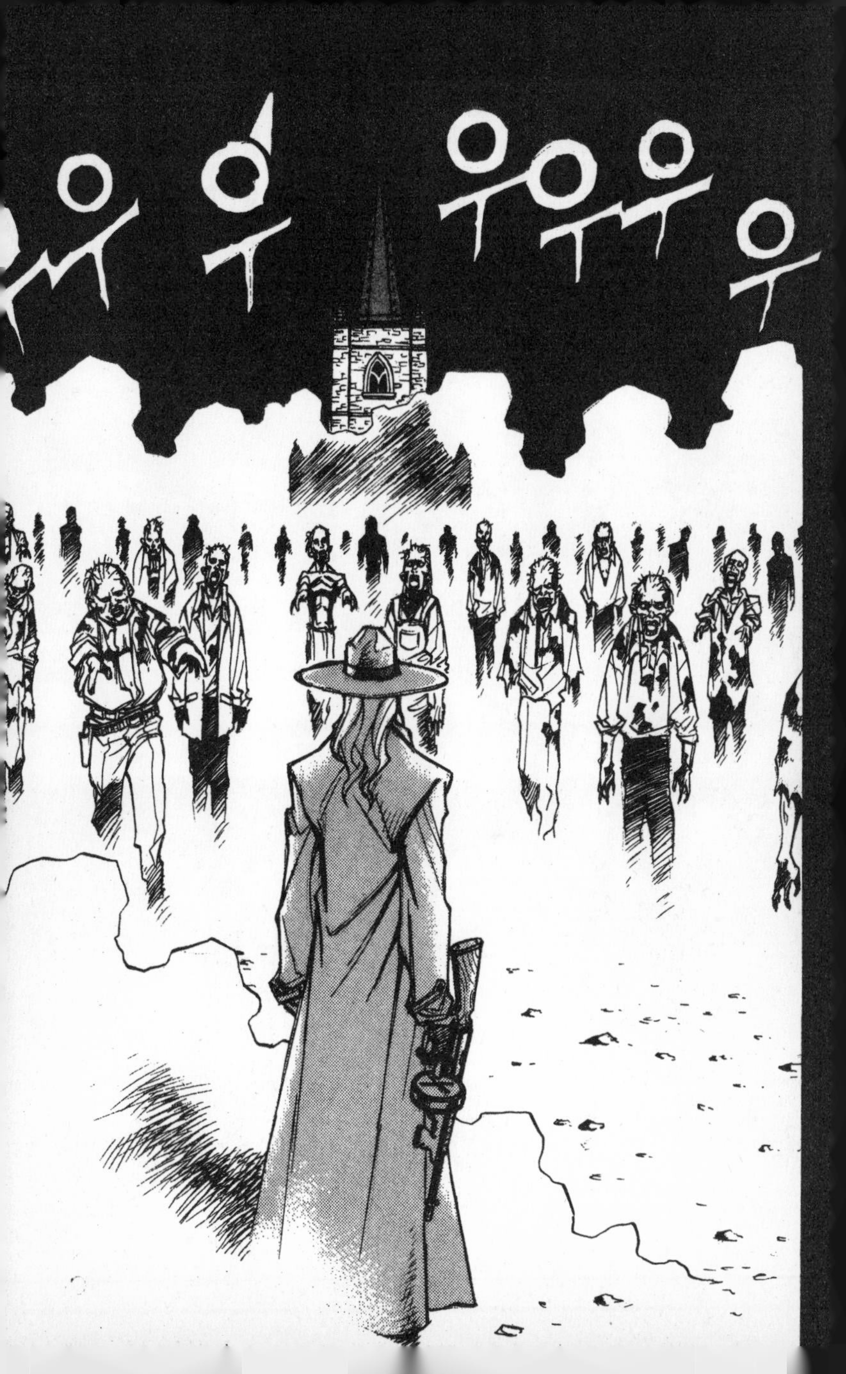

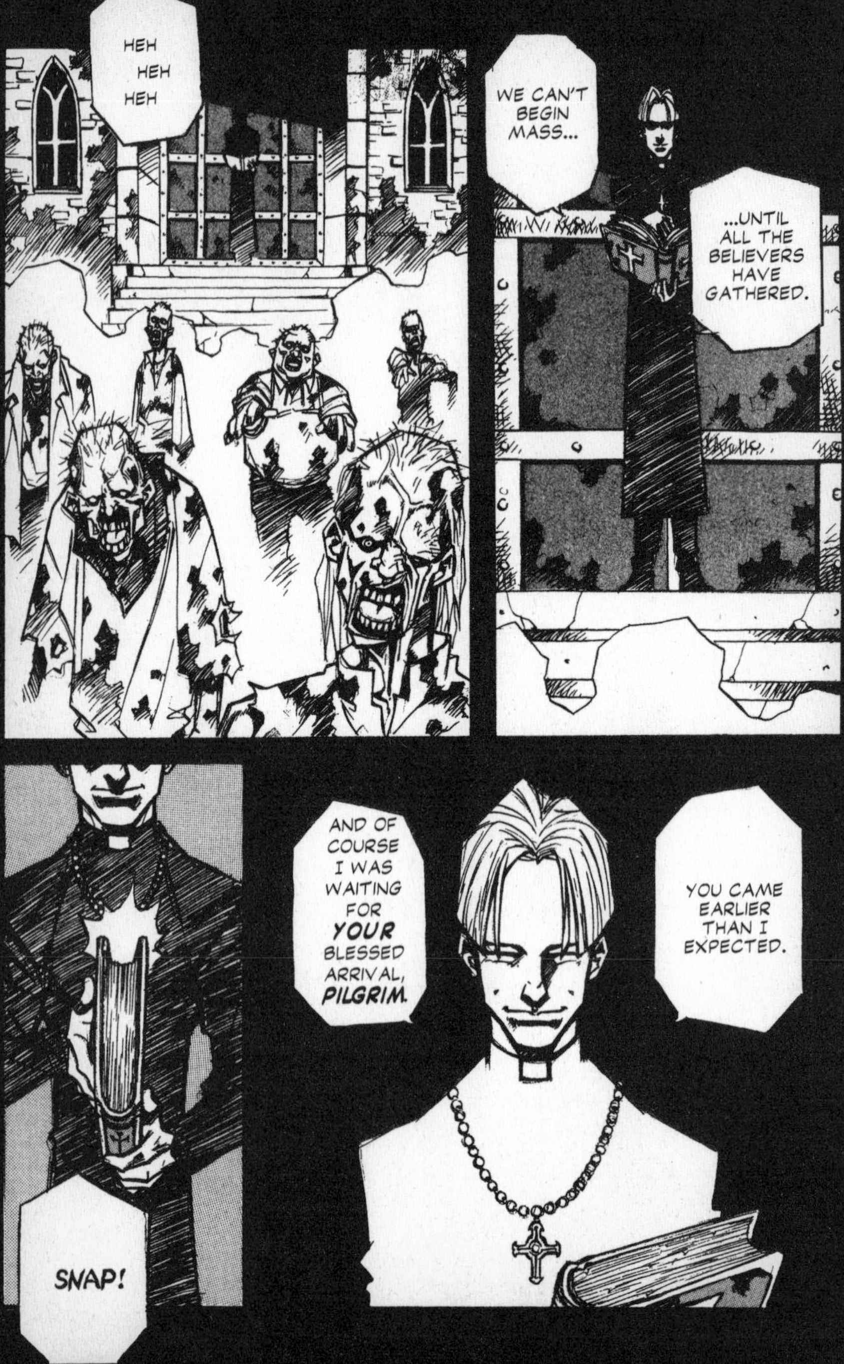
HEH HEH HEH
WE CAN'T BEGIN MASS...
...UNTIL ALL THE BELIEVERS HAVE GATHERED.
SNAP!
AND OF COURSE I WAS WAITING FOR YOUR BLESSED ARRIVAL, PILGRIM.
YOU CAME EARLIER THAN I EXPECTED.

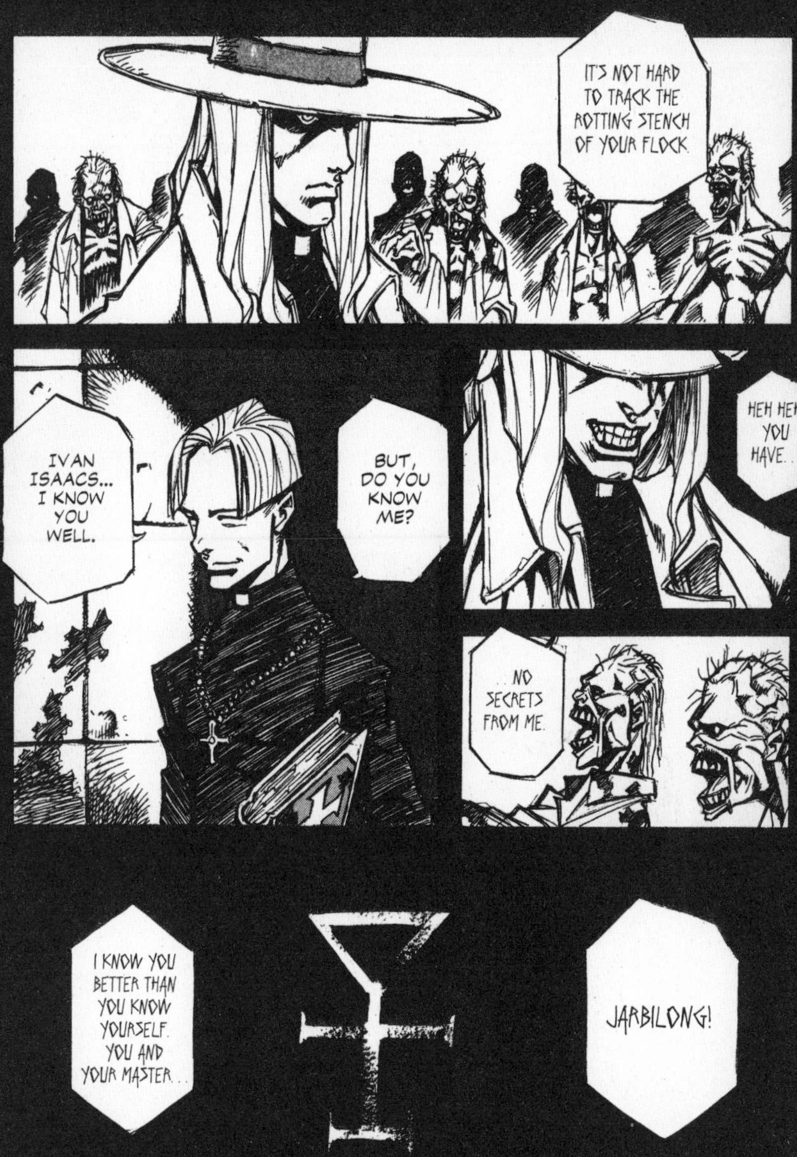
IT'S NOT HARD TO TRACK THE ROTTING STENCH OF YOUR FLOCK.
IVAN ISAACS... I KNOW YOU WELL.
BUT, DO YOU KNOW ME?
HEH HEH! YOU HAVE...
...NO SECRETS FROM ME.
I KNOW YOU BETTER THAN YOU KNOW YOURSELF. YOU AND YOUR MASTER...
JARBILONG!

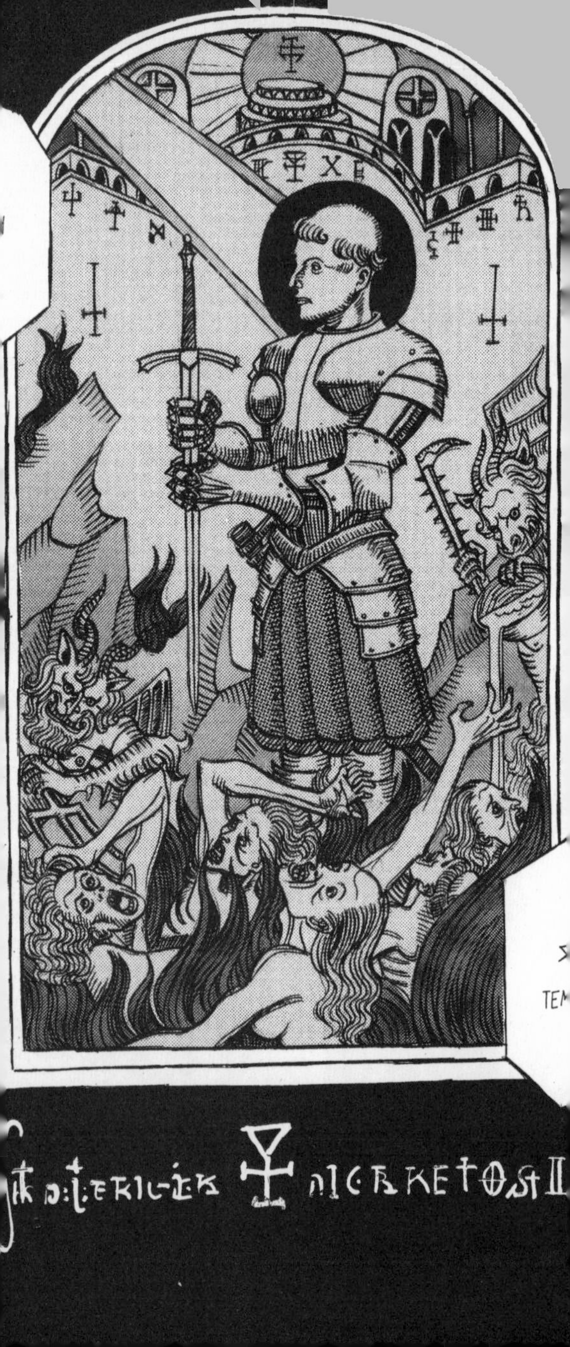

TEM

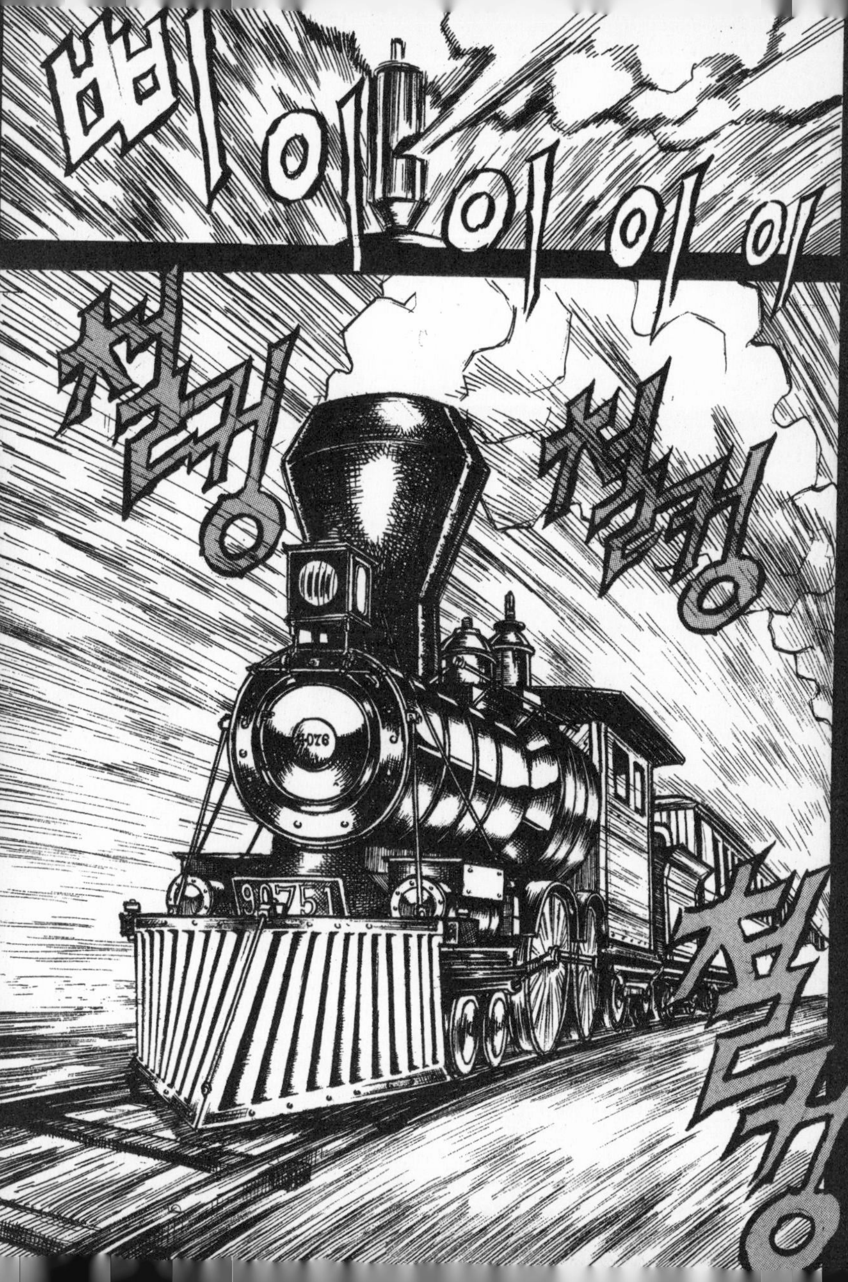

삐이이이이이
철컹
철컹
철컹

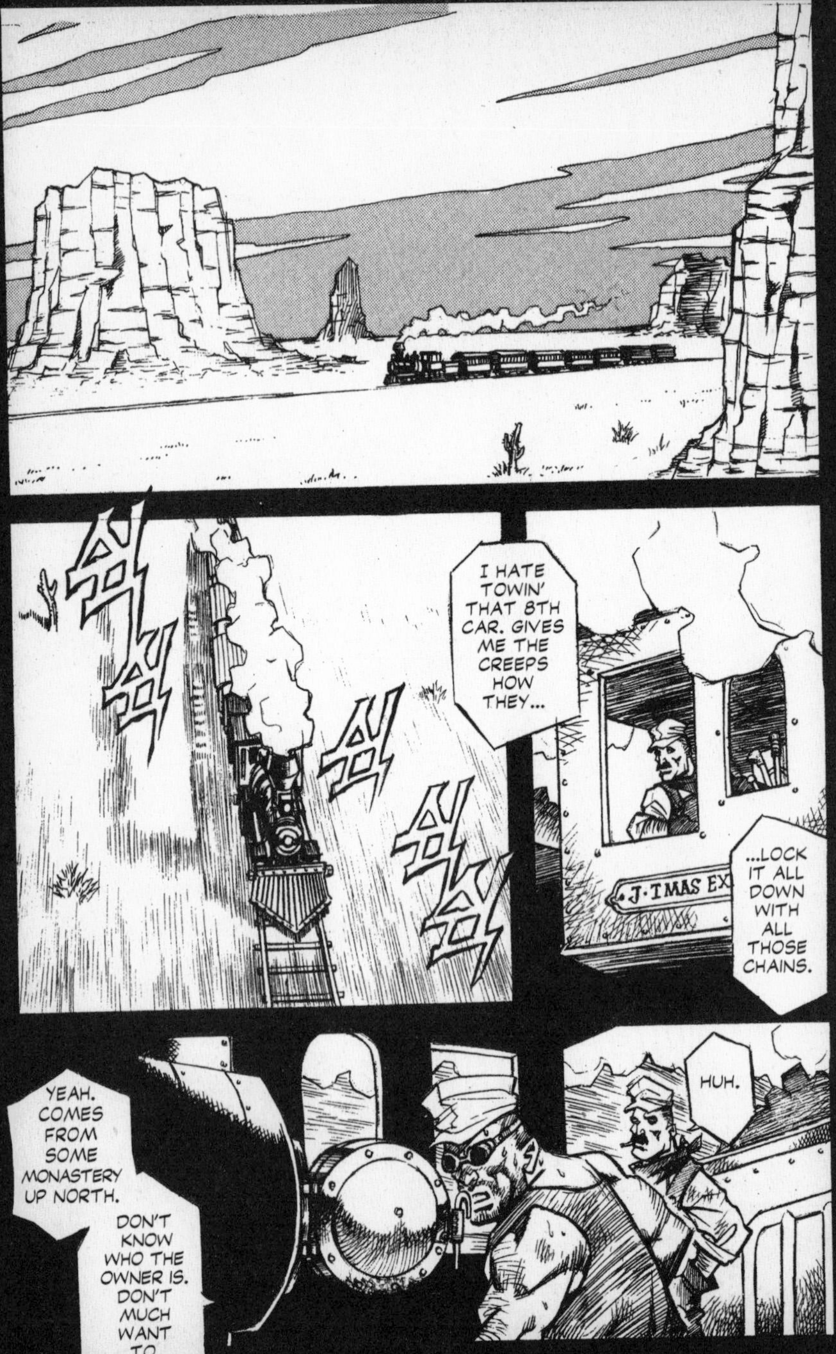
I HATE TOWIN' THAT 8TH CAR. GIVES ME THE CREEPS HOW THEY...
J·TMAS EX
...LOCK IT ALL DOWN WITH ALL THOSE CHAINS.
YEAH. COMES FROM SOME MONASTERY UP NORTH.
DON'T KNOW WHO THE OWNER IS. DON'T MUCH WANT TO.
HUH.

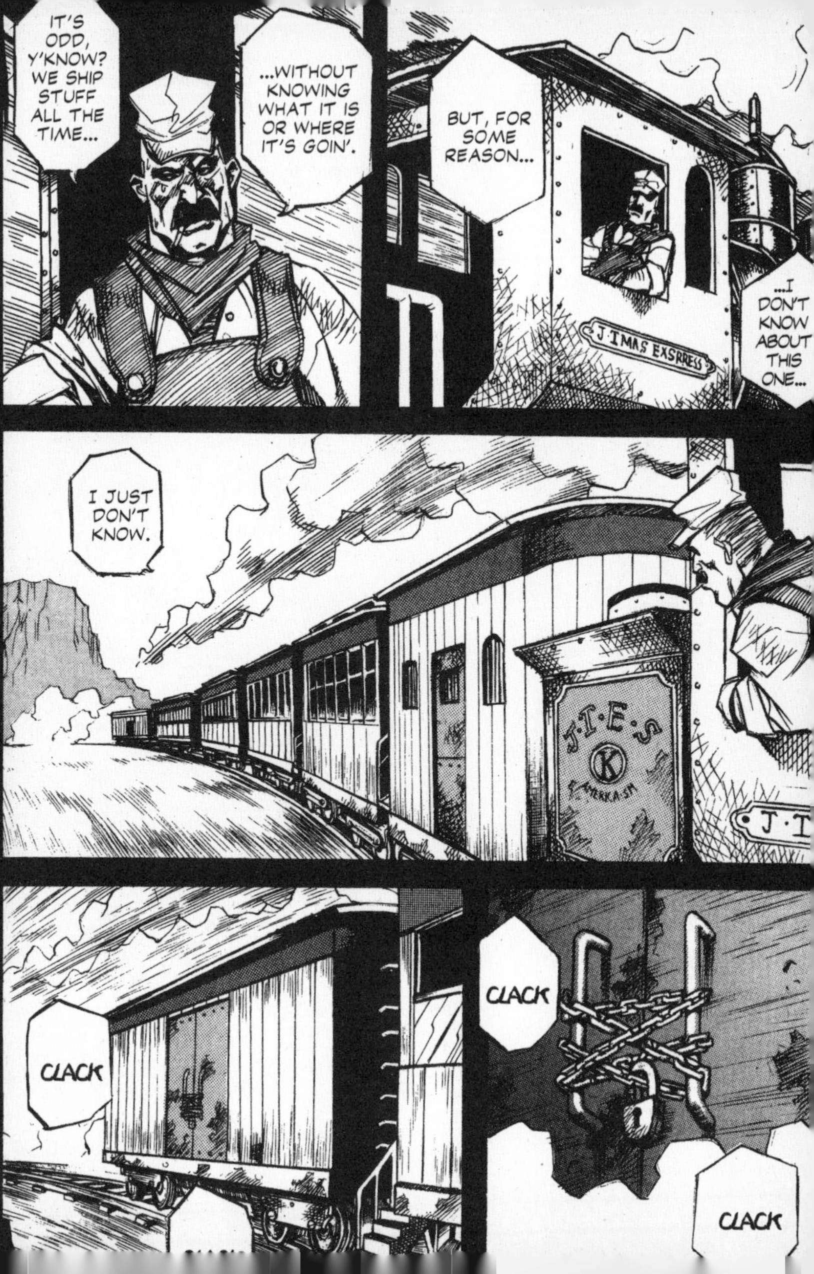
IT'S ODD, Y'KNOW? WE SHIP STUFF ALL THE TIME...
...WITHOUT KNOWING WHAT IT IS OR WHERE IT'S GOIN'.
BUT, FOR SOME REASON...
J·IMAS EXSRRESS
...I DON'T KNOW ABOUT THIS ONE...
I JUST DON'T KNOW.
CLACK
CLACK
CLACK

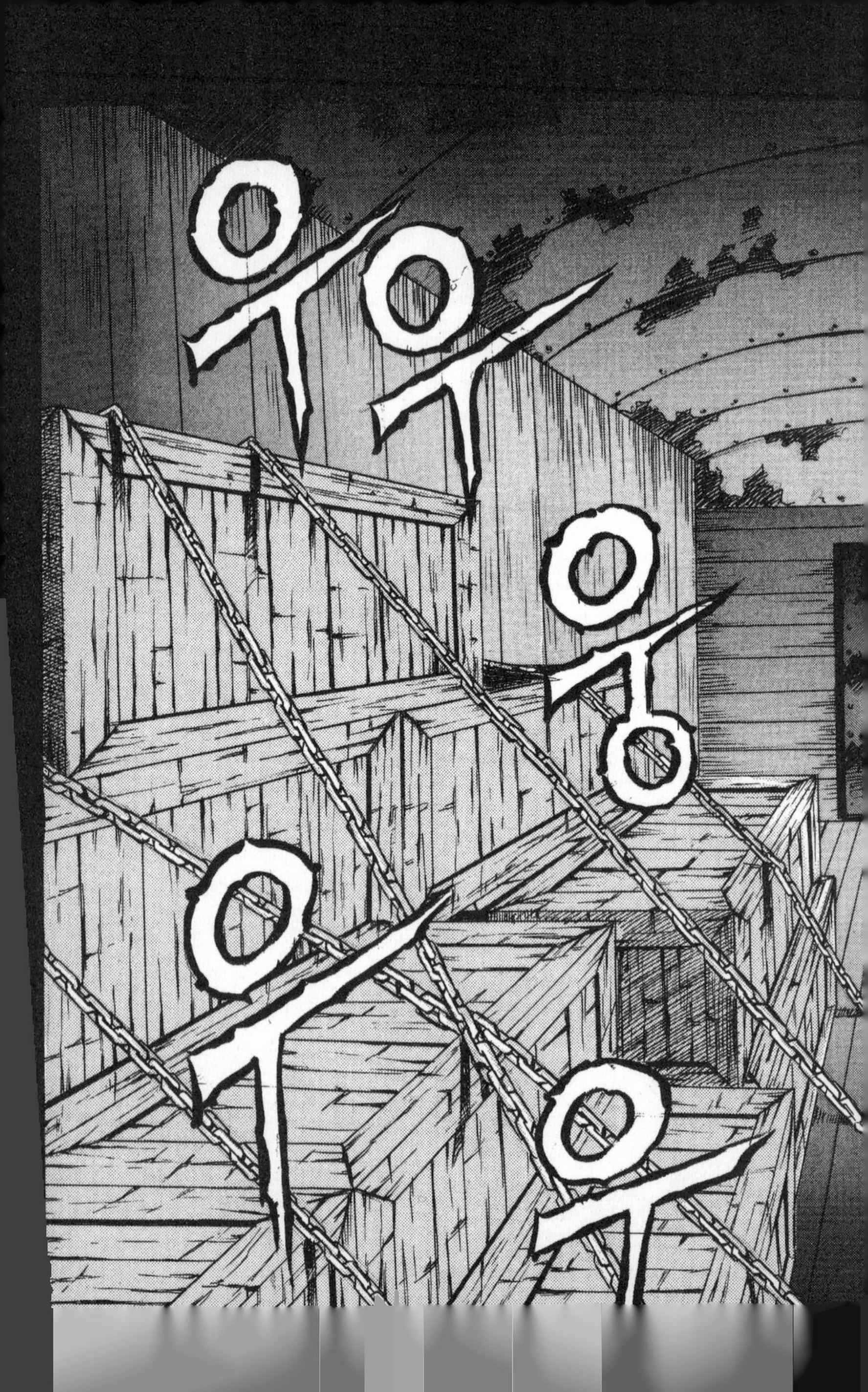

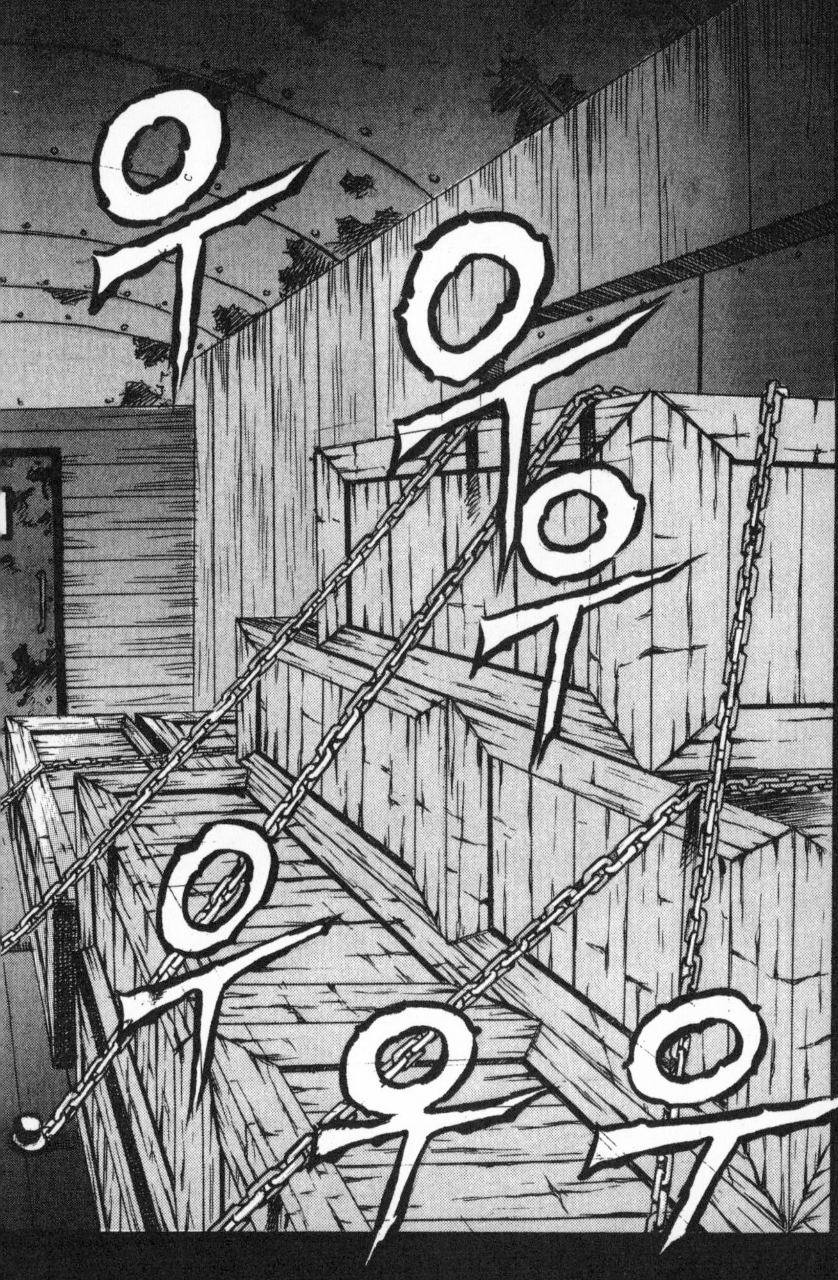
우우우우우우

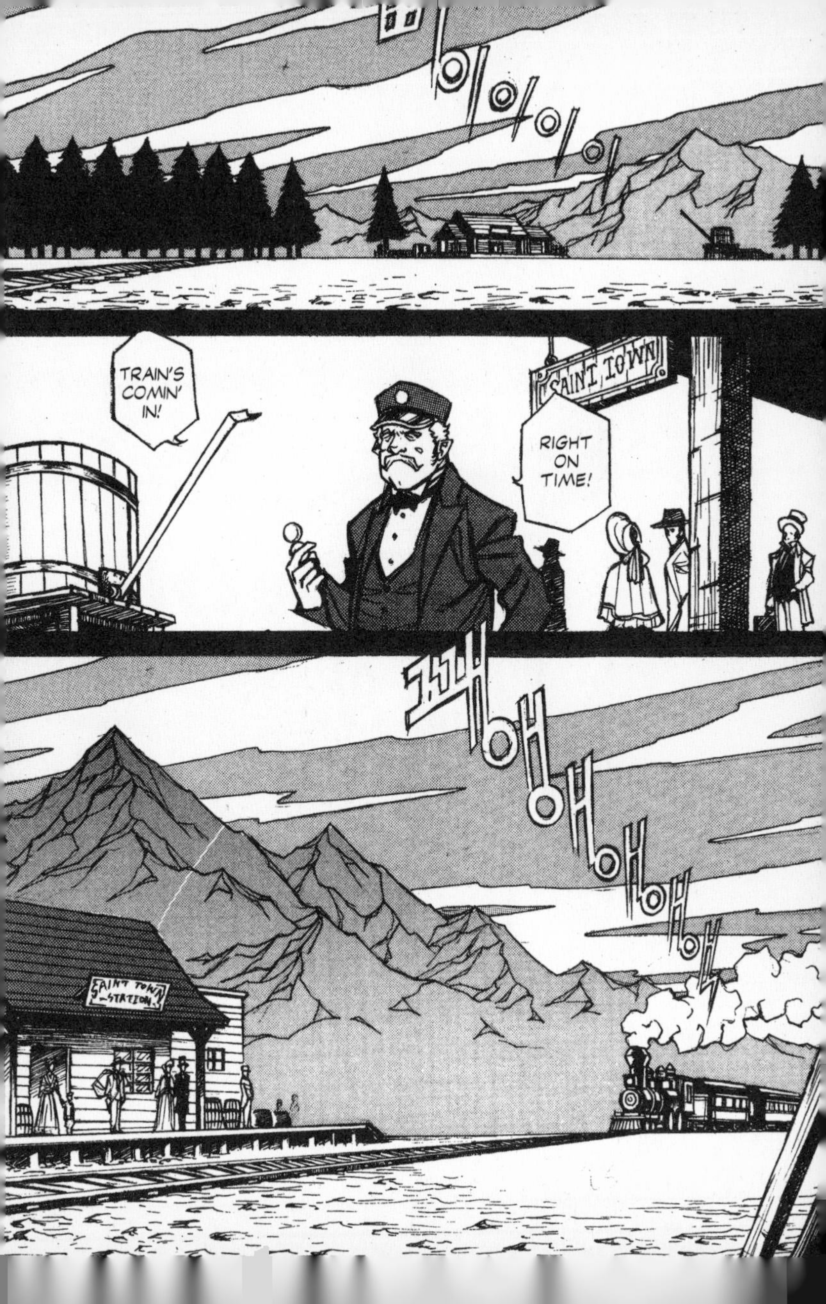
TRAIN'S COMIN' IN!
SAINT TOWN
RIGHT ON TIME!
SAINT TOWN STATION

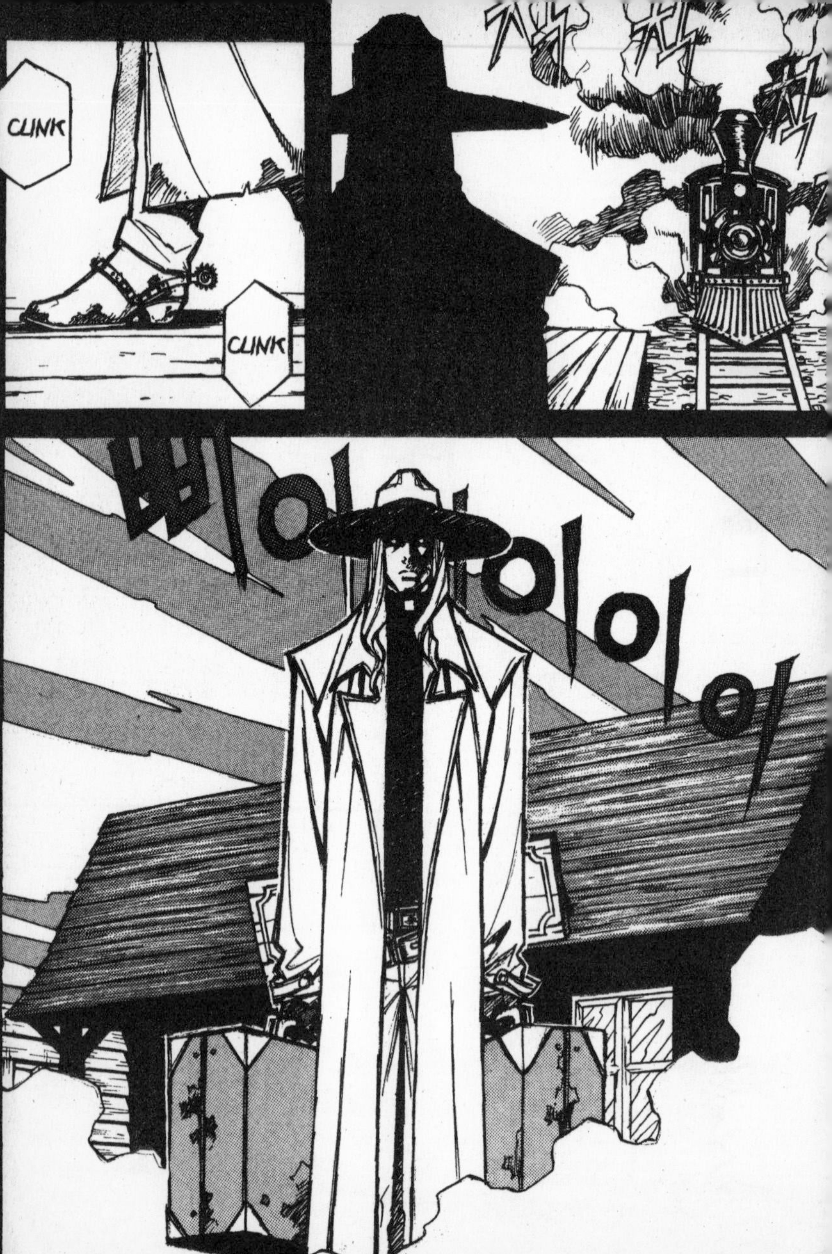
CLUNK
CLUNK

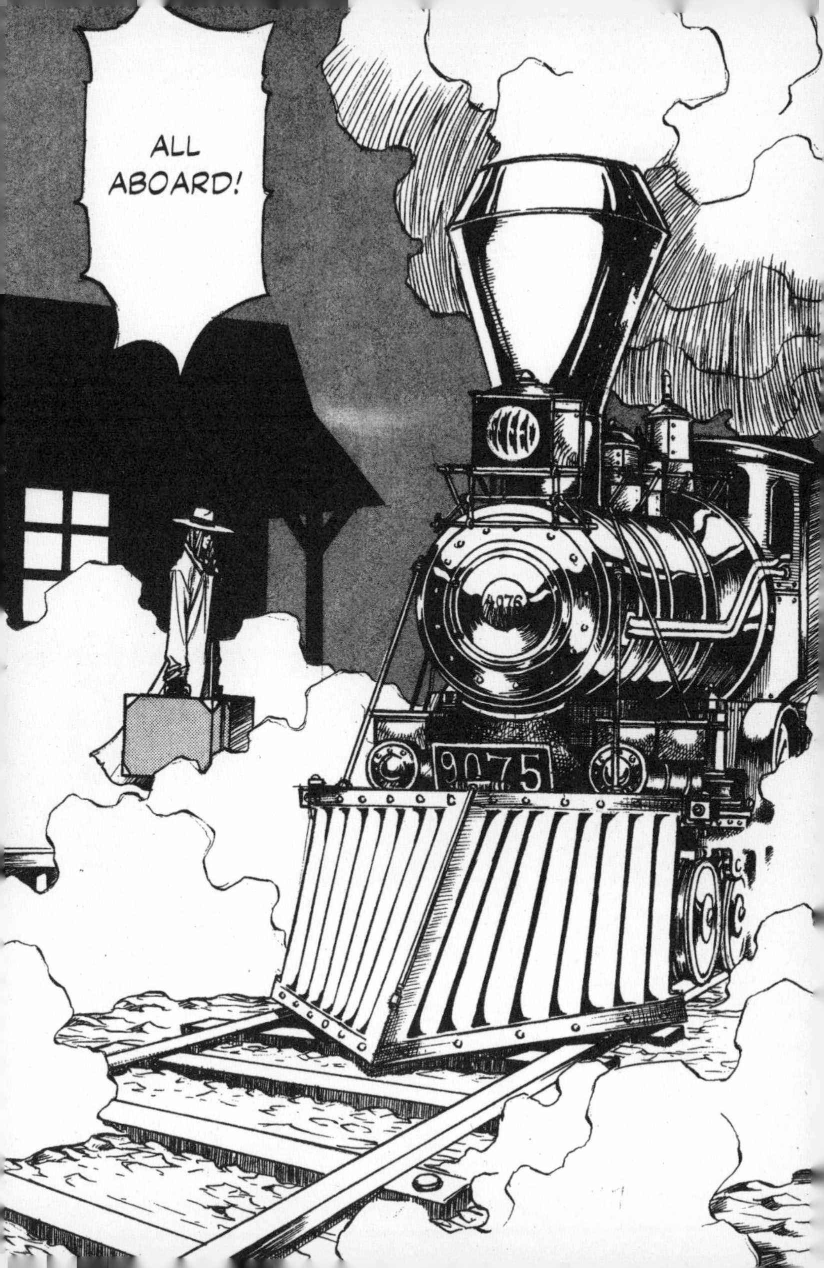
ALL ABOARD!
9075

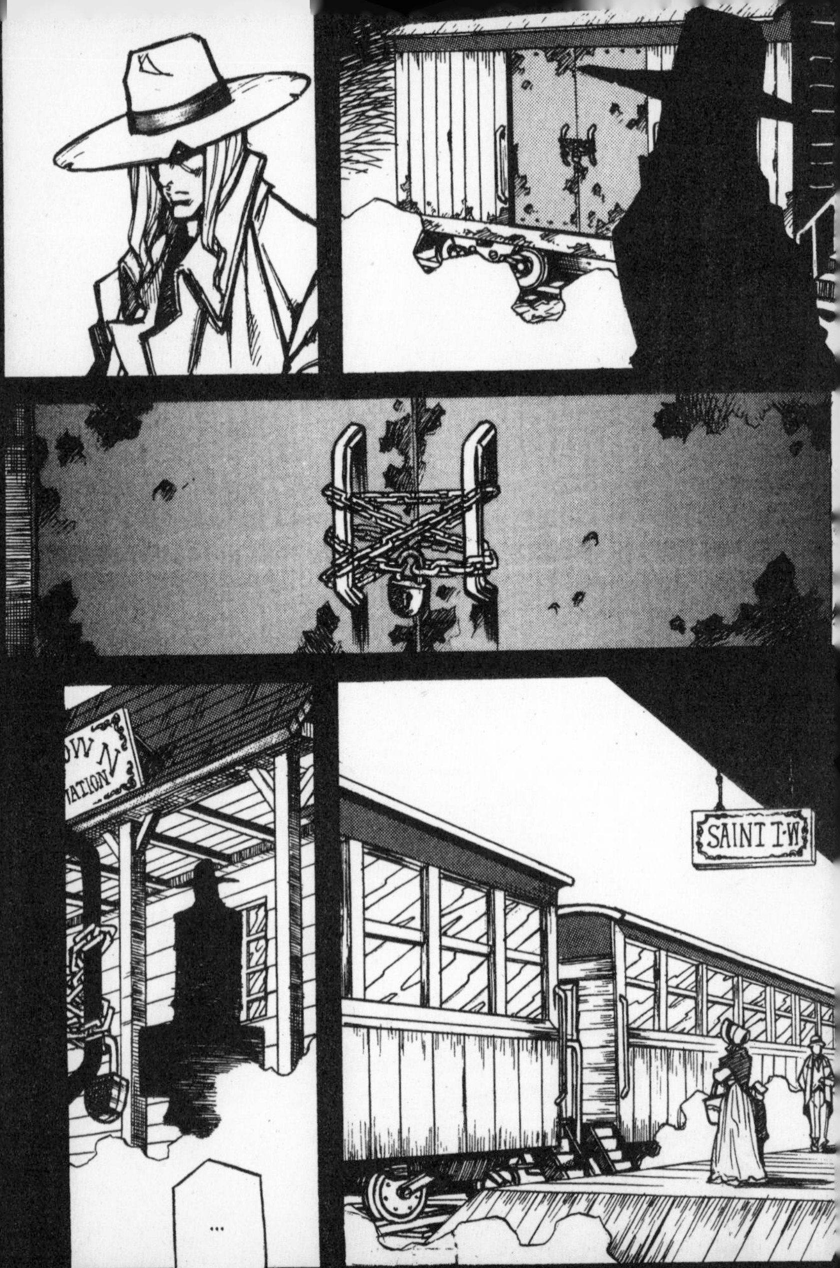
SAINT I·W
...

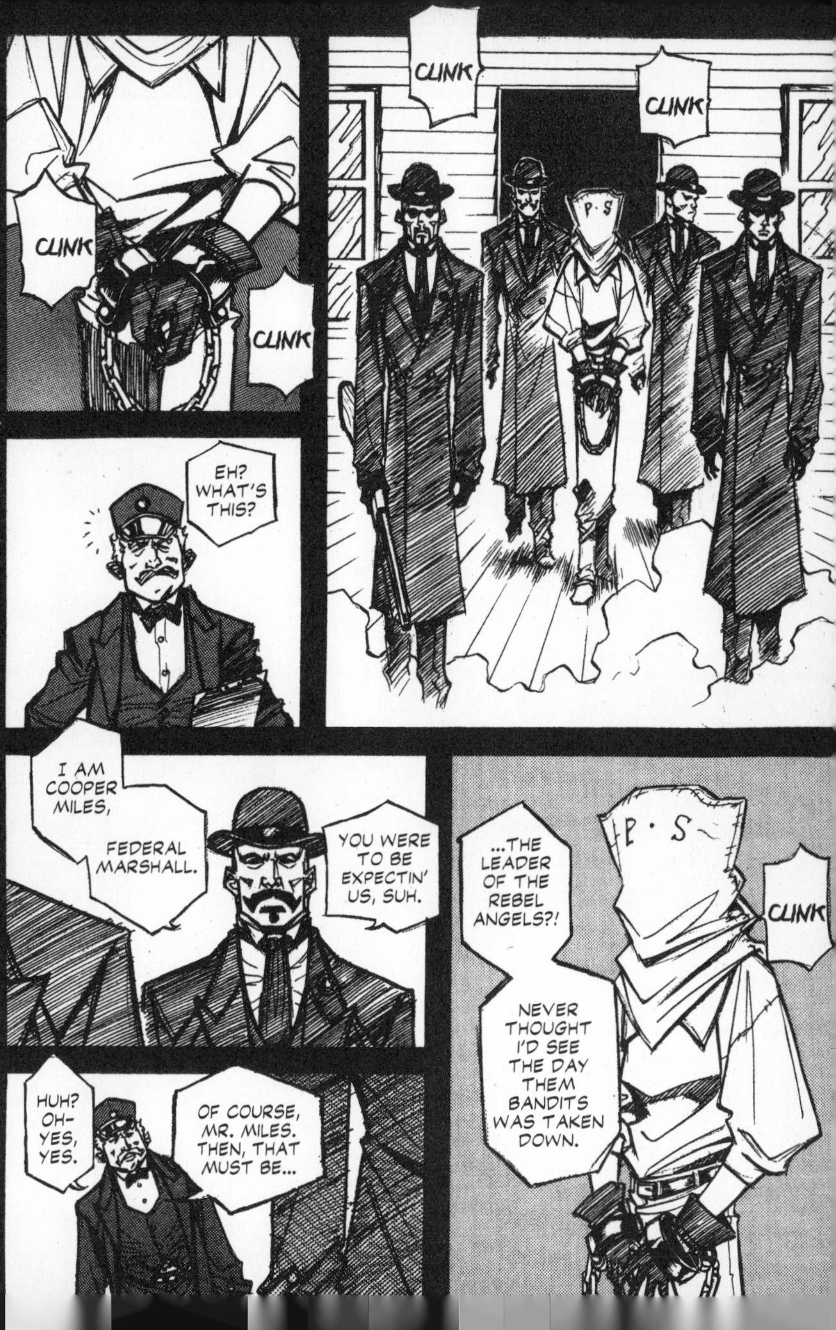
CLINK
CLINK
CLINK
CLINK
EH? WHAT'S THIS?
I AM COOPER MILES,
FEDERAL MARSHALL.
YOU WERE TO BE EXPECTIN' US, SUH.
HUH? OH- YES, YES.
OF COURSE, MR. MILES. THEN, THAT MUST BE...
...THE LEADER OF THE REBEL ANGELS?!
NEVER THOUGHT I'D SEE THE DAY THEM BANDITS WAS TAKEN DOWN.
CLINK

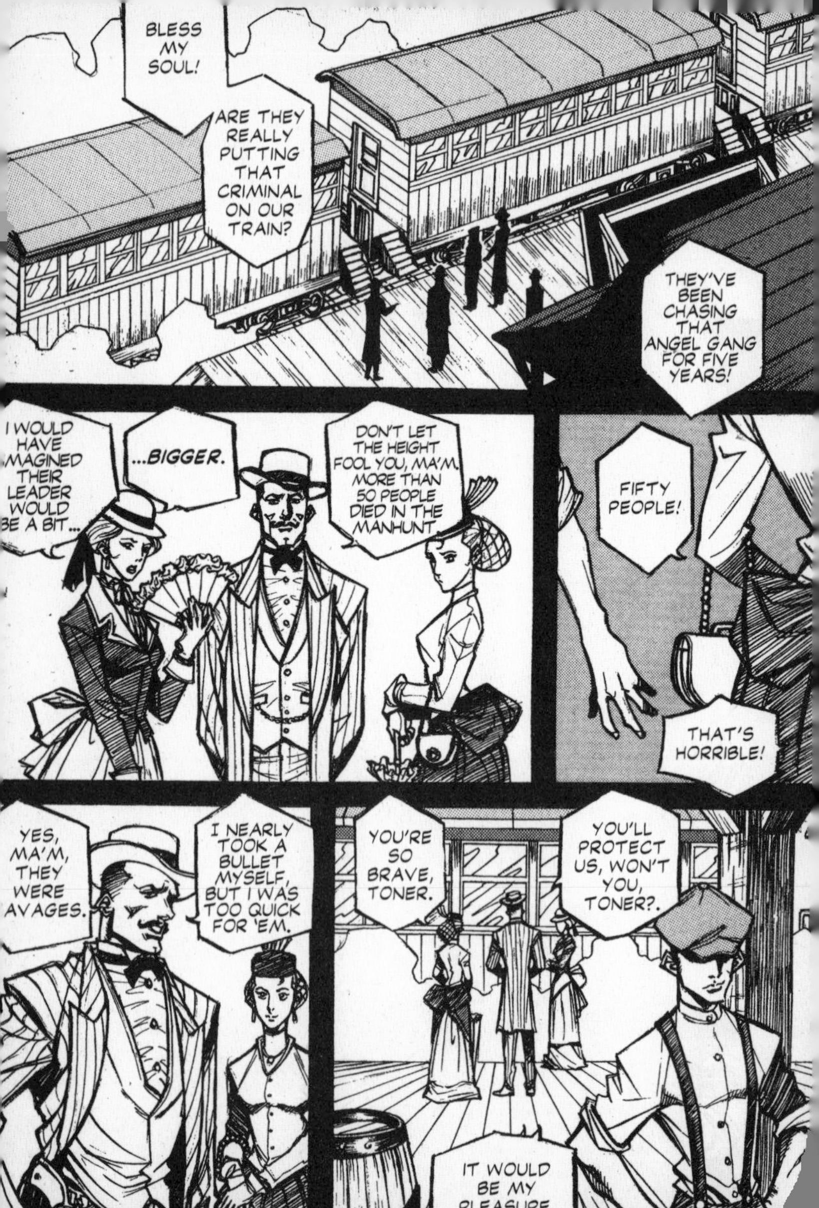
BLESS MY SOUL!
ARE THEY REALLY PUTTING THAT CRIMINAL ON OUR TRAIN?
THEY'VE BEEN CHASING THAT ANGEL GANG FOR FIVE YEARS!
I WOULD HAVE IMAGINED THEIR LEADER WOULD BE A BIT...
...BIGGER.
DON'T LET THE HEIGHT FOOL YOU, MA'M. MORE THAN 50 PEOPLE DIED IN THE MANHUNT.
FIFTY PEOPLE!
THAT'S HORRIBLE!
YES, MA'M, THEY WERE SAVAGES.
I NEARLY TOOK A BULLET MYSELF, BUT I WAS TOO QUICK FOR 'EM.
YOU'RE SO BRAVE, TONER.
YOU'LL PROTECT US, WON'T YOU, TONER?.
IT WOULD BE MY PLEASURE, LADIES.

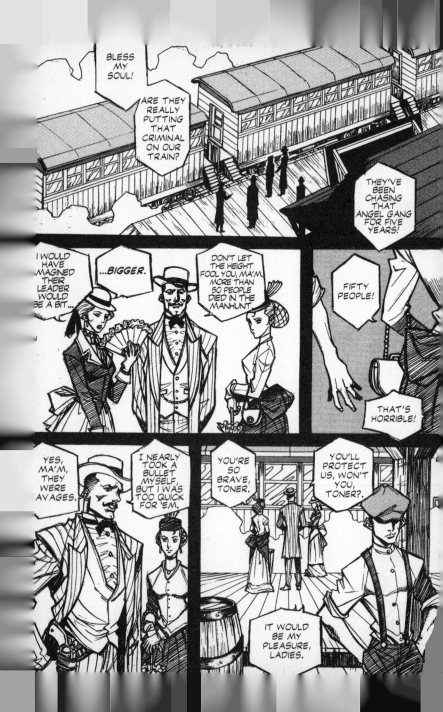

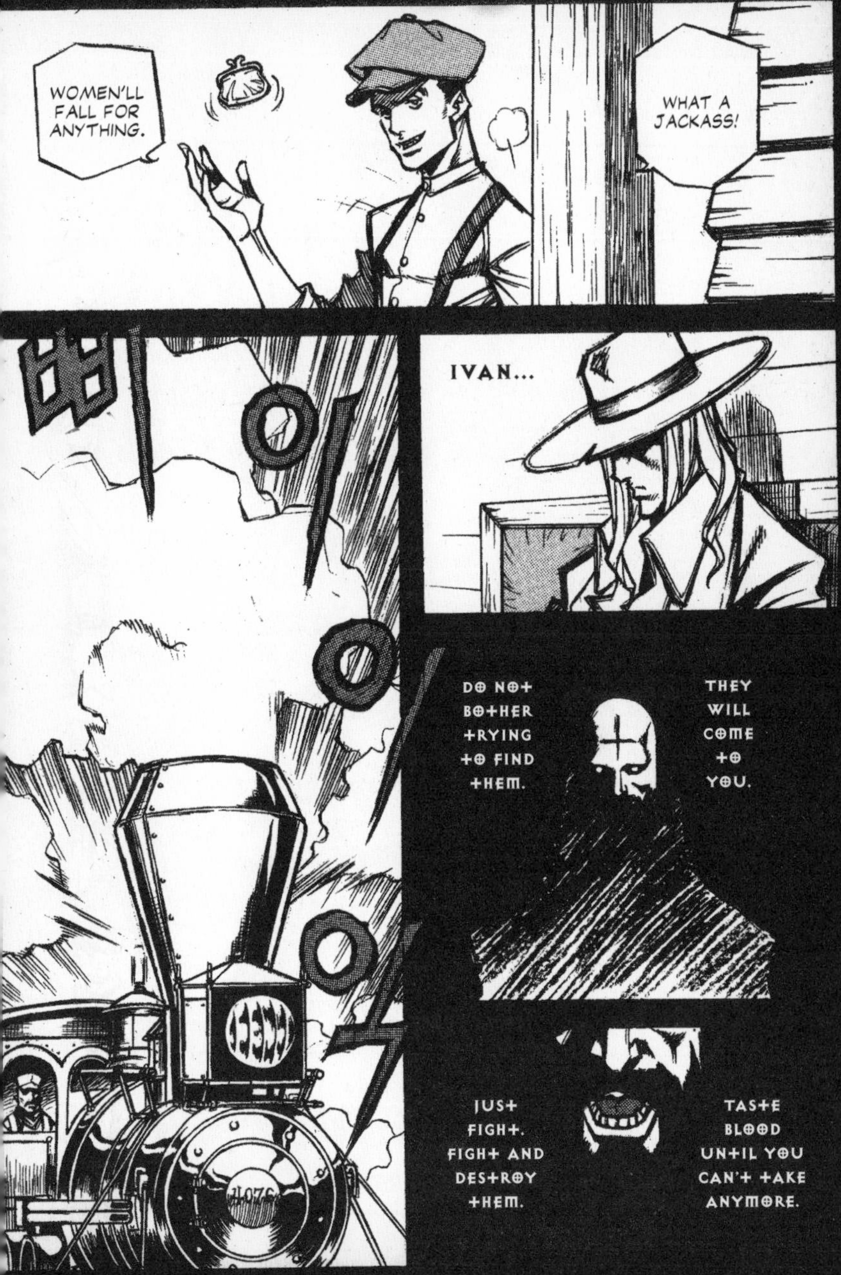
WOMEN'LL FALL FOR ANYTHING.
WHAT A JACKASS!
IVAN...
DO NOT BOTHER TRYING TO FIND THEM.
THEY WILL COME TO YOU.
JUST FIGHT. FIGHT AND DESTROY THEM.
TASTE BLOOD UNTIL YOU CAN'T TAKE ANYMORE.

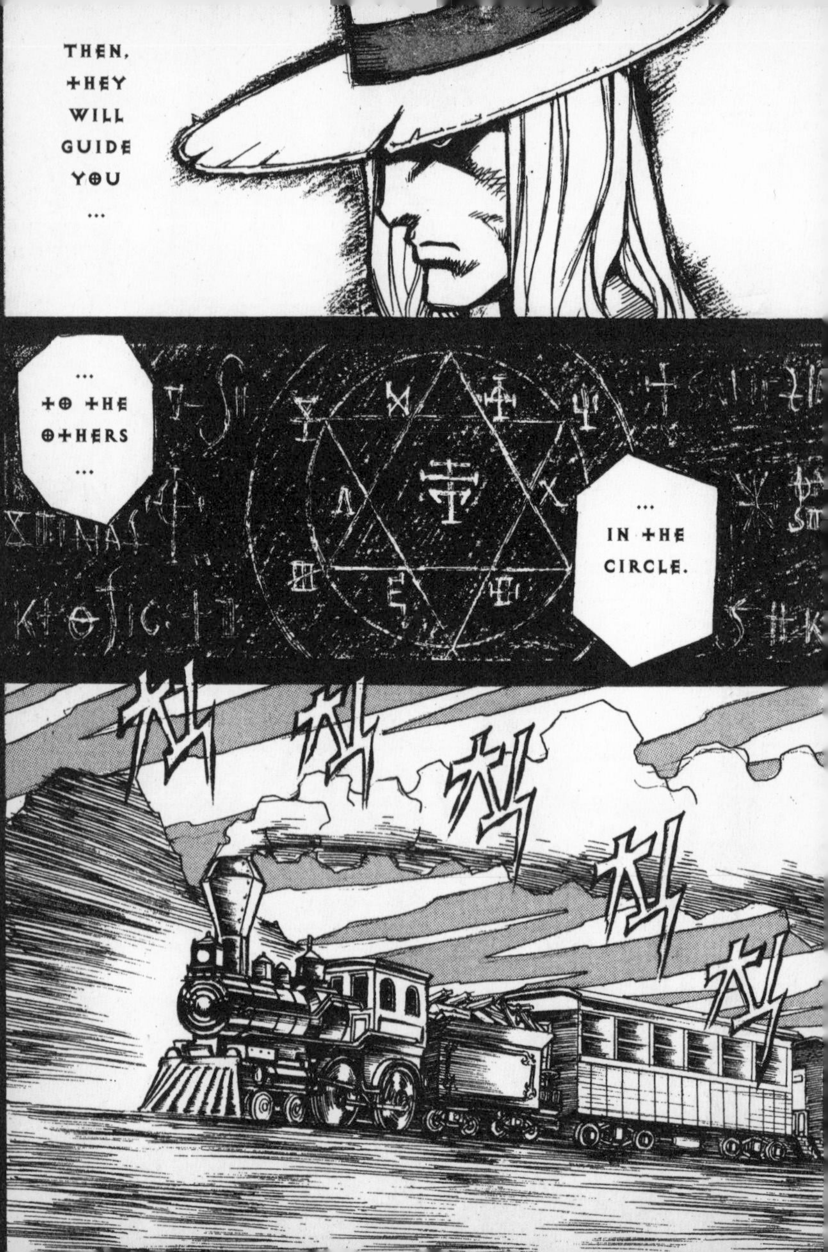
THEN, THEY WILL GUIDE YOU ...
... TO THE OTHERS ...
... IN THE CIRCLE.

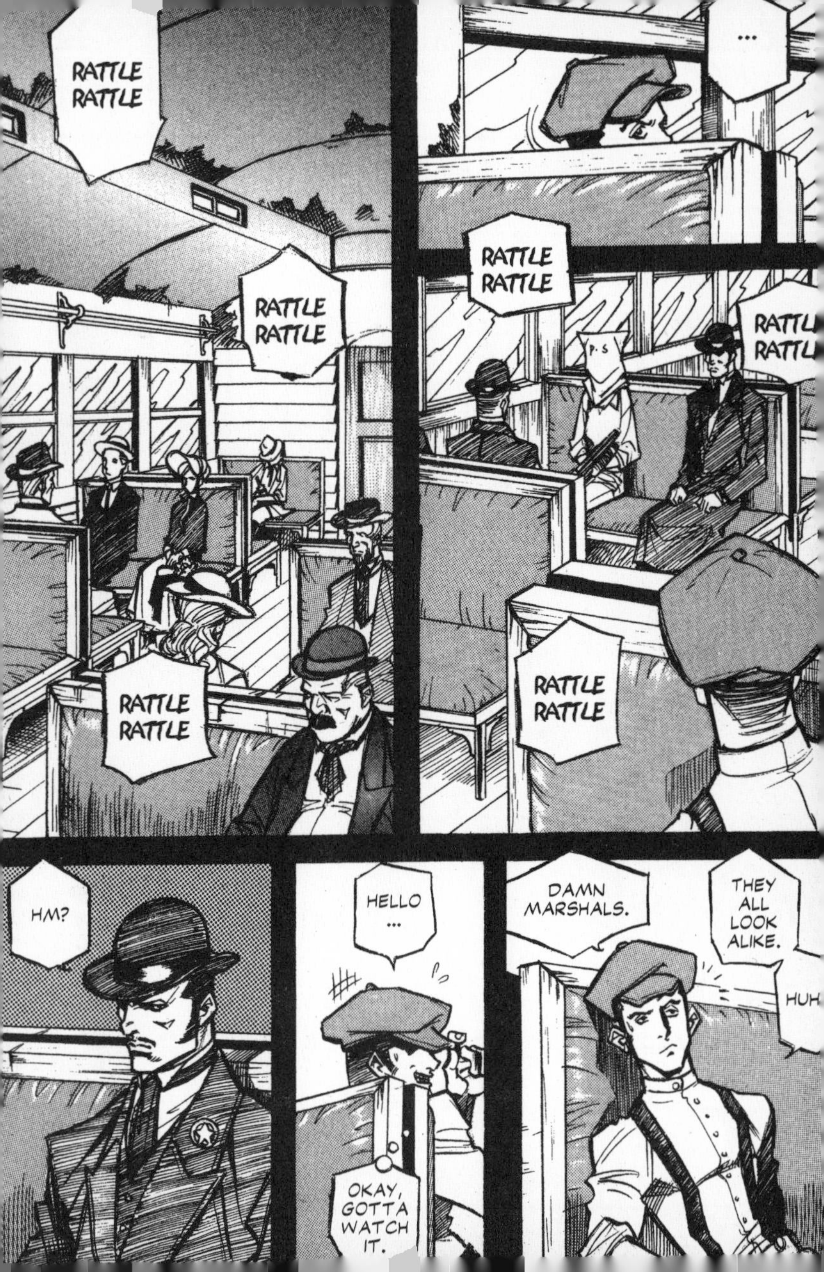
RATTLE RATTLE
RATTLE RATTLE
RATTLE RATTLE
...
RATTLE RATTLE
RATTL RATTL
RATTLE RATTLE
HM?
HELLO ...
OKAY, GOTTA WATCH IT.
DAMN MARSHALS.
THEY ALL LOOK ALIKE.
HUH

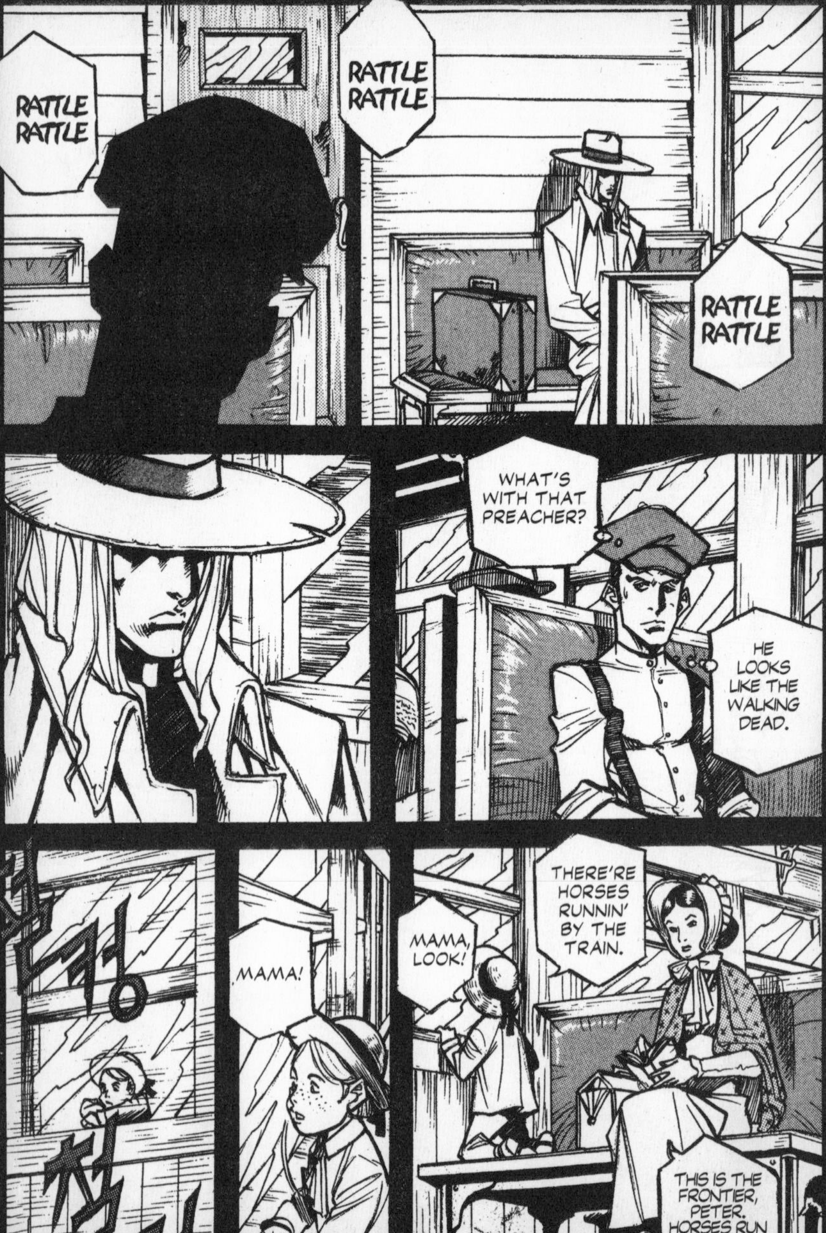
RATTLE RATTLE
RATTLE RATTLE
RATTLE RATTLE
WHAT'S WITH THAT PREACHER?
HE LOOKS LIKE THE WALKING DEAD.
MAMA!
MAMA, LOOK!
THERE'RE HORSES RUNNIN' BY THE TRAIN.
THIS IS THE FRONTIER, PETER. HORSES RUN WILD OUT HERE.

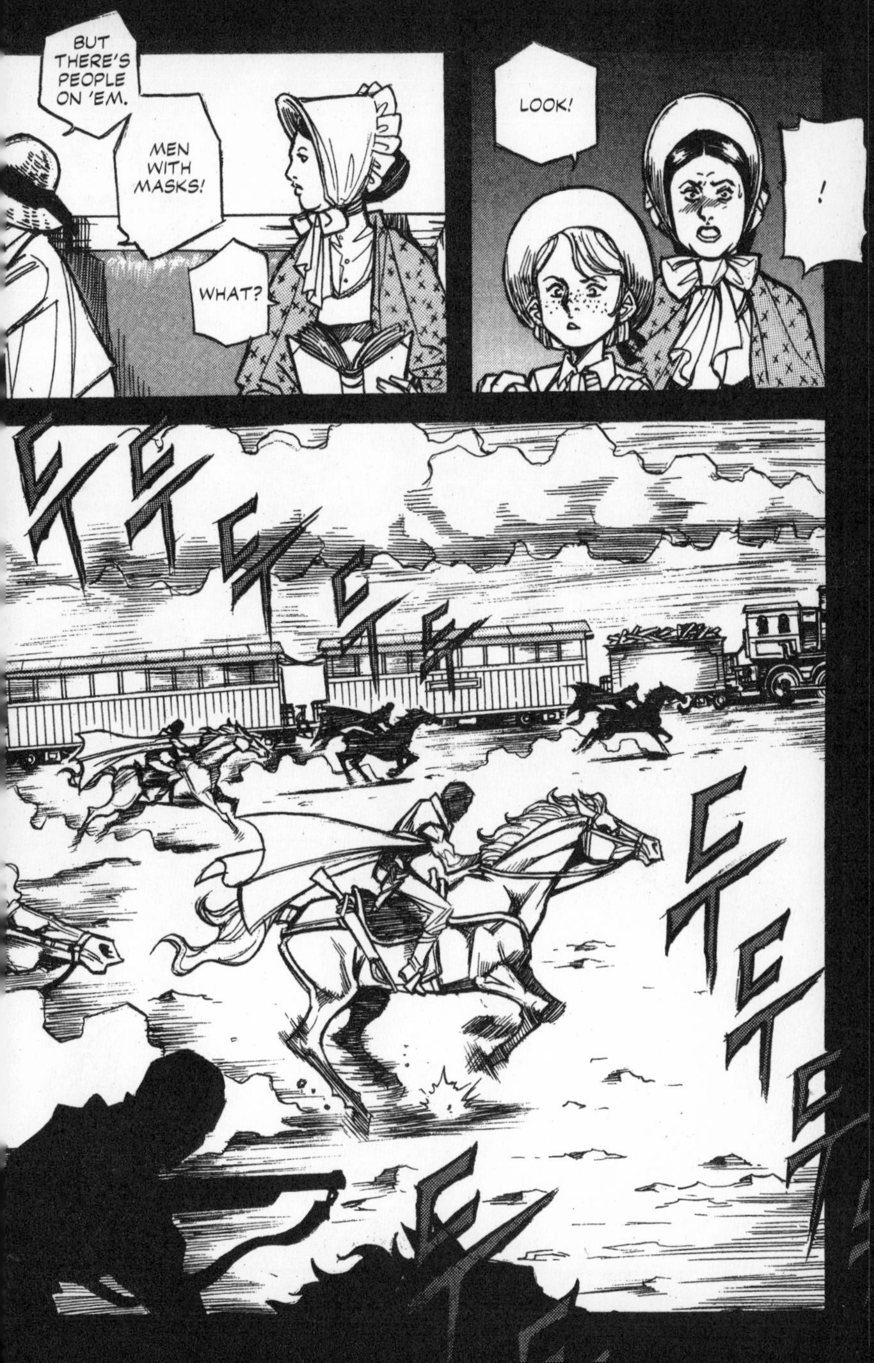
BUT THERE'S PEOPLE ON 'EM.
MEN WITH MASKS!
WHAT?
LOOK!
!

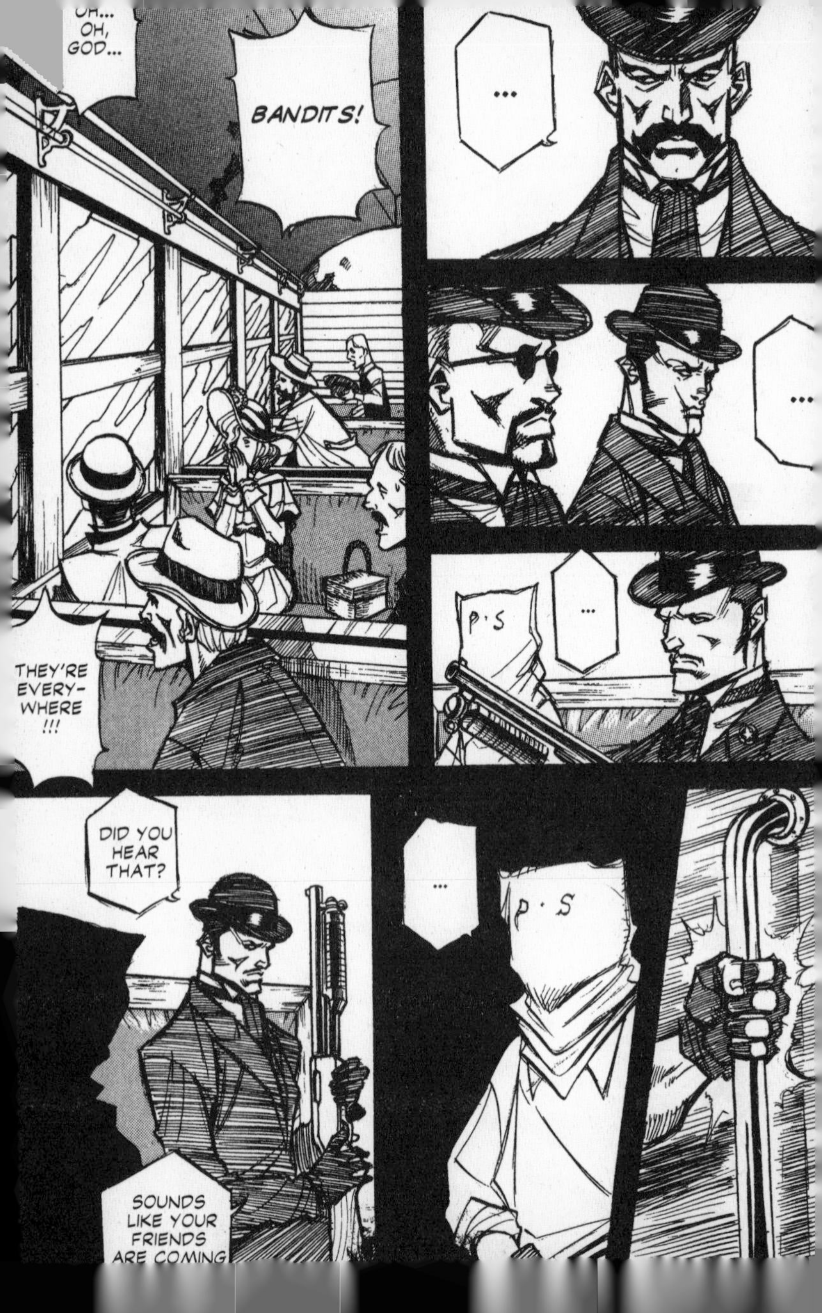
OH... OH, GOD...
BANDITS!
THEY'RE EVERY-WHERE !!!
...
...
P·S
...
DID YOU HEAR THAT?
SOUNDS LIKE YOUR FRIENDS ARE COMING
...
P·S

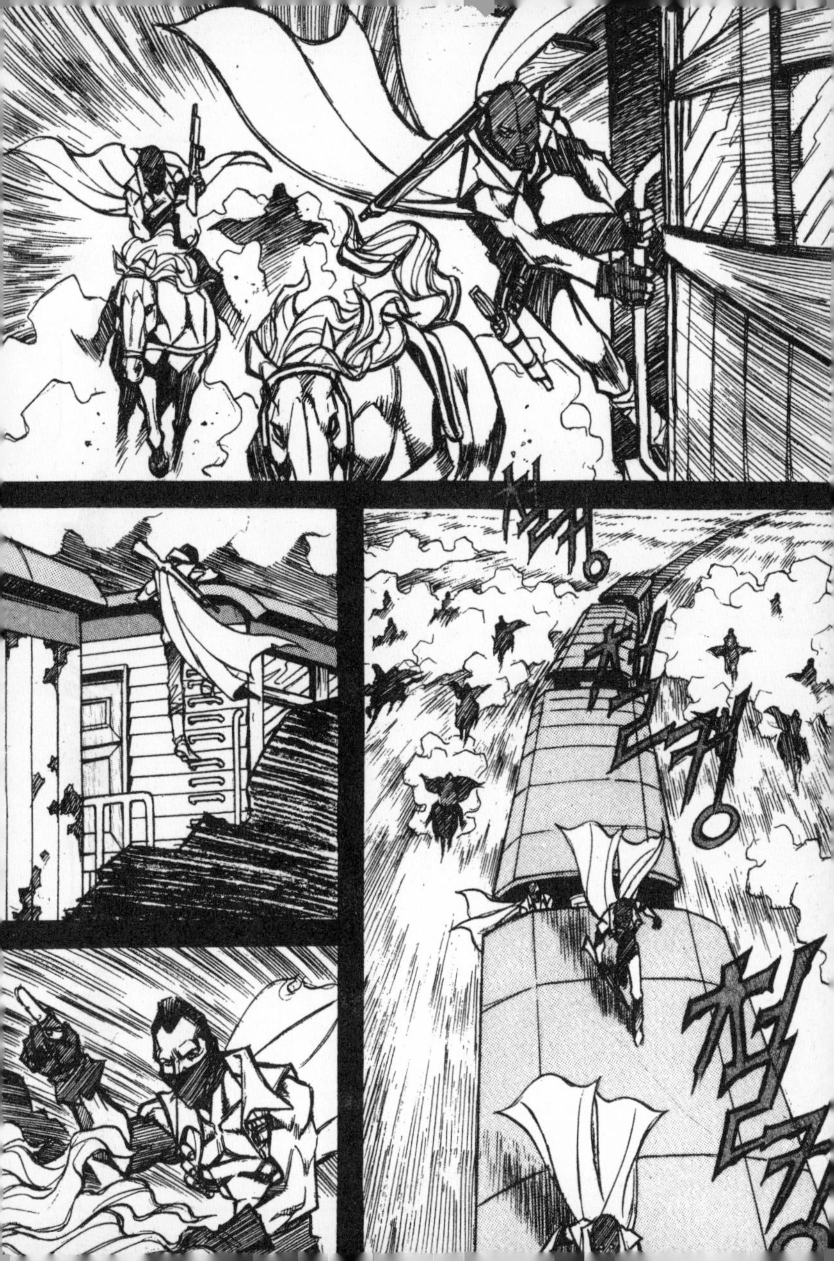

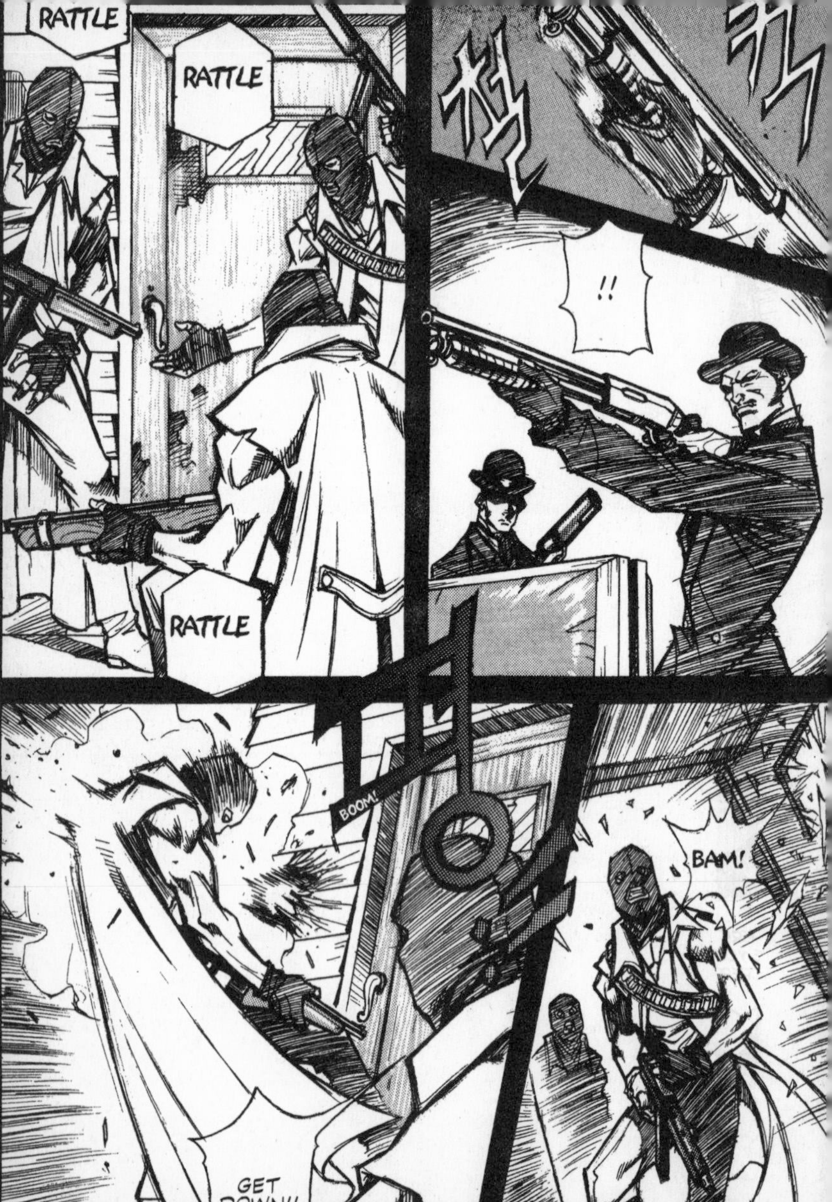
RATTLE
RATTLE
RATTLE
!!
BOOM!
GET DOWN!!
BAM!

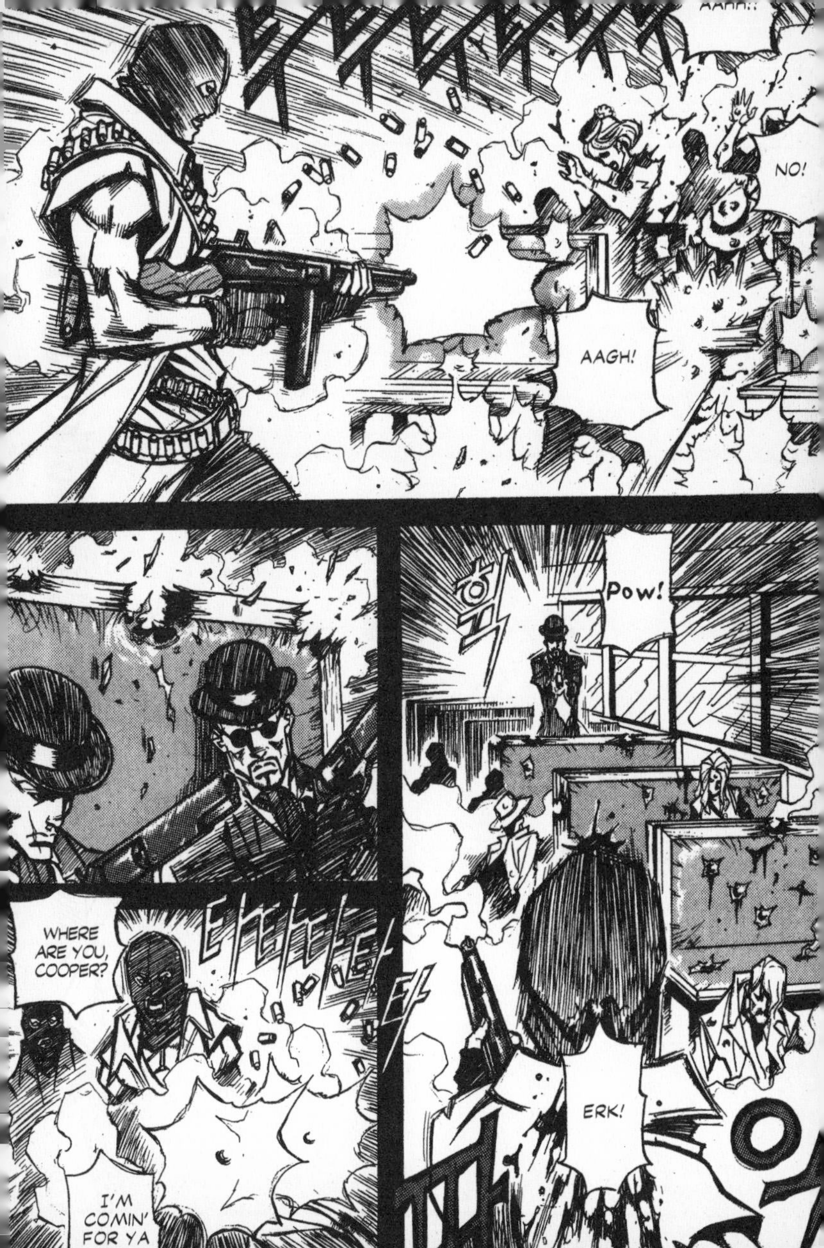
AAHH!!
NO!
AAGH!
WHERE ARE YOU, COOPER?
I'M COMIN' FOR YA
Pow!
ERK!

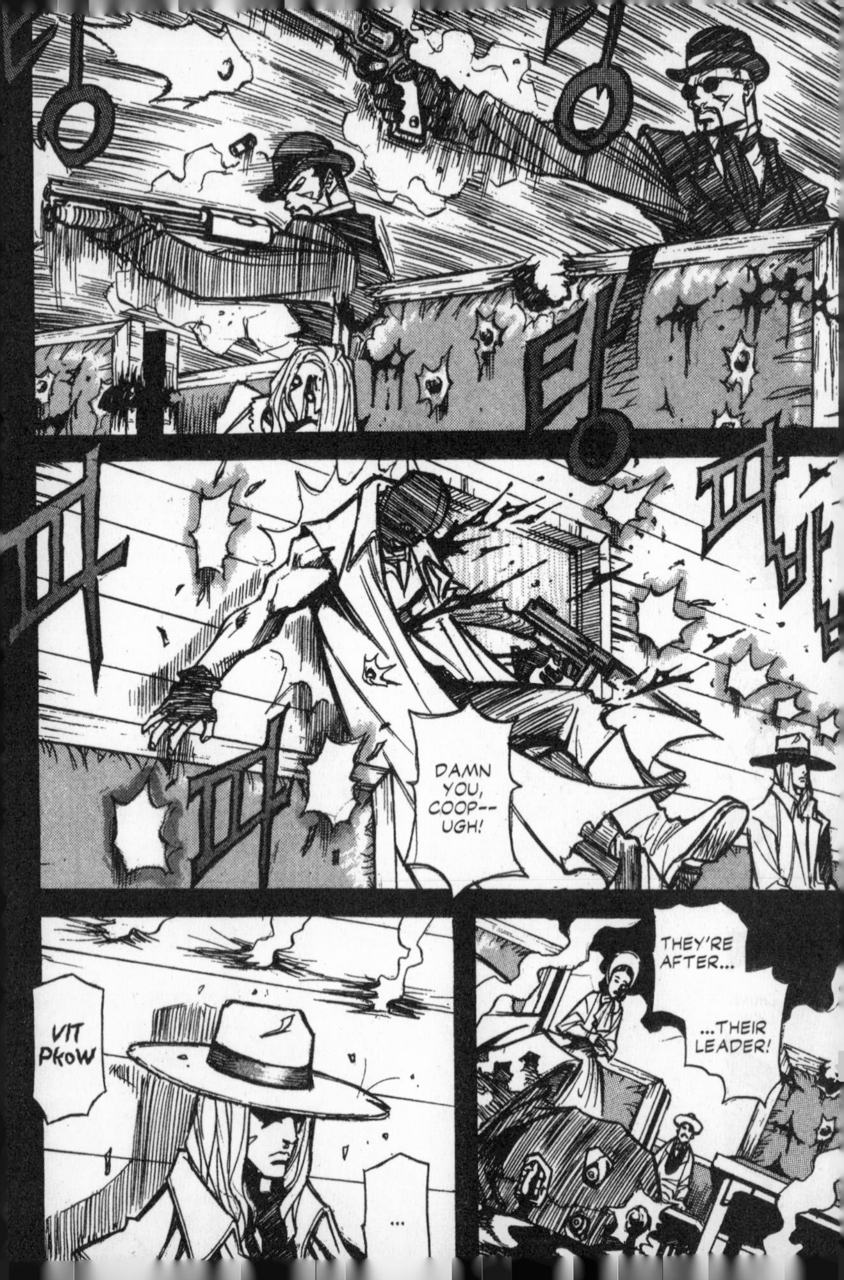
DAMN YOU, COOP-- UGH!
VIT PKOW
...
THEY'RE AFTER...
...THEIR LEADER!

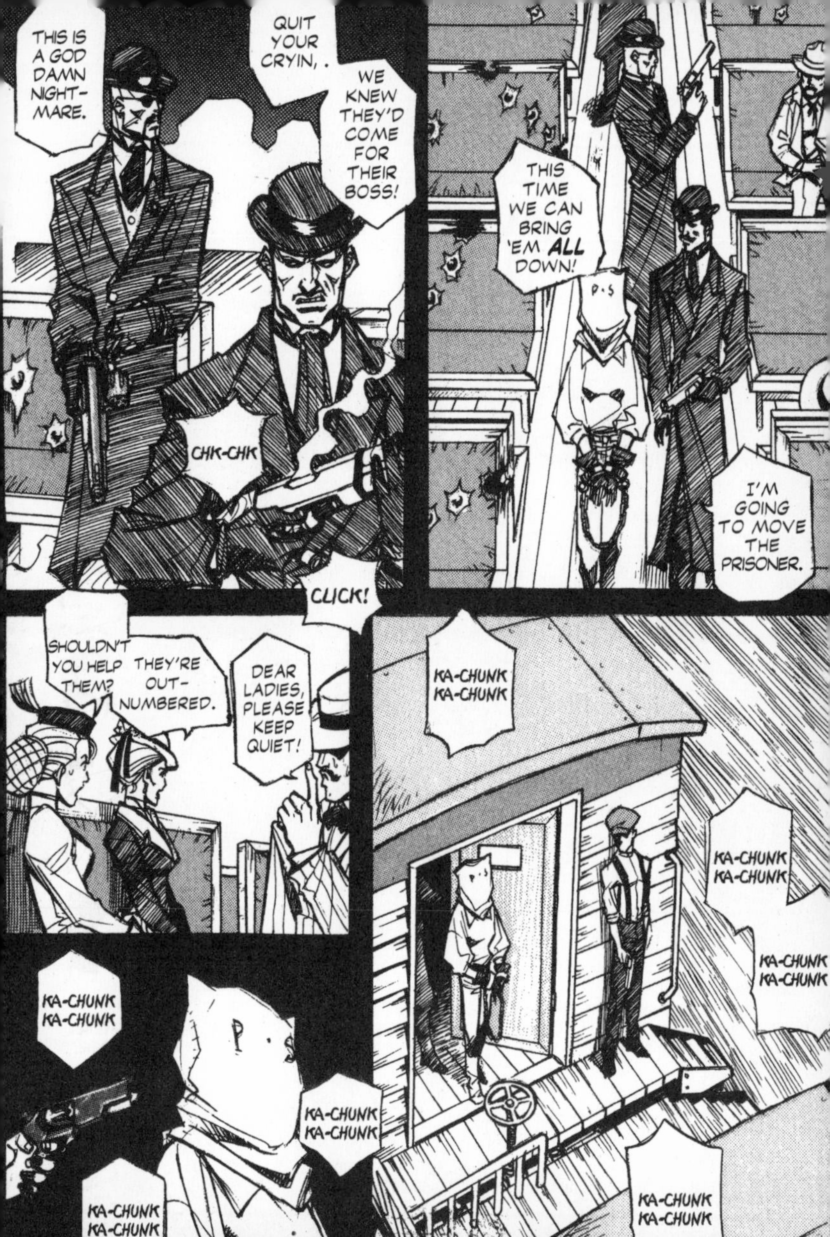
THIS IS A GOD DAMN NIGHT-MARE.
QUIT YOUR CRYIN, .
WE KNEW THEY'D COME FOR THEIR BOSS!
CHK-CHK
CLICK!
THIS TIME WE CAN BRING 'EM ALL DOWN!
P·S
I'M GOING TO MOVE THE PRISONER.
SHOULDN'T YOU HELP THEM?
THEY'RE OUT-NUMBERED.
DEAR LADIES, PLEASE KEEP QUIET!
KA-CHUNK KA-CHUNK
P·S
KA-CHUNK KA-CHUNK
KA-CHUNK KA-CHUNK
KA-CHUNK KA-CHUNK
P·S
KA-CHUNK KA-CHUNK
KA-CHUNK KA-CHUNK
KA-CHUNK KA-CHUNK

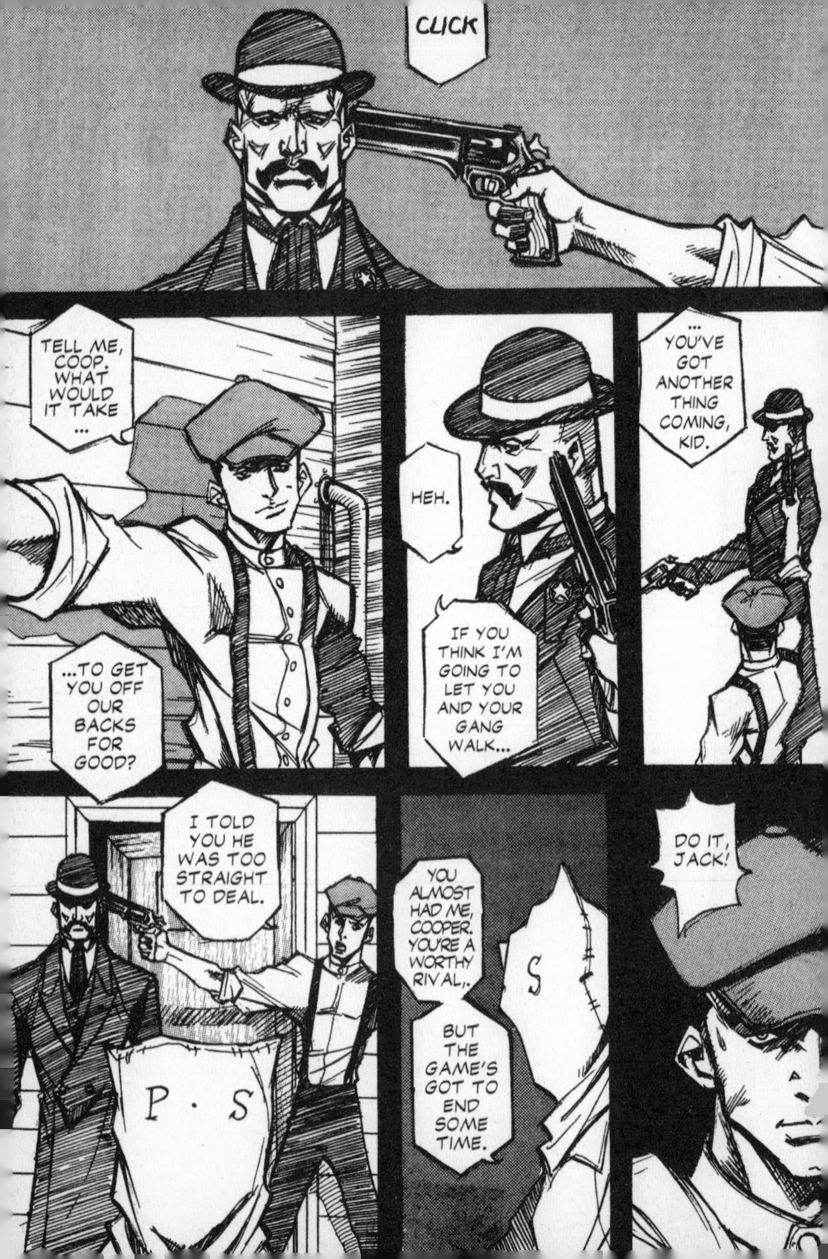
CLICK
TELL ME, COOP. WHAT WOULD IT TAKE ...
...TO GET YOU OFF OUR BACKS FOR GOOD?
HEH.
IF YOU THINK I'M GOING TO LET YOU AND YOUR GANG WALK...
... YOU'VE GOT ANOTHER THING COMING, KID.
I TOLD YOU HE WAS TOO STRAIGHT TO DEAL.
P · S
YOU ALMOST HAD ME, COOPER. YOU'RE A WORTHY RIVAL,.
BUT THE GAME'S GOT TO END SOME TIME.
S
DO IT, JACK!

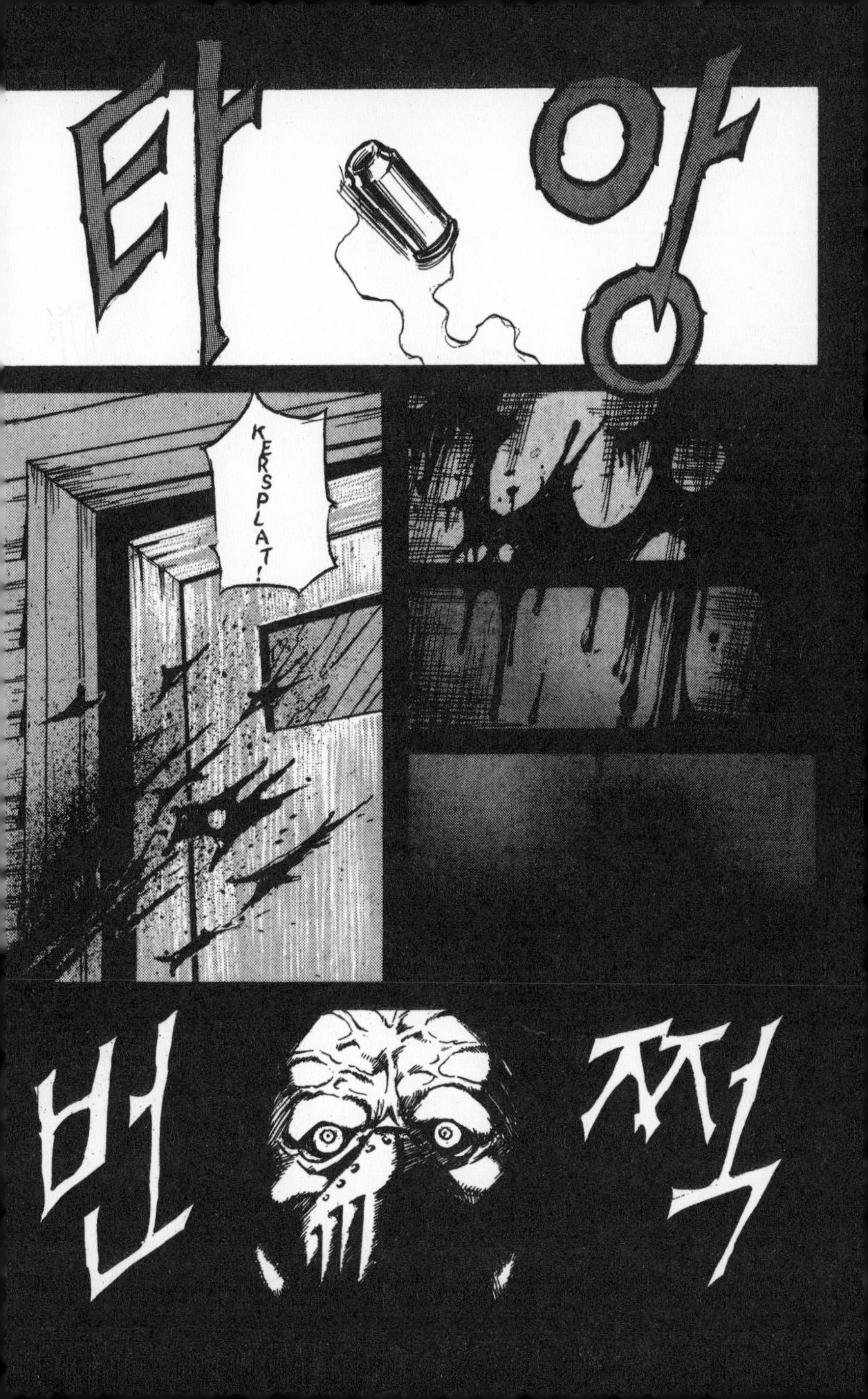
타앙
KERSPLAT!
번쩍

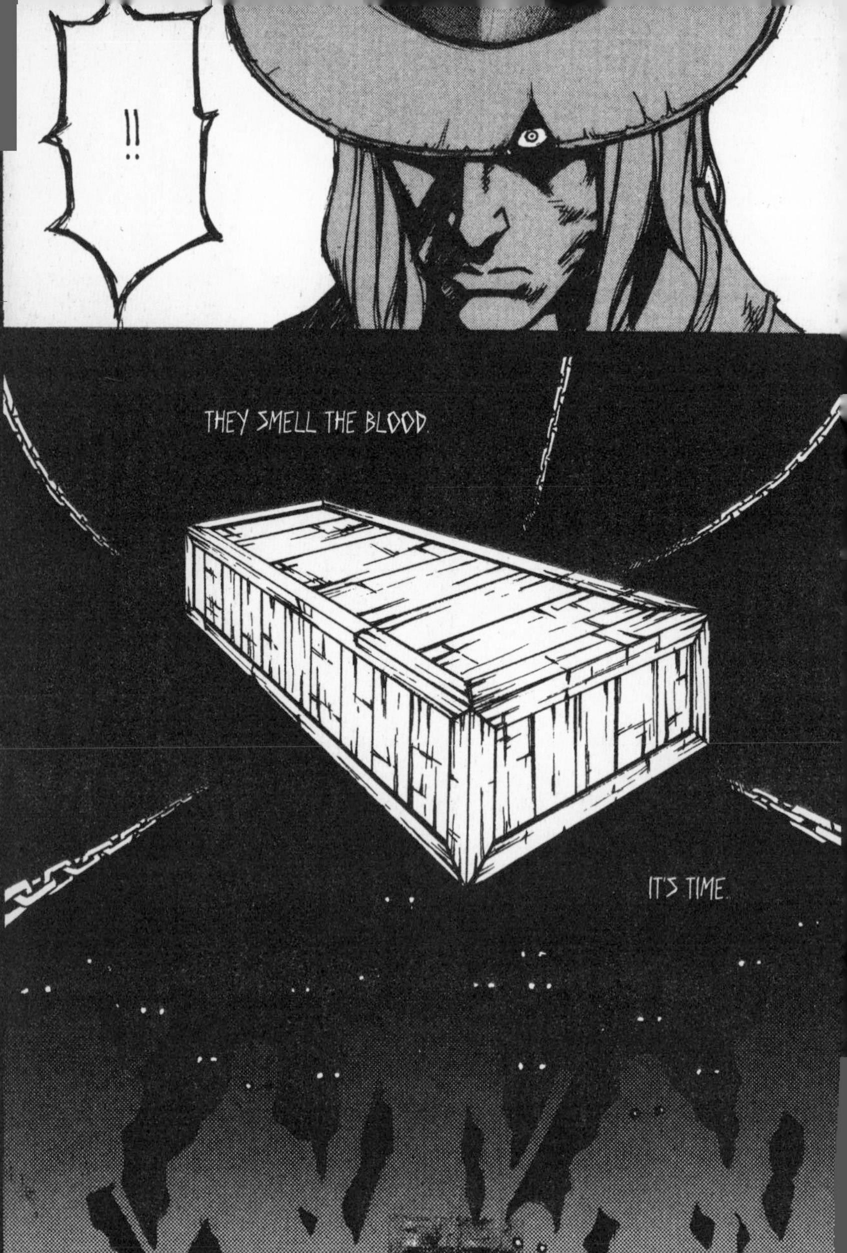
!!
THEY SMELL THE BLOOD.
IT'S TIME.

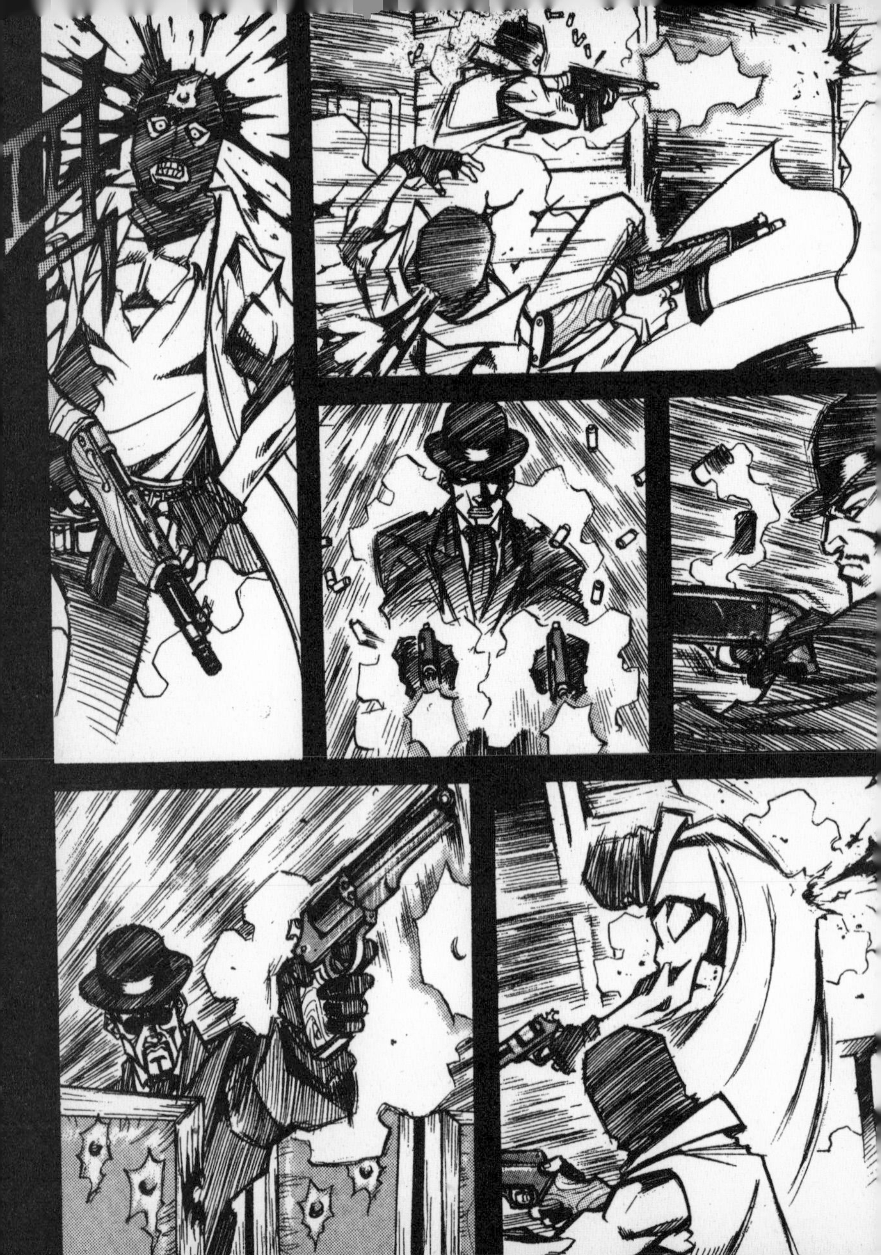

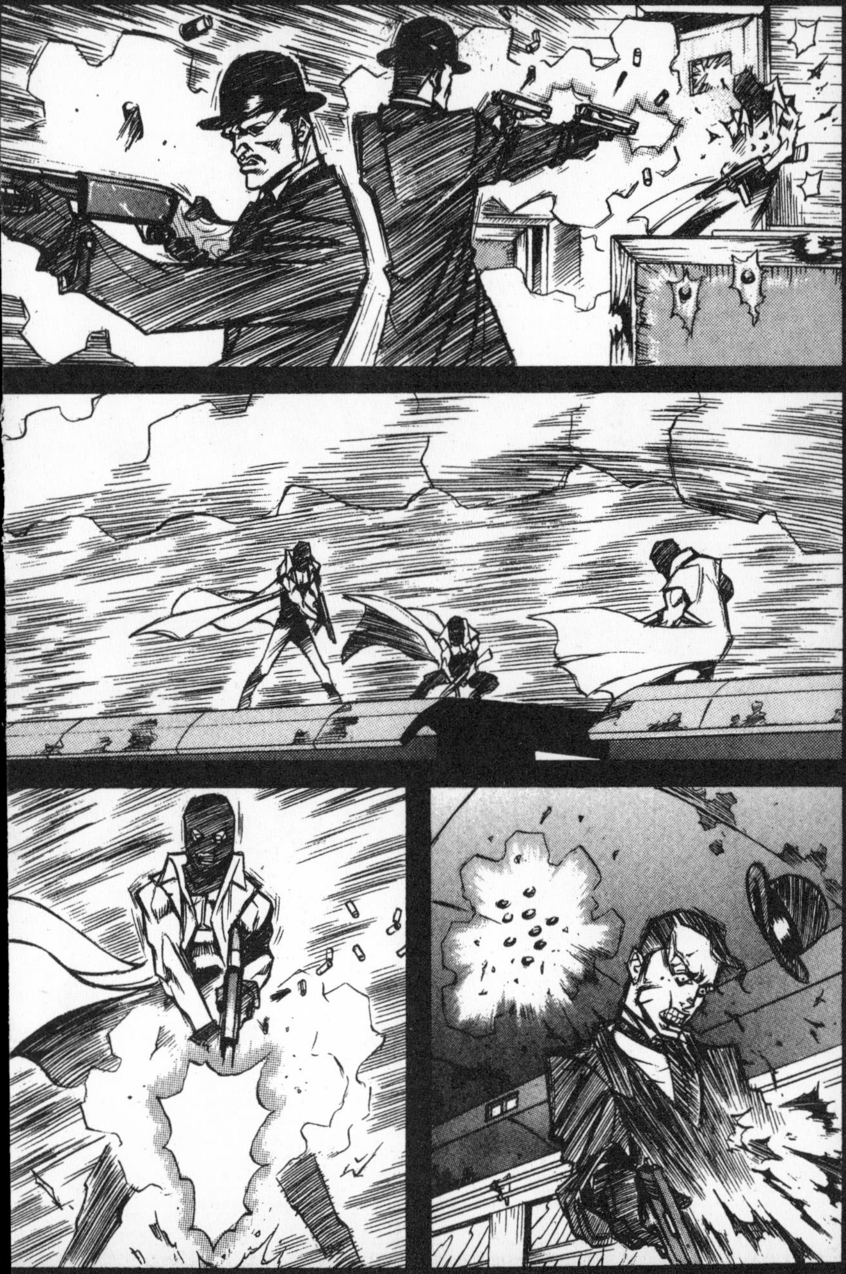

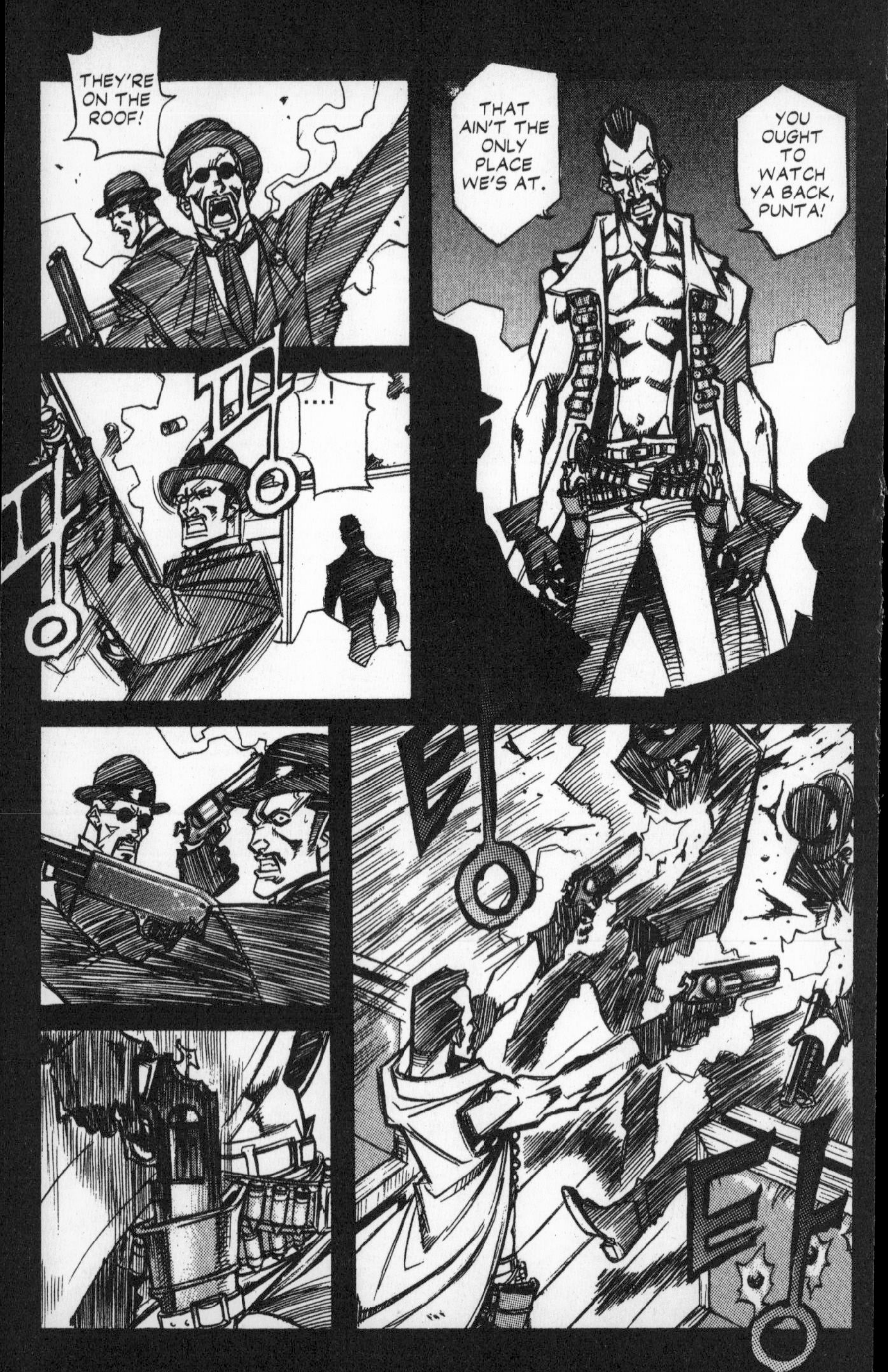
THEY'RE ON THE ROOF!
...!
THAT AIN'T THE ONLY PLACE WE'S AT.
YOU OUGHT TO WATCH YA BACK, PUNTA!

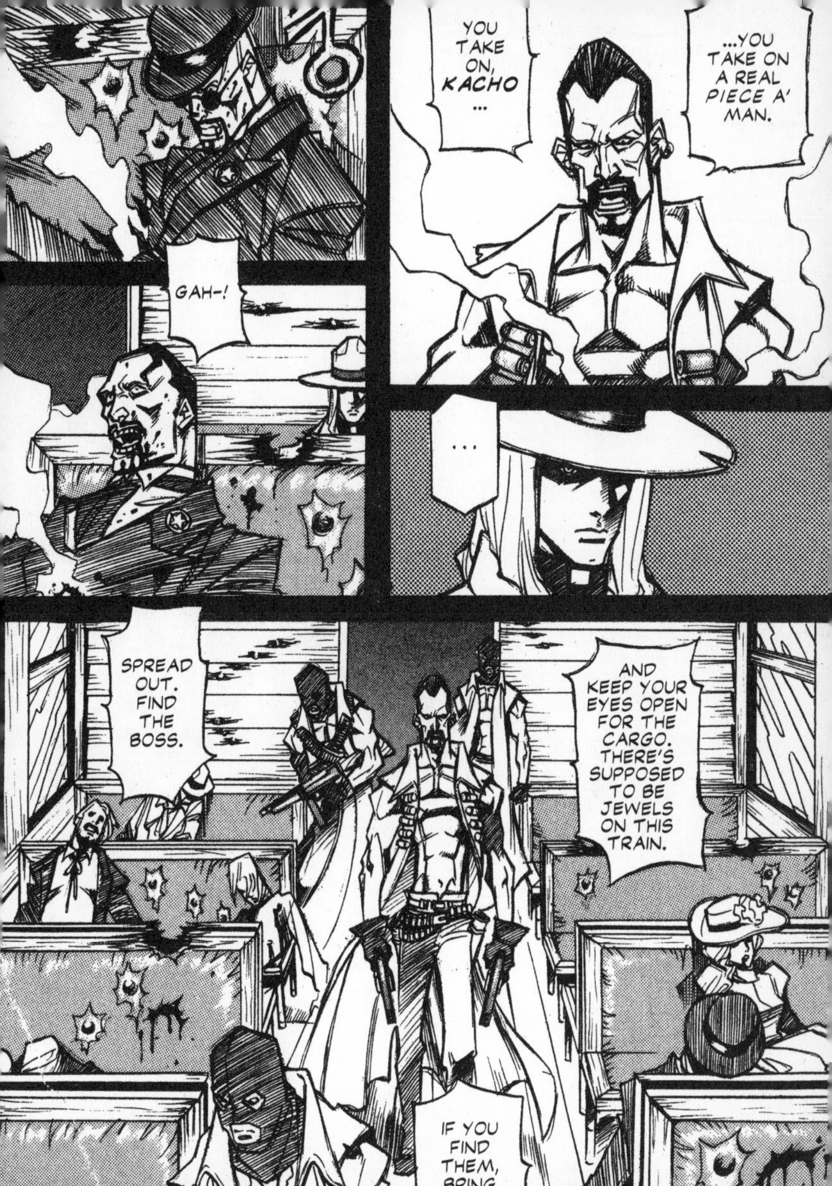
GAH-!
YOU TAKE ON, KACHO ...
...YOU TAKE ON A REAL PIECE A' MAN.
...
SPREAD OUT. FIND THE BOSS.
AND KEEP YOUR EYES OPEN FOR THE CARGO. THERE'S SUPPOSED TO BE JEWELS ON THIS TRAIN.
IF YOU FIND THEM, BRING 'EM TO ME.

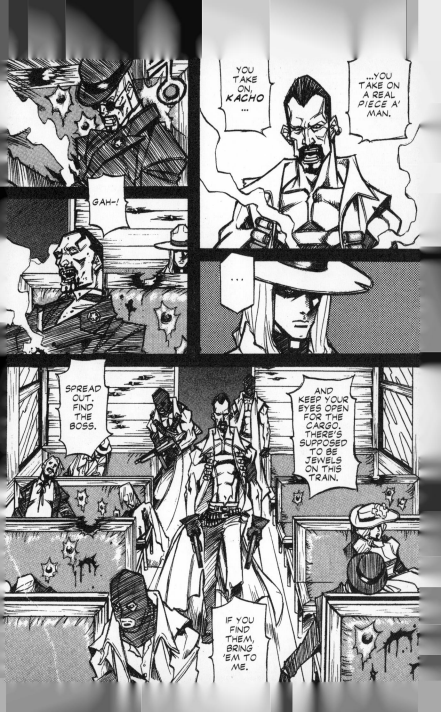

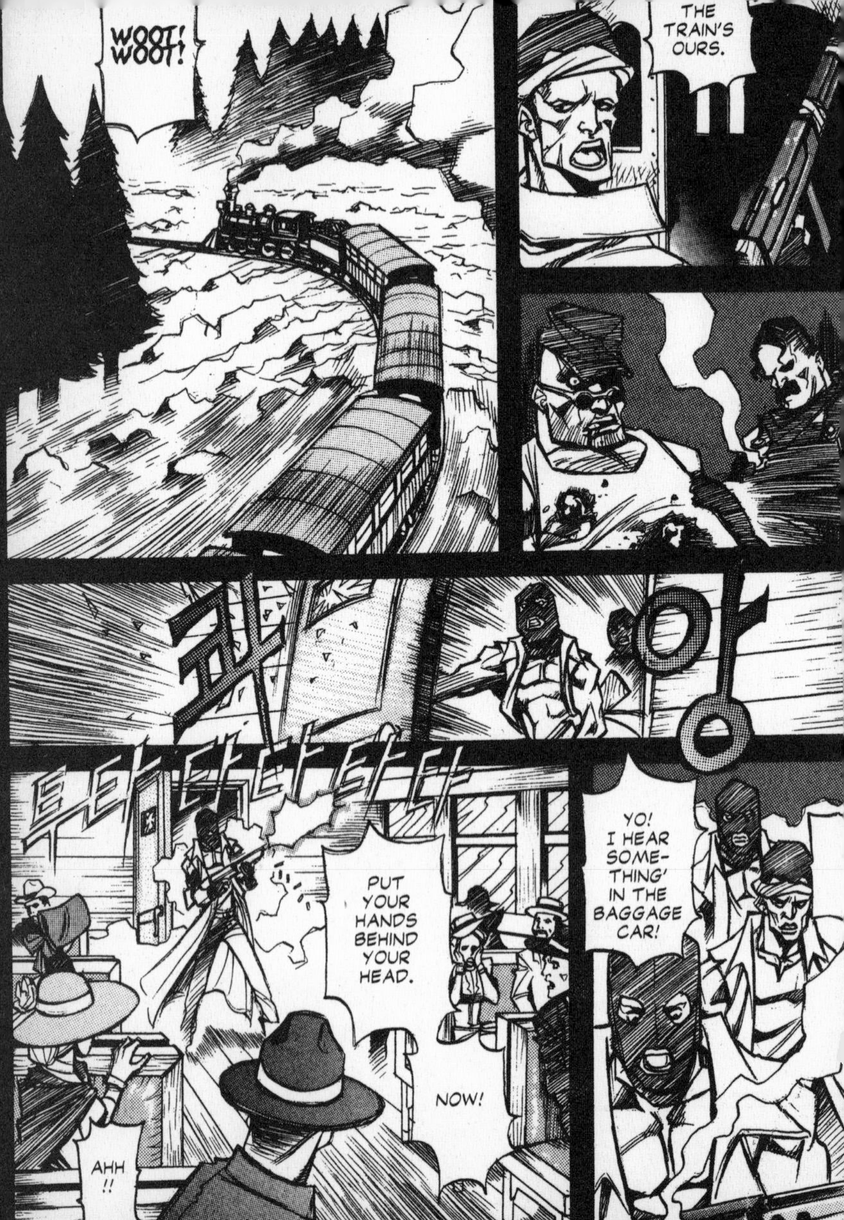

WOOT! WOOT!
THE TRAIN'S OURS.
PUT YOUR HANDS BEHIND YOUR HEAD.
NOW!
AHH!!
YO! I HEAR SOME-THING' IN THE BAGGAGE CAR!

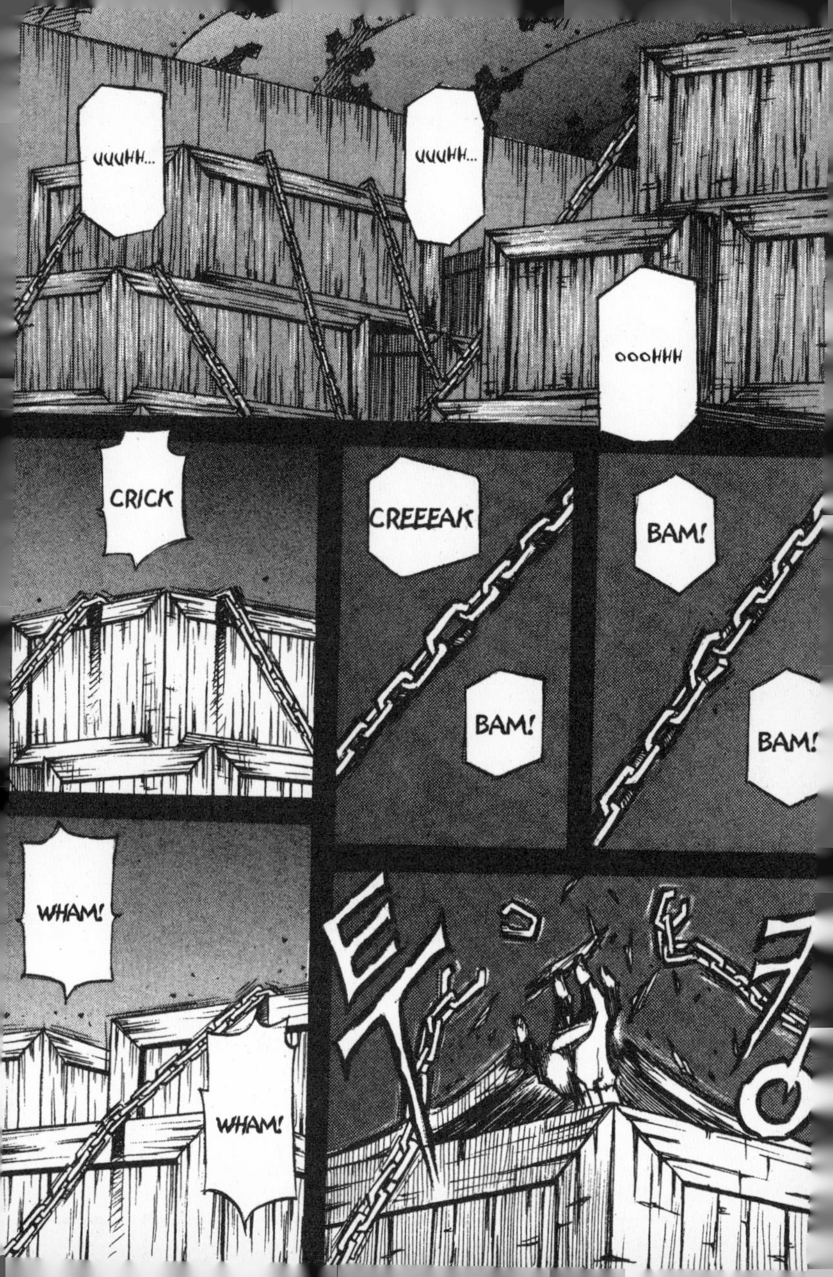
UUUHH...
UUUHH...
oooHHH
CRICK
CREEEAK
BAM!
BAM!
BAM!
WHAM!
WHAM!

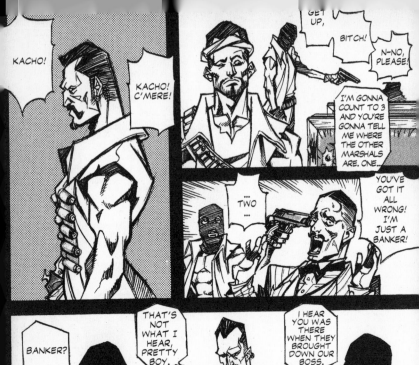

KACHO!

KACHO! C'MERE!

GET UP, BITCH!

N-NO, PLEASE!

I'M GONNA COUNT TO 3 AND YOU'RE GONNA TELL ME WHERE THE OTHER MARSHALS ARE. ONE...

... TWO ...

YOU'VE GOT IT ALL WRONG! I'M JUST A BANKER!

BANKER?

THAT'S NOT WHAT I HEAR, PRETTY BOY.

I HEAR YOU WAS THERE WHEN THEY BROUGHT DOWN OUR BOSS.

W-WHERE DID YOU HEAR THAT?

LADIES, PLEASE!

TELL HIM I'M JUST A BANKER!

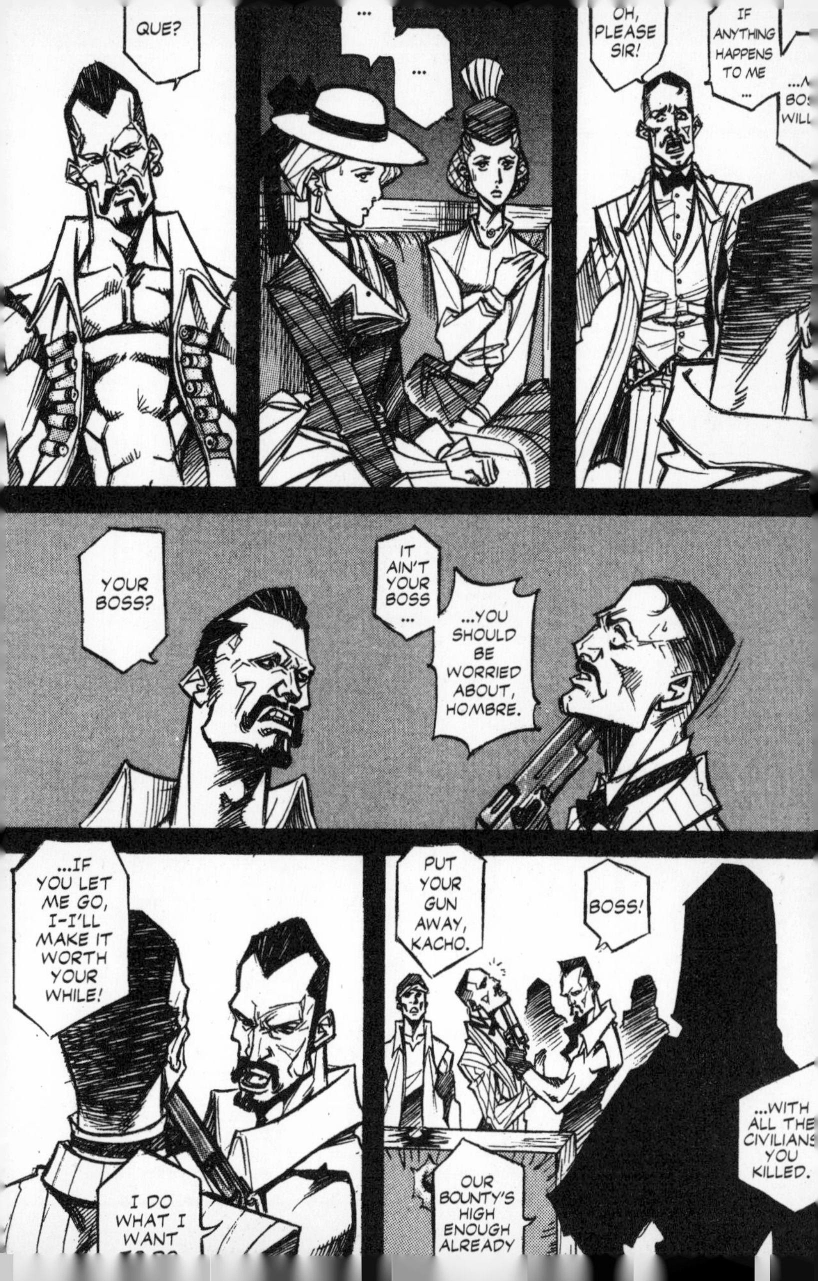
QUE?
...
...
OH, PLEASE SIR!
IF ANYTHING HAPPENS TO ME ...
YOUR BOSS?
IT AIN'T YOUR BOSS ...
...YOU SHOULD BE WORRIED ABOUT, HOMBRE.
...IF YOU LET ME GO, I-I'LL MAKE IT WORTH YOUR WHILE!
I DO WHAT I WANT
PUT YOUR GUN AWAY, KACHO.
BOSS!
OUR BOUNTY'S HIGH ENOUGH ALREADY
...WITH ALL THE CIVILIANS YOU KILLED.

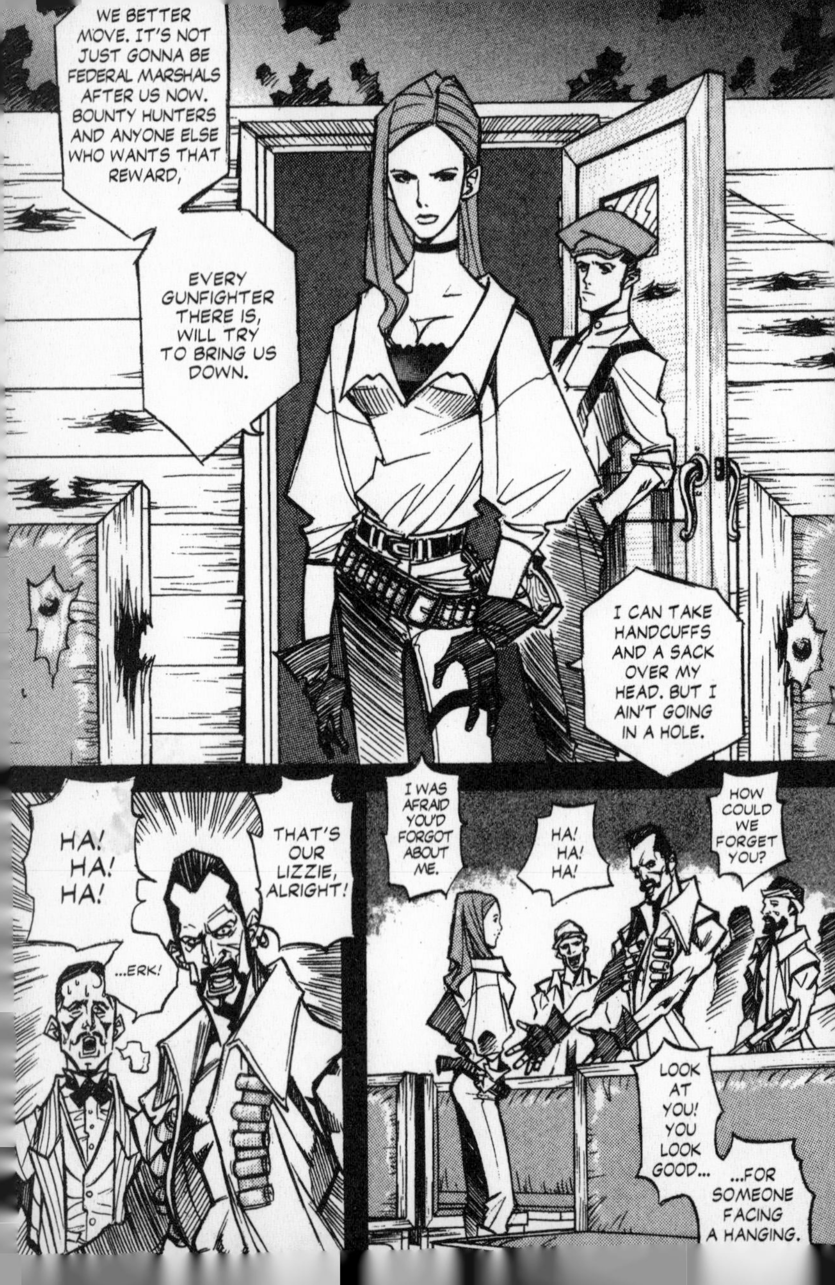
WE BETTER MOVE. IT'S NOT JUST GONNA BE FEDERAL MARSHALS AFTER US NOW. BOUNTY HUNTERS AND ANYONE ELSE WHO WANTS THAT REWARD,
EVERY GUNFIGHTER THERE IS, WILL TRY TO BRING US DOWN.
I CAN TAKE HANDCUFFS AND A SACK OVER MY HEAD. BUT I AIN'T GOING IN A HOLE.
HA! HA! HA!
THAT'S OUR LIZZIE, ALRIGHT!
...ERK!
I WAS AFRAID YOU'D FORGOT ABOUT ME.
HA! HA! HA!
HOW COULD WE FORGET YOU?
LOOK AT YOU! YOU LOOK GOOD...
...FOR SOMEONE FACING A HANGING.

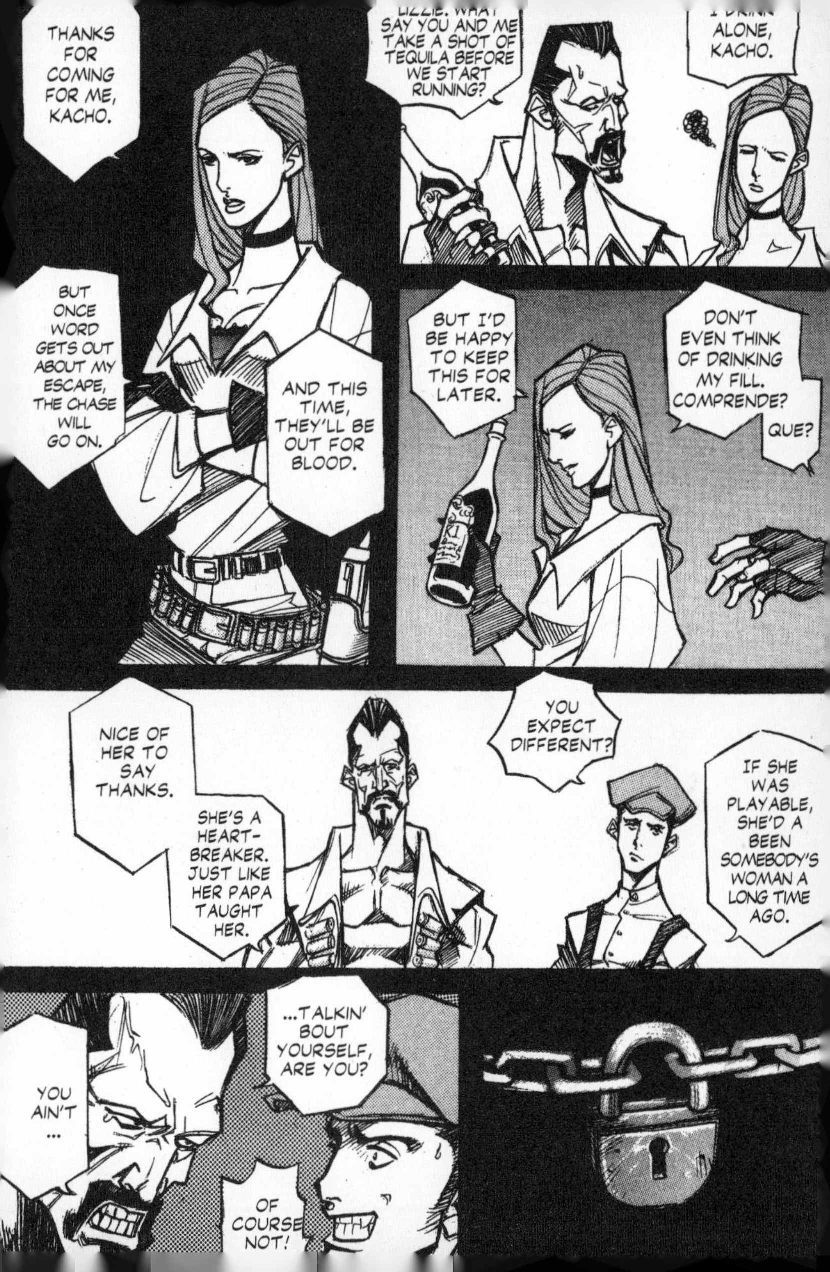
THANKS FOR COMING FOR ME, KACHO.
BUT ONCE WORD GETS OUT ABOUT MY ESCAPE, THE CHASE WILL GO ON.
AND THIS TIME, THEY'LL BE OUT FOR BLOOD.
SAY YOU AND ME TAKE A SHOT OF TEQUILA BEFORE WE START RUNNING?
ALONE, KACHO.
BUT I'D BE HAPPY TO KEEP THIS FOR LATER.
DON'T EVEN THINK OF DRINKING MY FILL. COMPRENDE?
QUE?
NICE OF HER TO SAY THANKS.
SHE'S A HEART-BREAKER. JUST LIKE HER PAPA TAUGHT HER.
YOU EXPECT DIFFERENT?
IF SHE WAS PLAYABLE, SHE'D A BEEN SOMEBODY'S WOMAN A LONG TIME AGO.
YOU AIN'T ...
...TALKIN' BOUT YOURSELF, ARE YOU?
OF COURSE NOT!

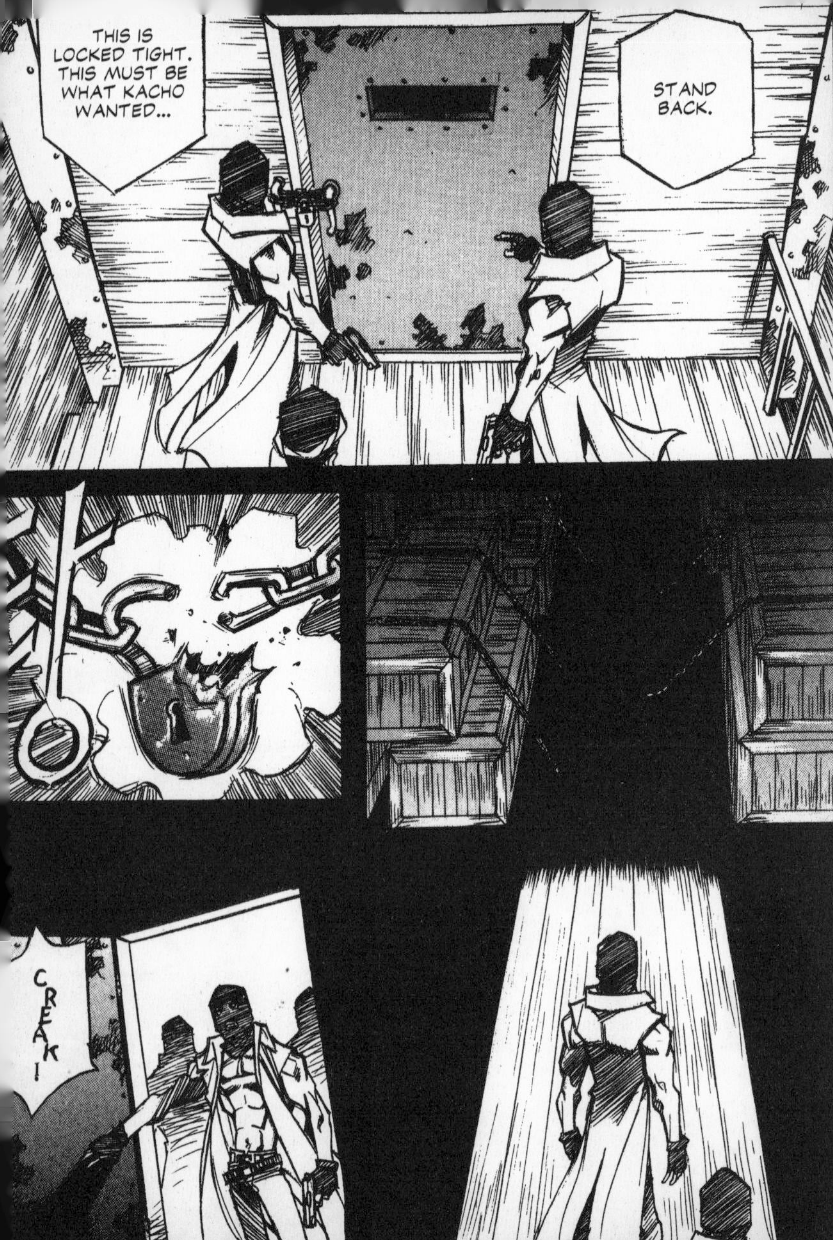
THIS IS LOCKED TIGHT. THIS MUST BE WHAT KACHO WANTED...
STAND BACK.
CREAK!

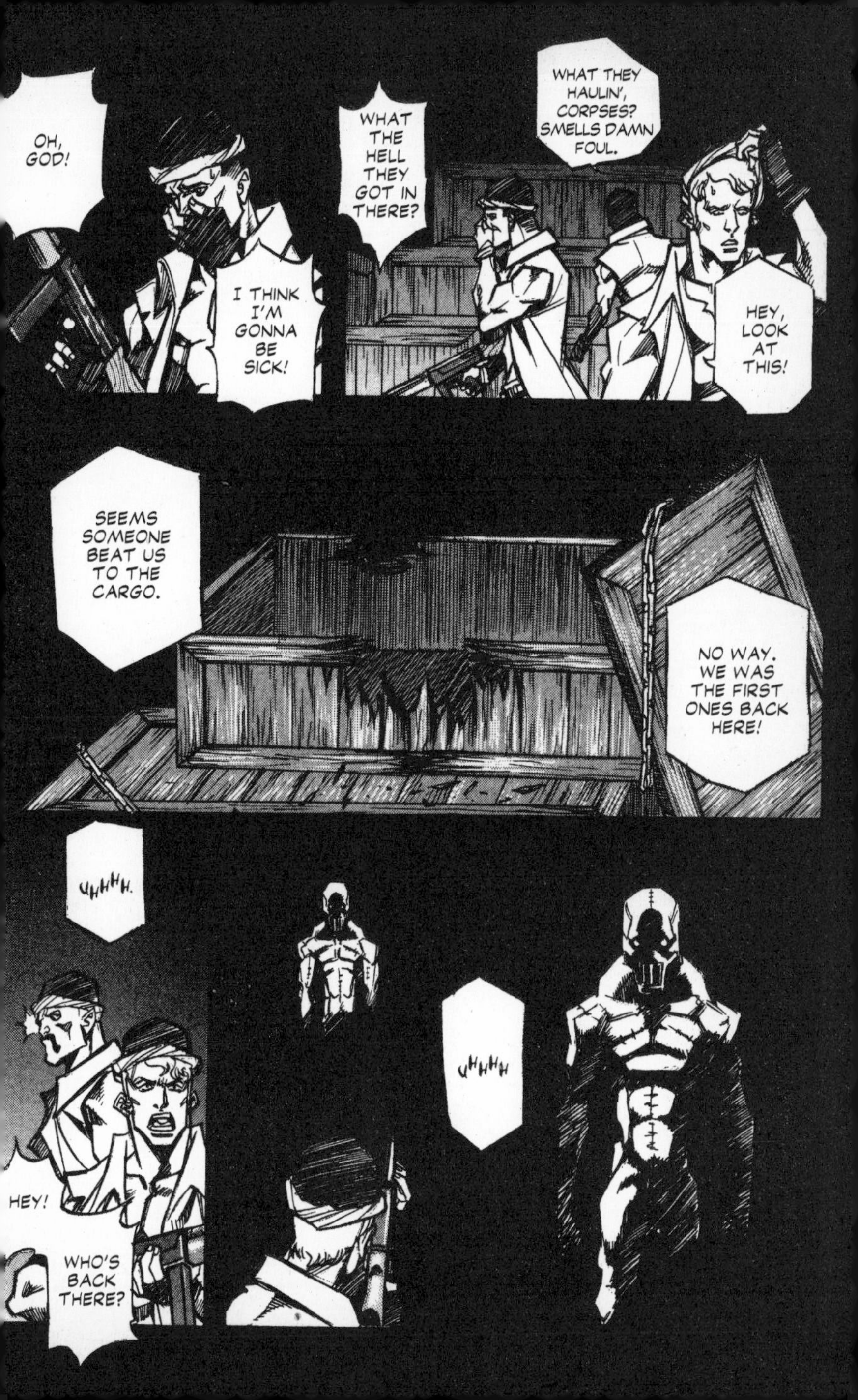
OH, GOD!
I THINK I'M GONNA BE SICK!
WHAT THE HELL THEY GOT IN THERE?
WHAT THEY HAULIN', CORPSES? SMELLS DAMN FOUL.
HEY, LOOK AT THIS!
SEEMS SOMEONE BEAT US TO THE CARGO.
NO WAY. WE WAS THE FIRST ONES BACK HERE!
UHHHH.
HEY!
WHO'S BACK THERE?
UHHHH

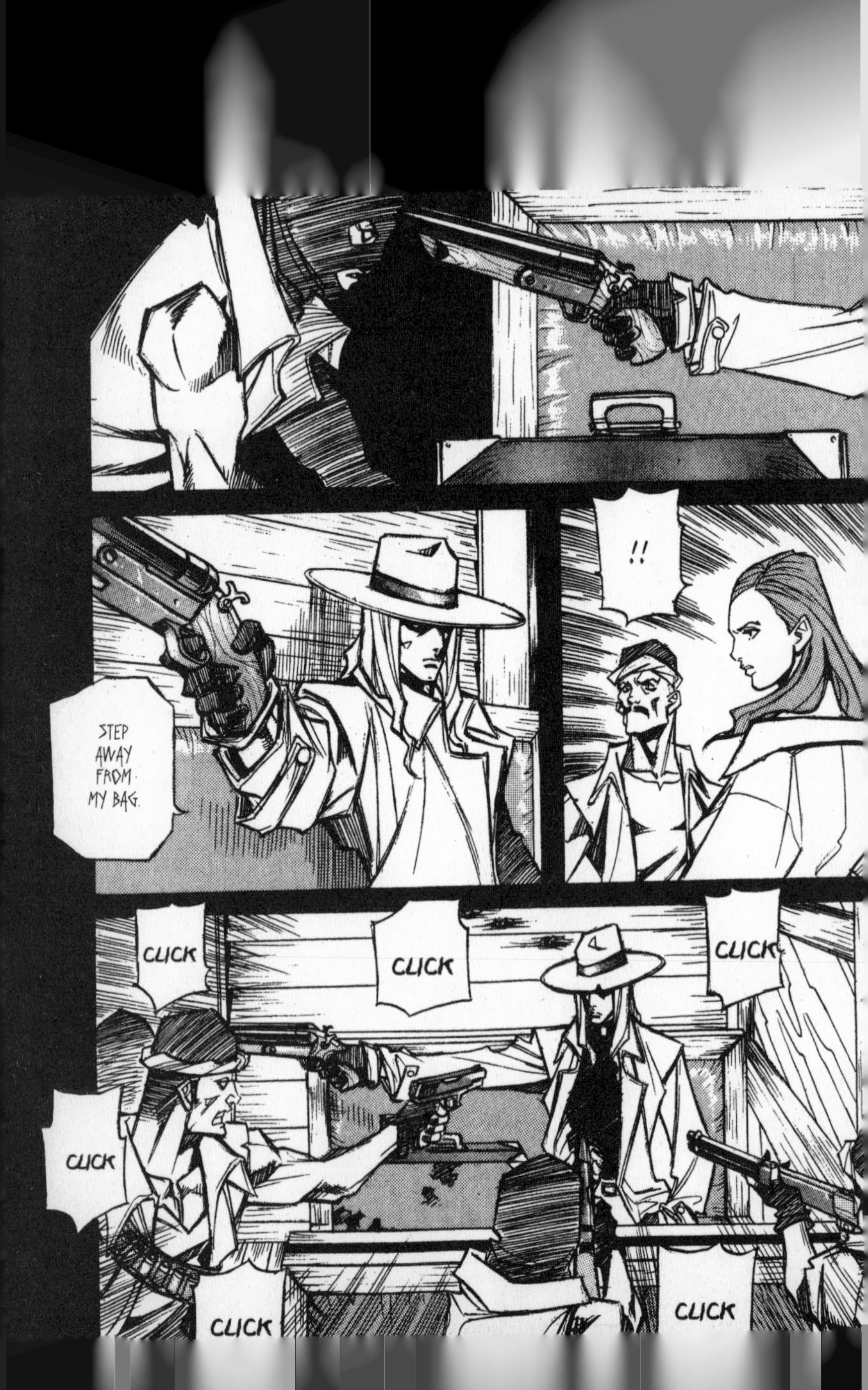
STEP AWAY FROM MY BAG.
!!
CLICK
CLICK
CLICK
CLICK
CLICK
CLICK

WHAT DO WE HAVE HERE?

I DIDN'T KNOW THE CHURCH WAS TRADING IN BIBLES FOR GUNS.

IF YOU DON'T WANT TO DIE...

...TAKE FLOCK LEAVE NO

I THOUGHT YOU WAS A PILGRIM, SO I WAS GONNA LEAVE YOU BE...

...BU KAC DON TA THRE FRO NO C

YOU WANT A *SERMON*, PREACHER MAN? I'LL GIVE YOU A SERMON.

SAY YOUR PRAYERS!

WA

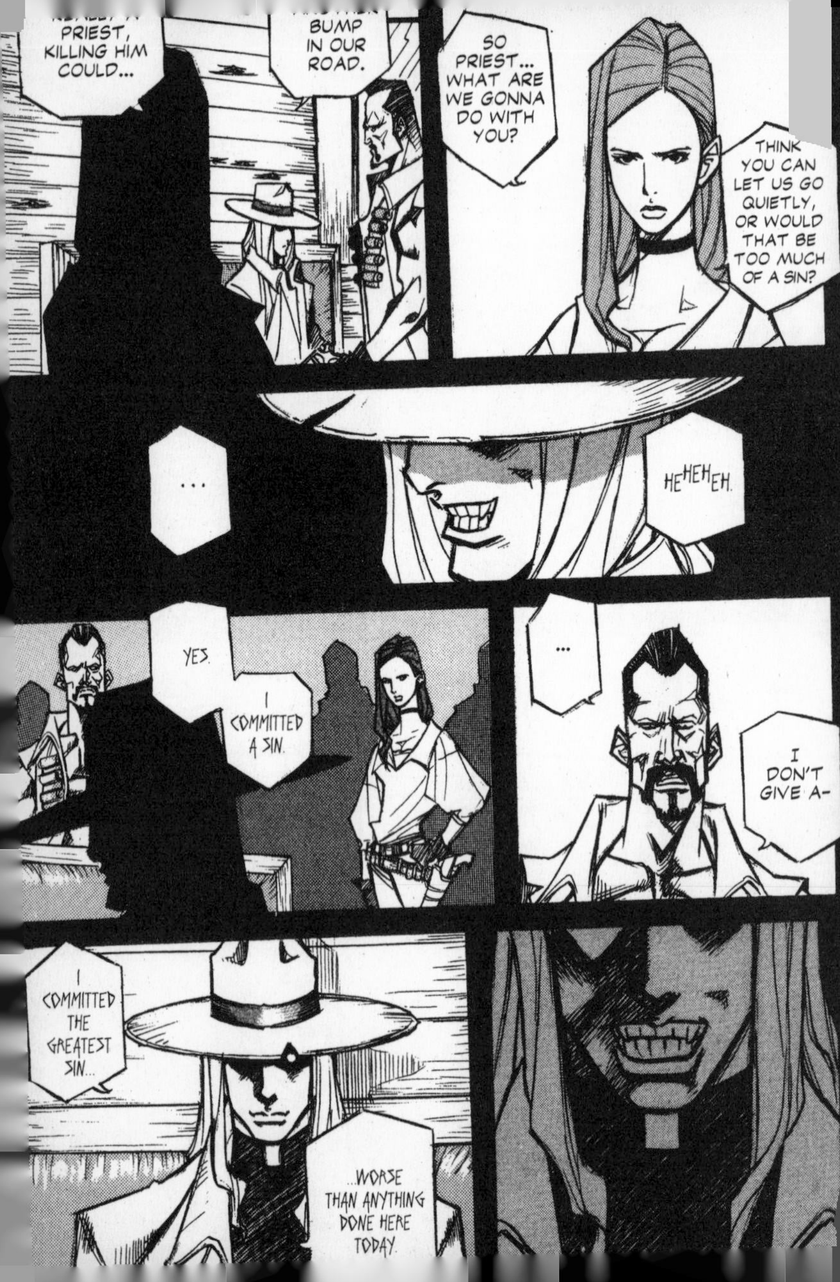

PRIEST, KILLING HIM COULD...
BUMP IN OUR ROAD.
SO PRIEST... WHAT ARE WE GONNA DO WITH YOU?
THINK YOU CAN LET US GO QUIETLY, OR WOULD THAT BE TOO MUCH OF A SIN?
...
HEHEHEH.
YES.
I COMMITTED A SIN.
...
I DON'T GIVE A-
I COMMITTED THE GREATEST SIN...
...WORSE THAN ANYTHING DONE HERE TODAY.

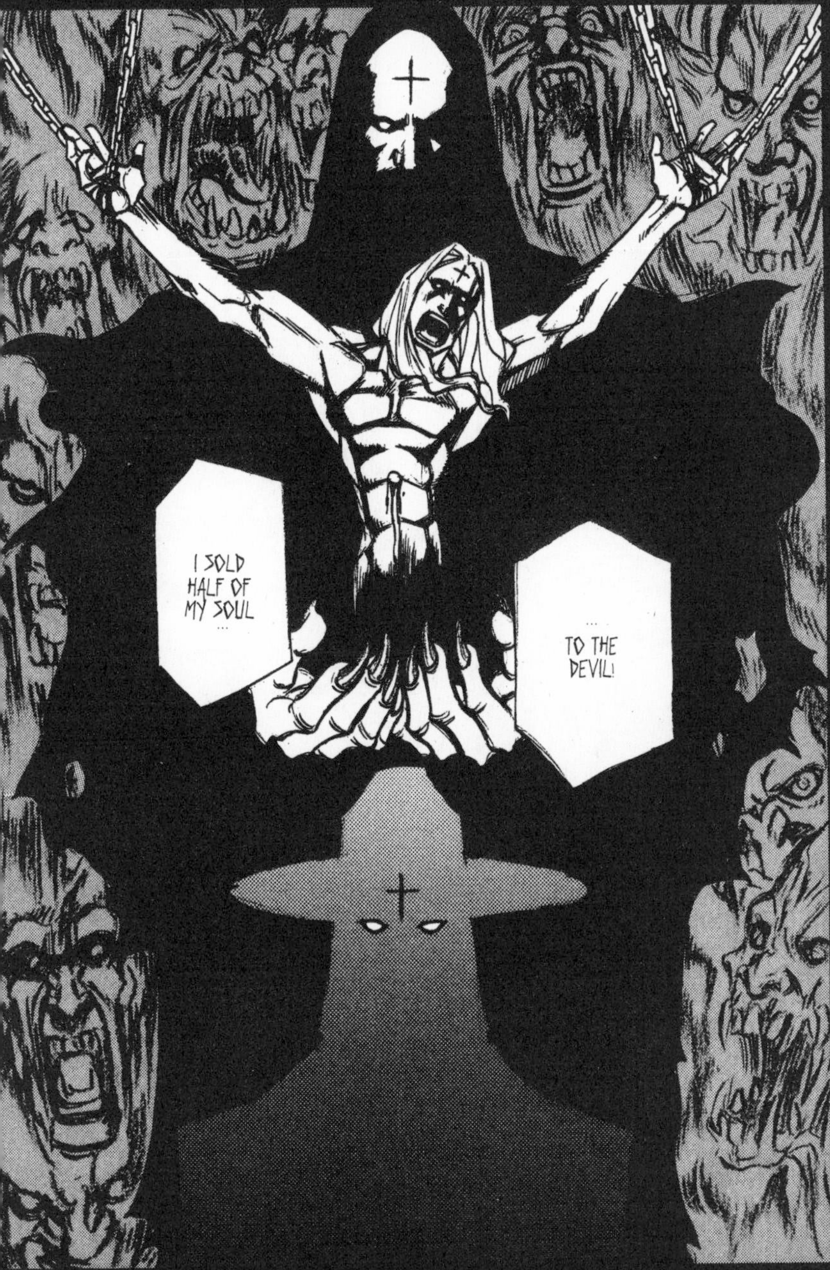
I SOLD HALF OF MY SOUL ...
... TO THE DEVIL!

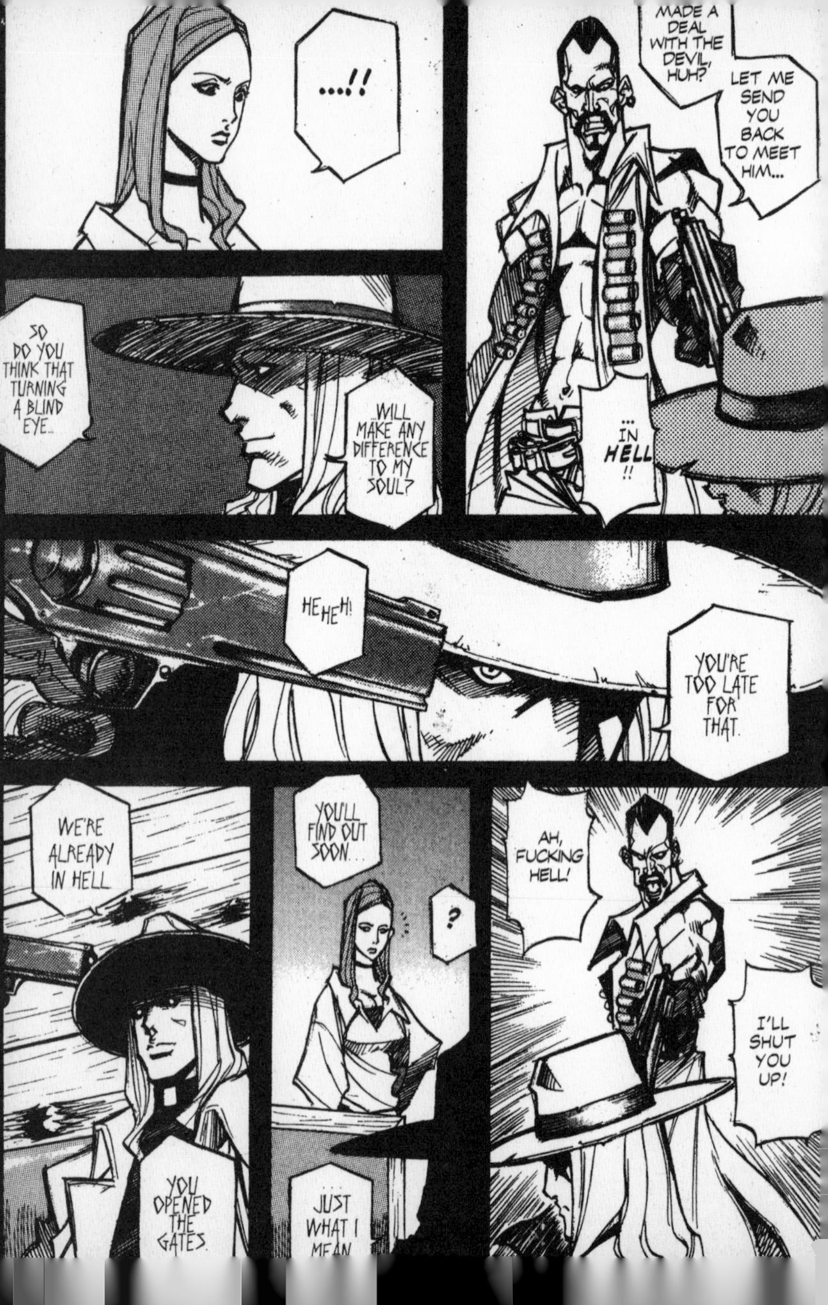
...!!
SO DO YOU THINK THAT TURNING A BLIND EYE...
...WILL MAKE ANY DIFFERENCE TO MY SOUL?
MADE A DEAL WITH THE DEVIL, HUH?
LET ME SEND YOU BACK TO MEET HIM...
... IN HELL !!
HEHEH!
YOU'RE TOO LATE FOR THAT.
WE'RE ALREADY IN HELL.
YOU OPENED THE GATES.
YOU'LL FIND OUT SOON...
?
... JUST WHAT I MEAN
AH, FUCKING HELL!
I'LL SHUT YOU UP!

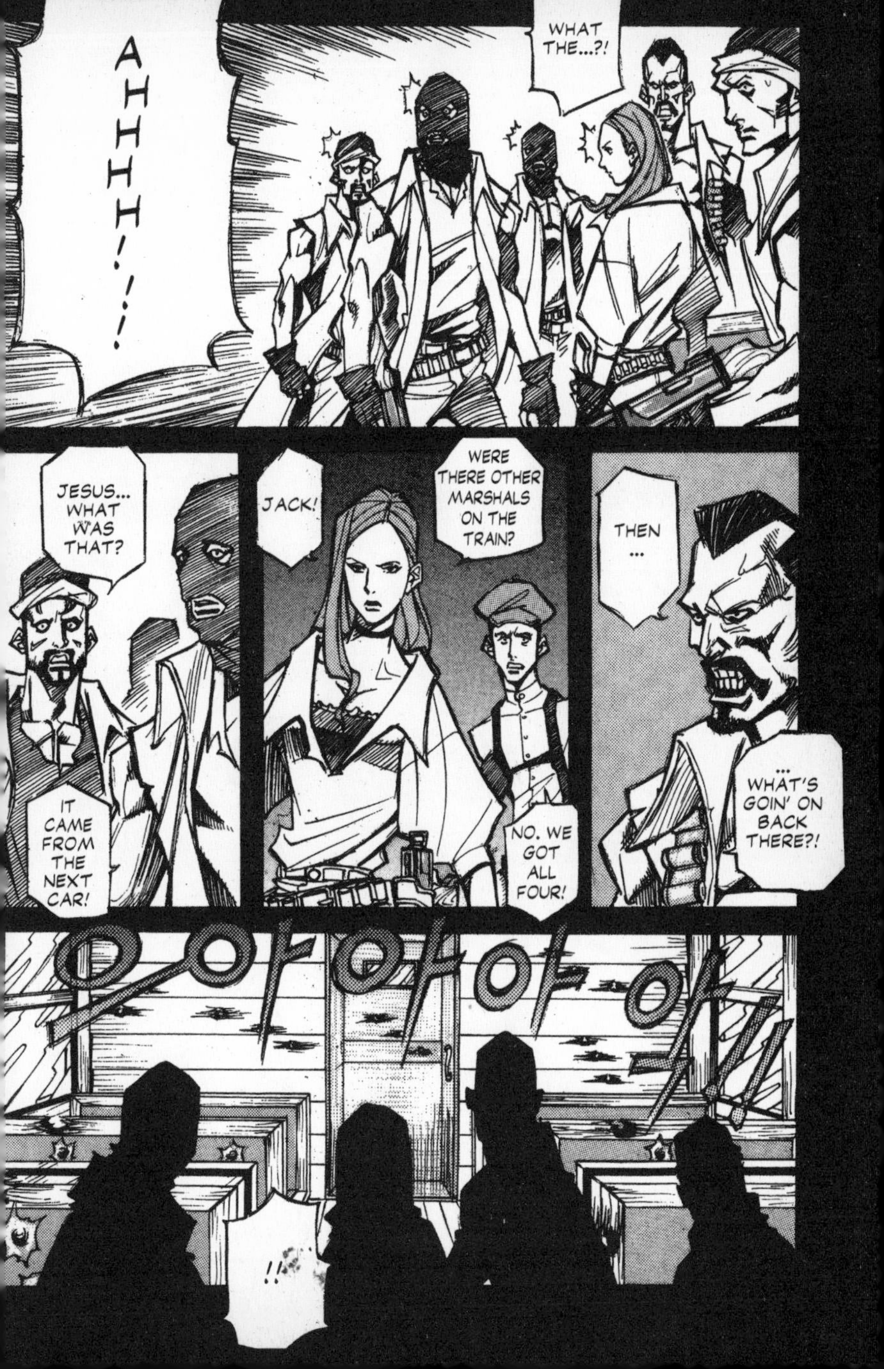
AHHHH!!!
WHAT THE...?!
JESUS... WHAT WAS THAT?
IT CAME FROM THE NEXT CAR!
JACK!
WERE THERE OTHER MARSHALS ON THE TRAIN?
NO. WE GOT ALL FOUR!
THEN ...
... WHAT'S GOIN' ON BACK THERE?!
OOF OOF OOF!!!
!!

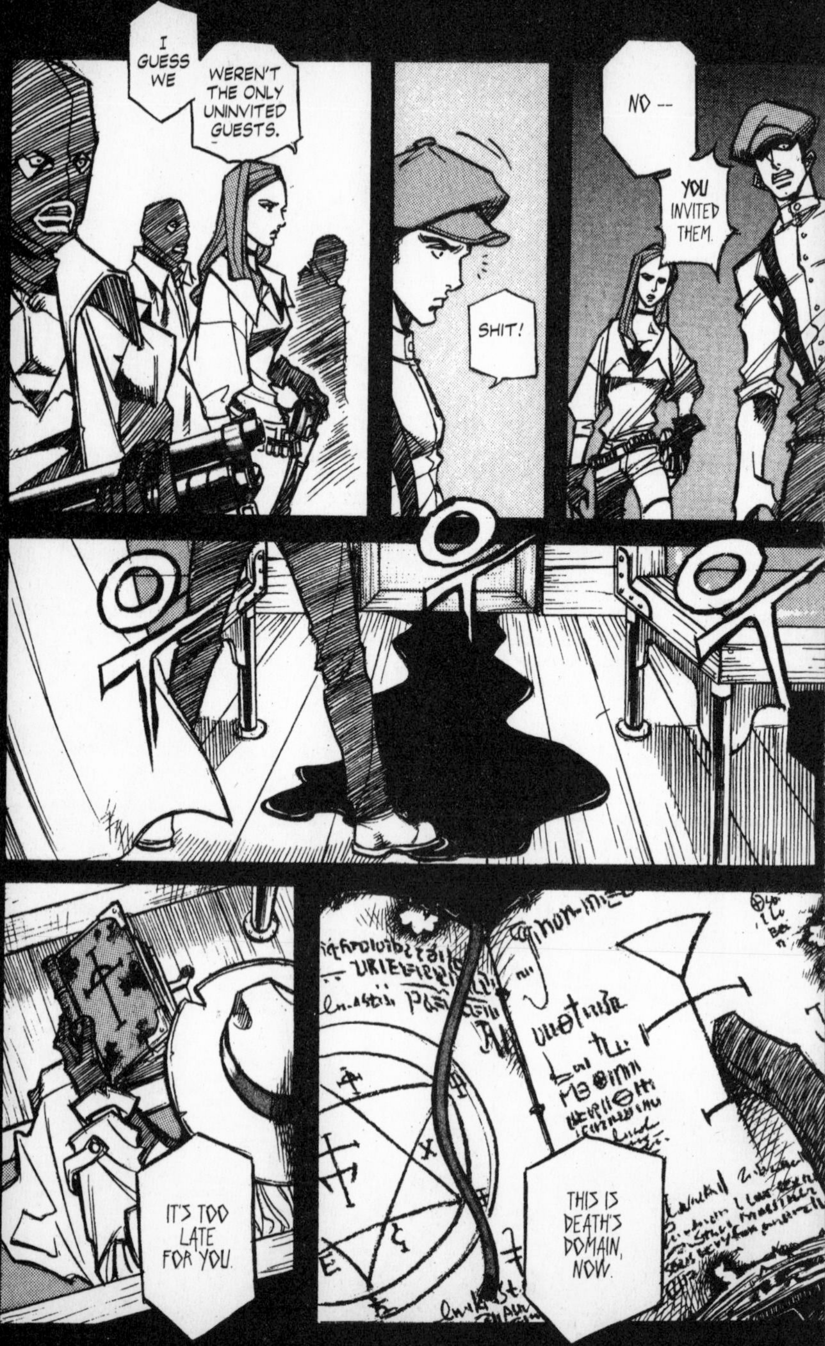
I GUESS WE
WEREN'T THE ONLY UNINVITED GUESTS.
SHIT!
NO --
YOU INVITED THEM.
IT'S TOO LATE FOR YOU.
THIS IS DEATH'S DOMAIN, NOW.

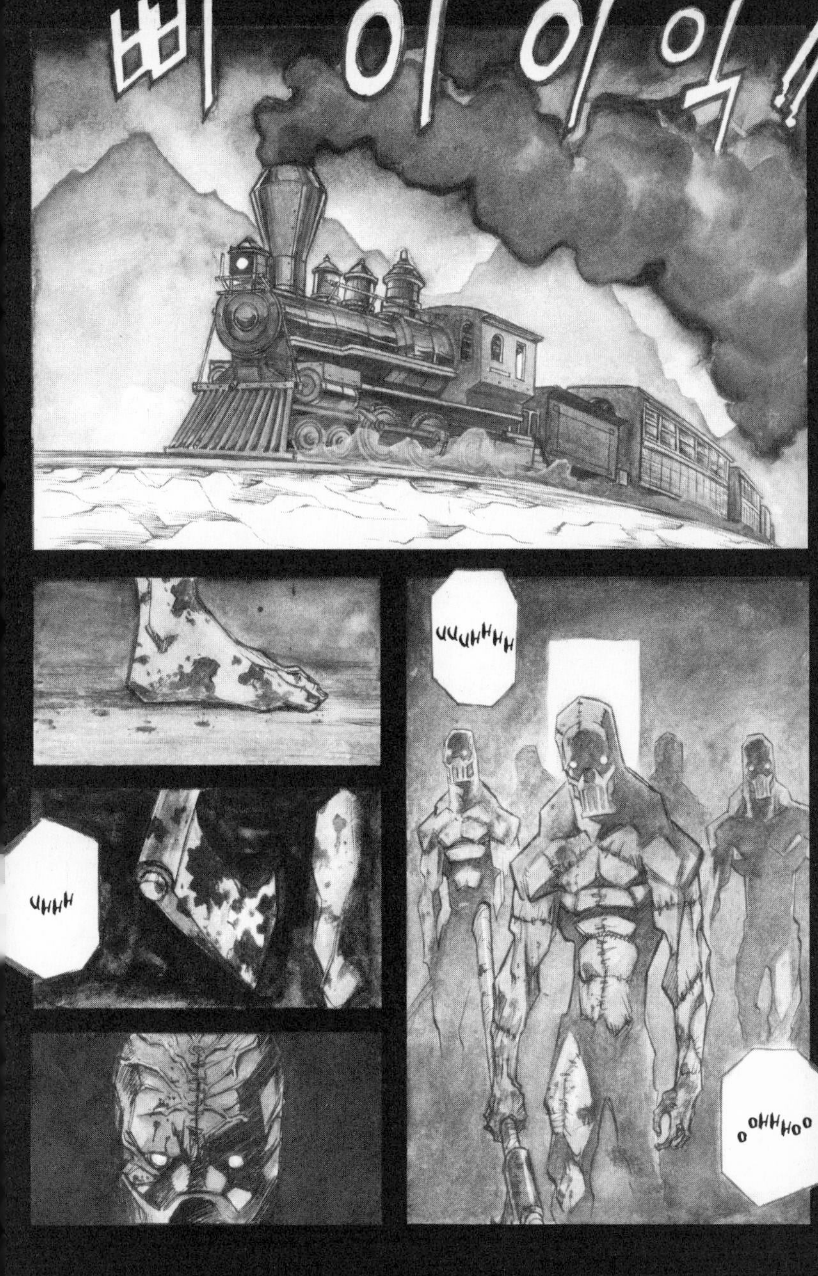
삐이이익!
UHHH
UUUHHHH
OOHHHOO

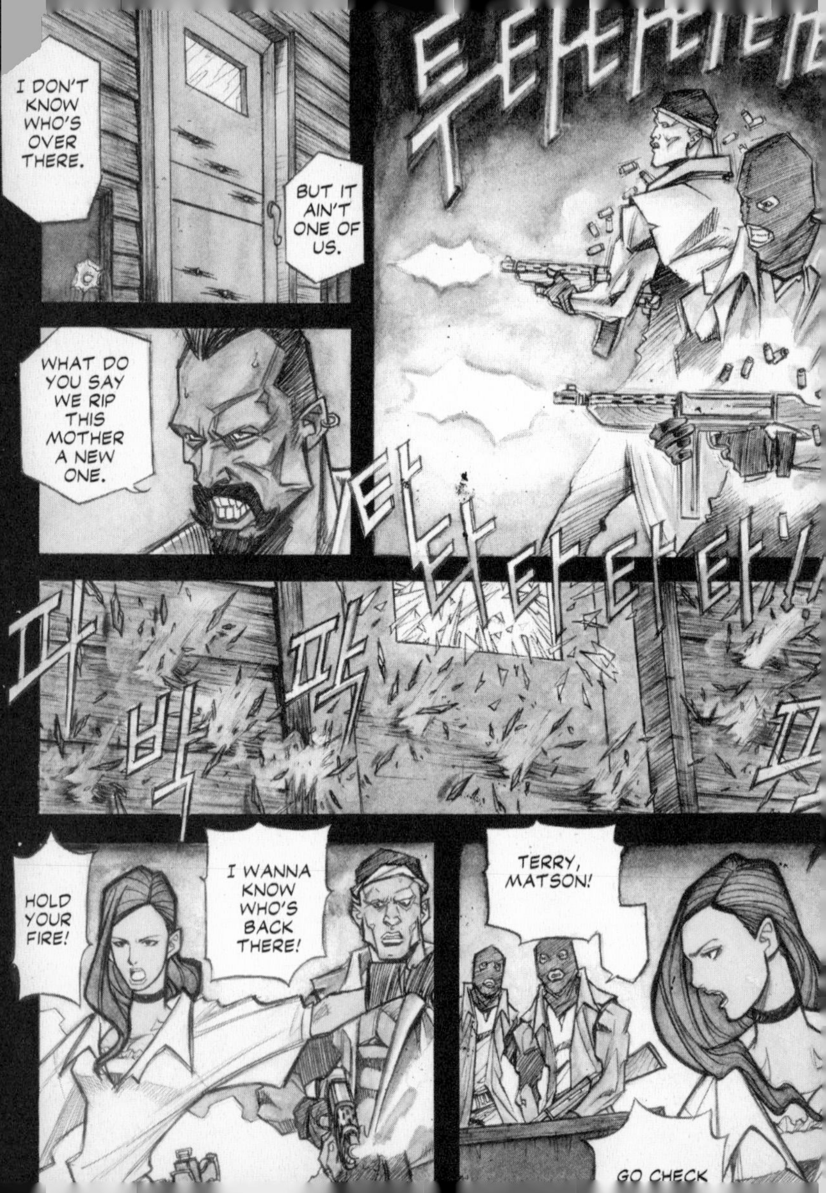
I DON'T KNOW WHO'S OVER THERE.
BUT IT AIN'T ONE OF US.
WHAT DO YOU SAY WE RIP THIS MOTHER A NEW ONE.
HOLD YOUR FIRE!
I WANNA KNOW WHO'S BACK THERE!
TERRY, MATSON!
GO CHECK

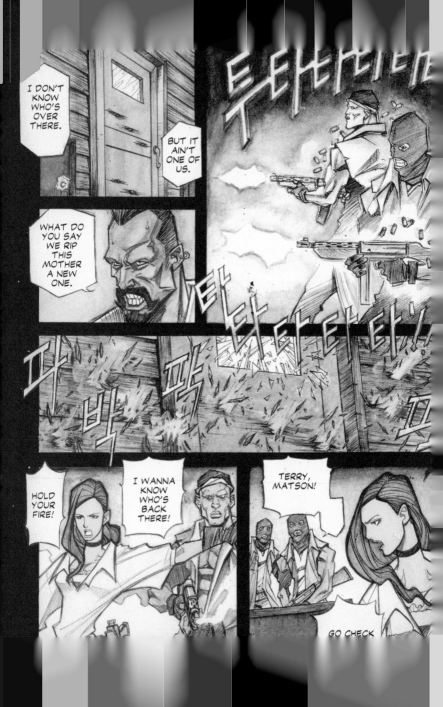

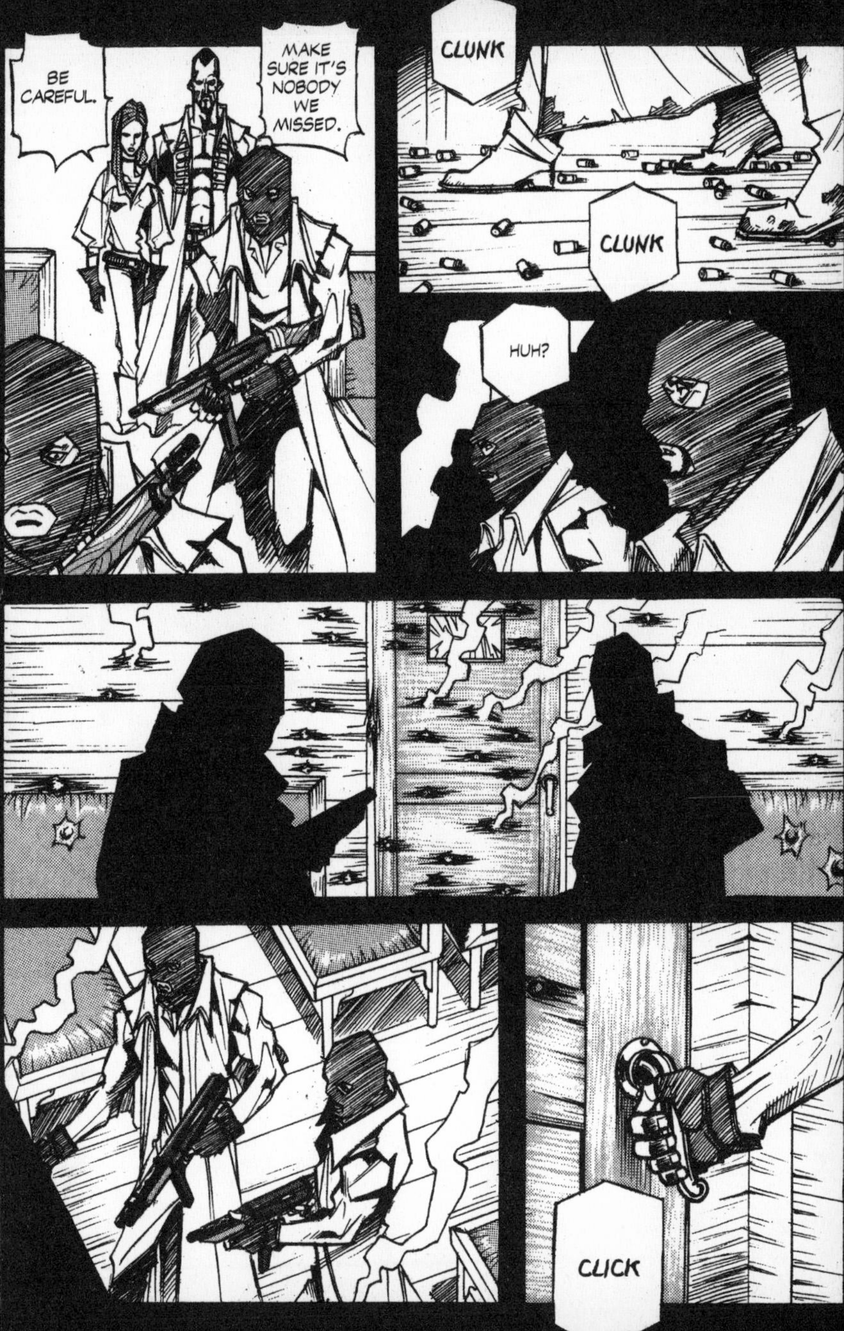
BE CAREFUL.
MAKE SURE IT'S NOBODY WE MISSED.
CLUNK
CLUNK
HUH?
CLICK

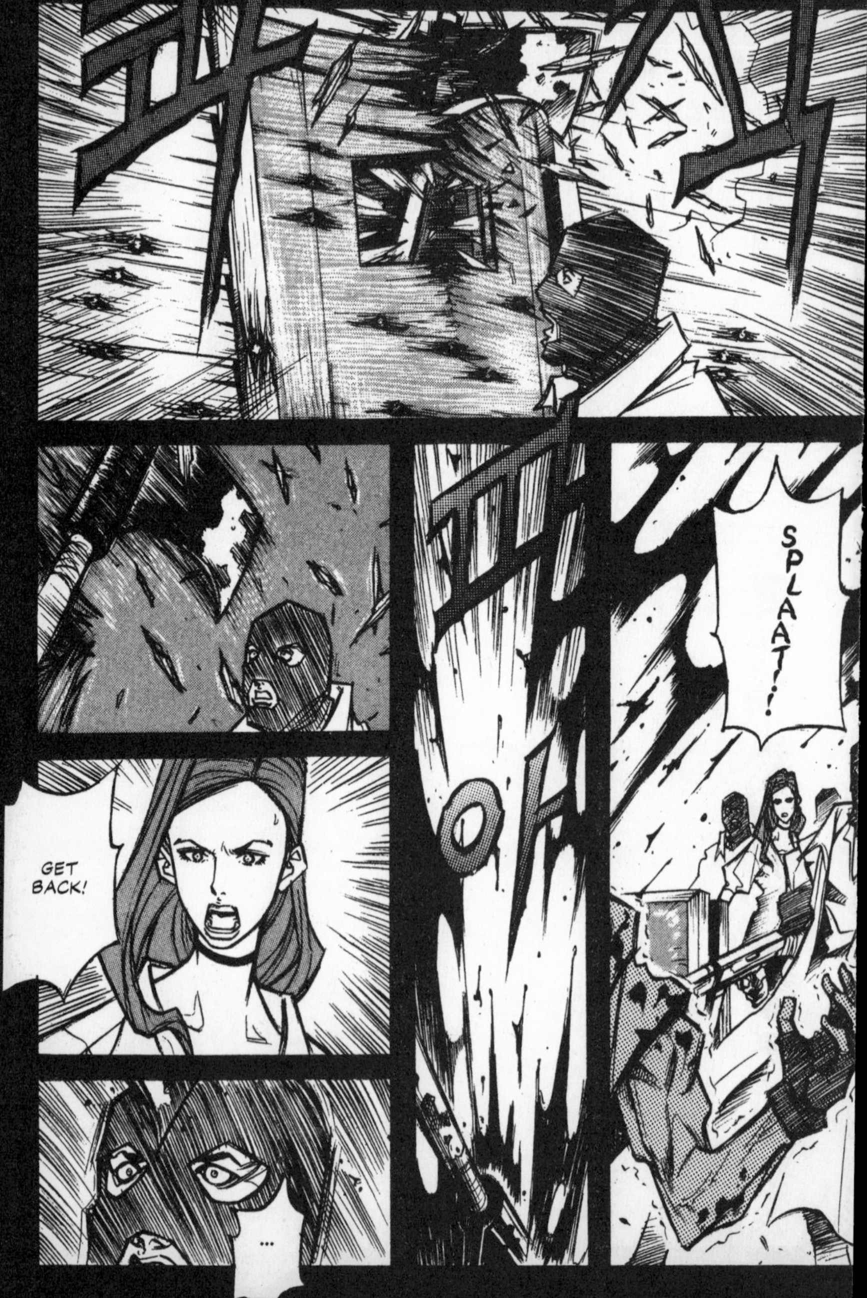
GET BACK!
...
SPLAAT!!!

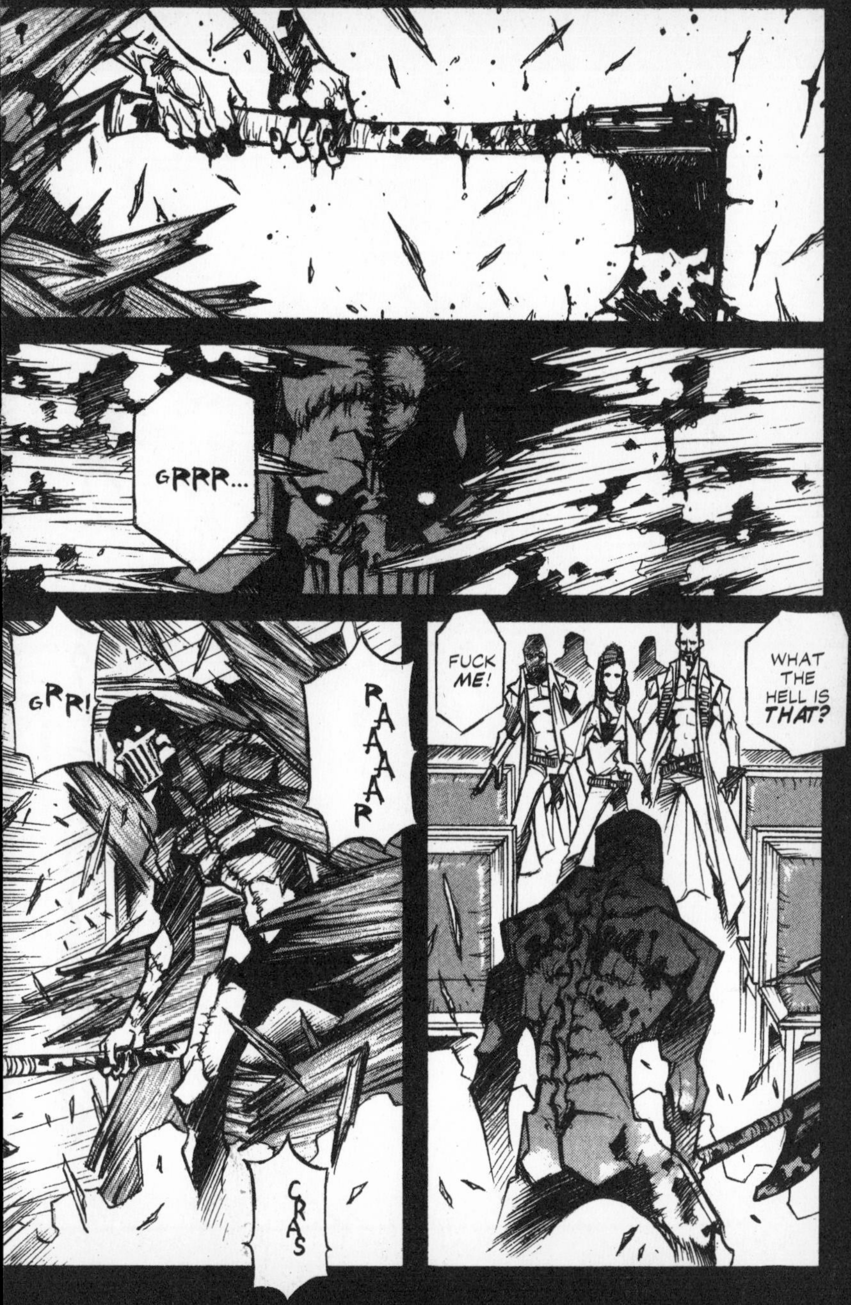
GRRR...
GRR!
RAAAAR
CRAS
FUCK ME!
WHAT THE HELL IS THAT?

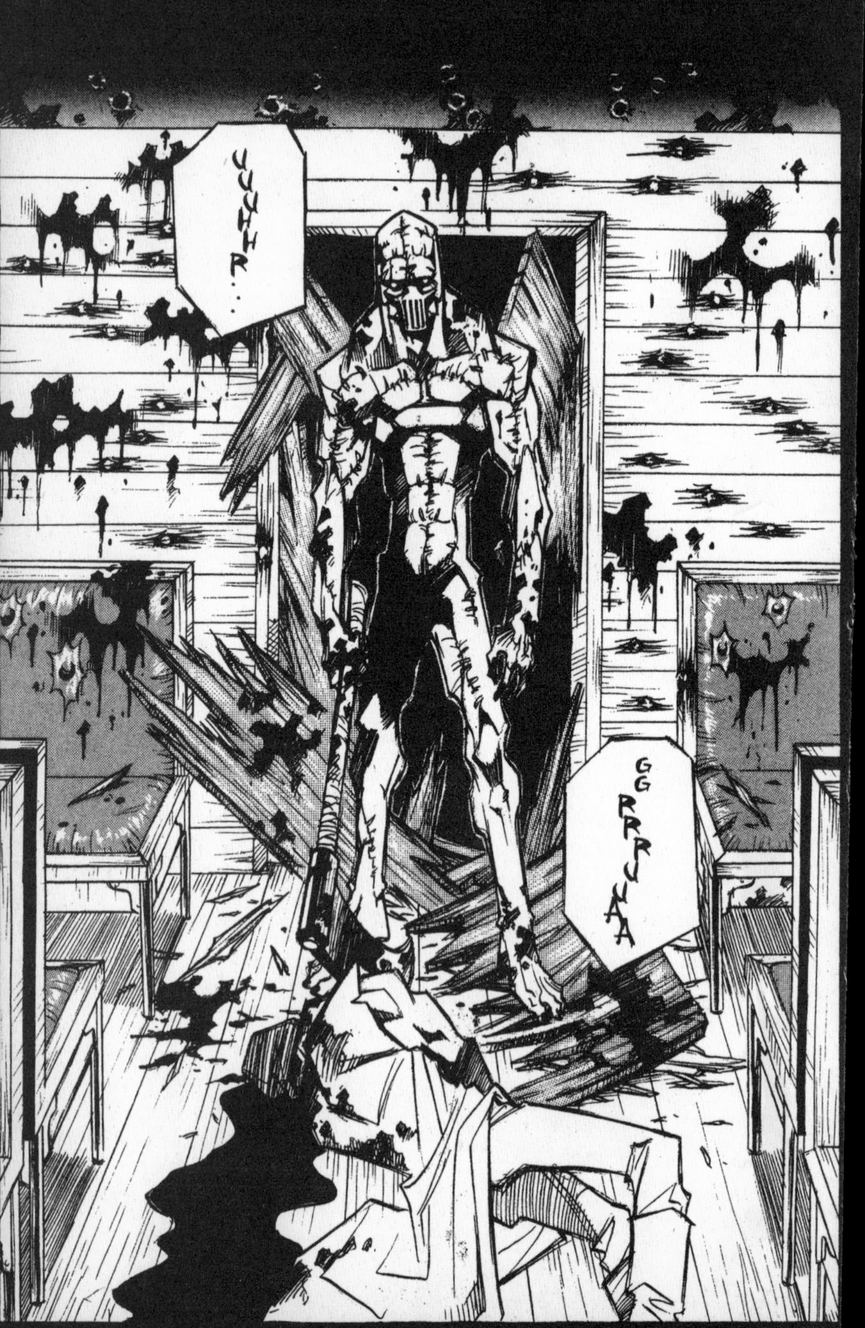
UUUHHR...
GGRRRUUAA

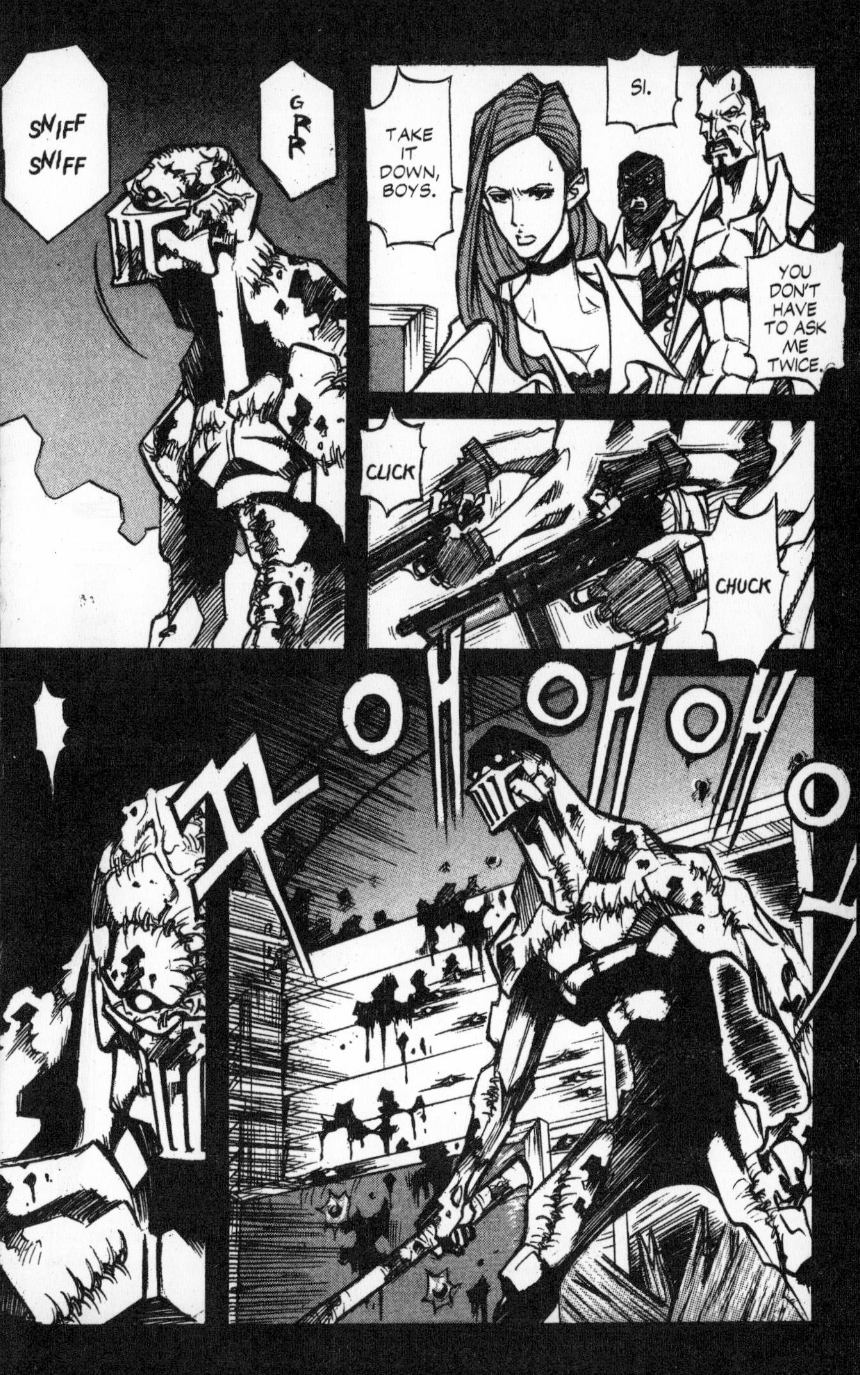
SNIFF SNIFF
GRR
TAKE IT DOWN, BOYS.
SI.
YOU DON'T HAVE TO ASK ME TWICE.
CLICK
CHUCK

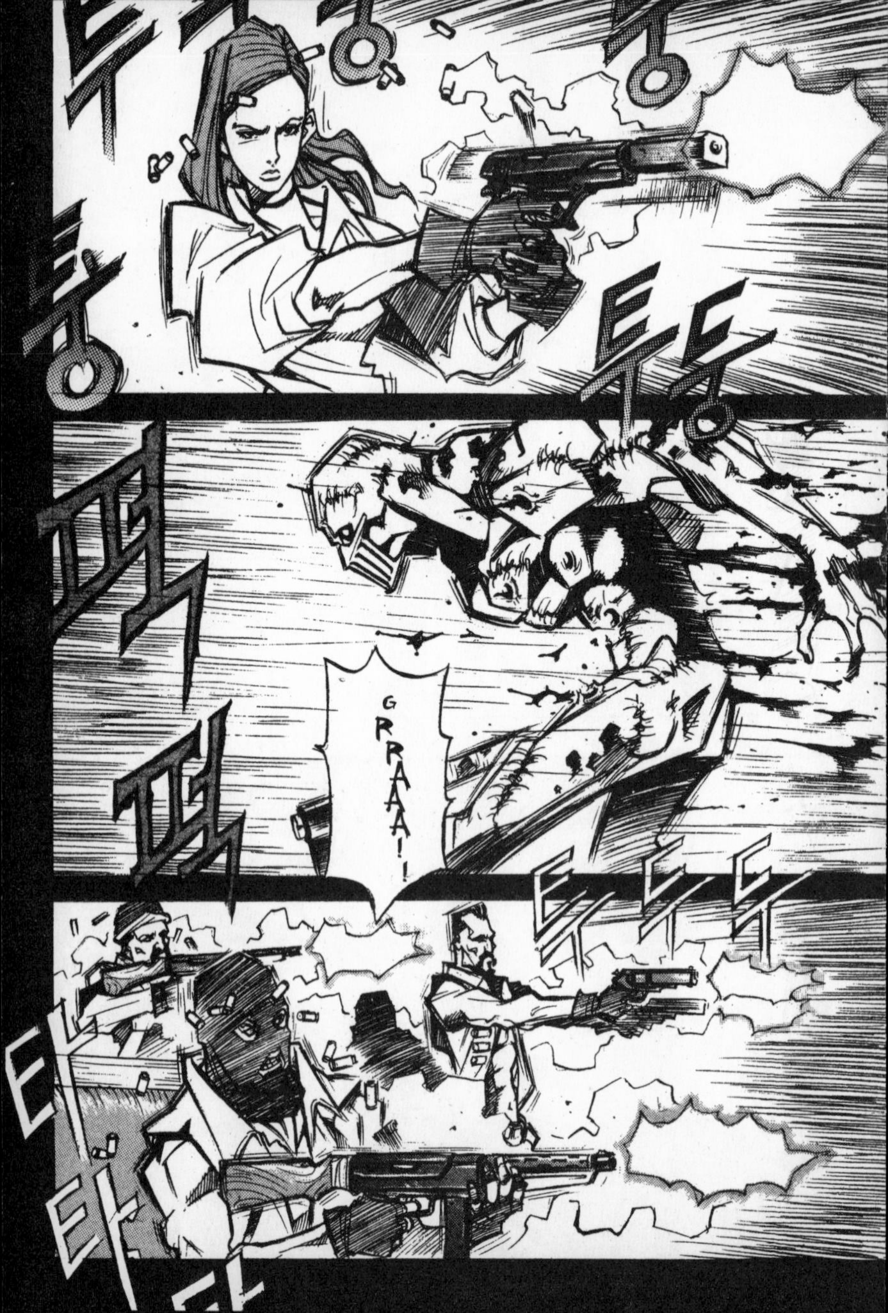
GRRAAA!!

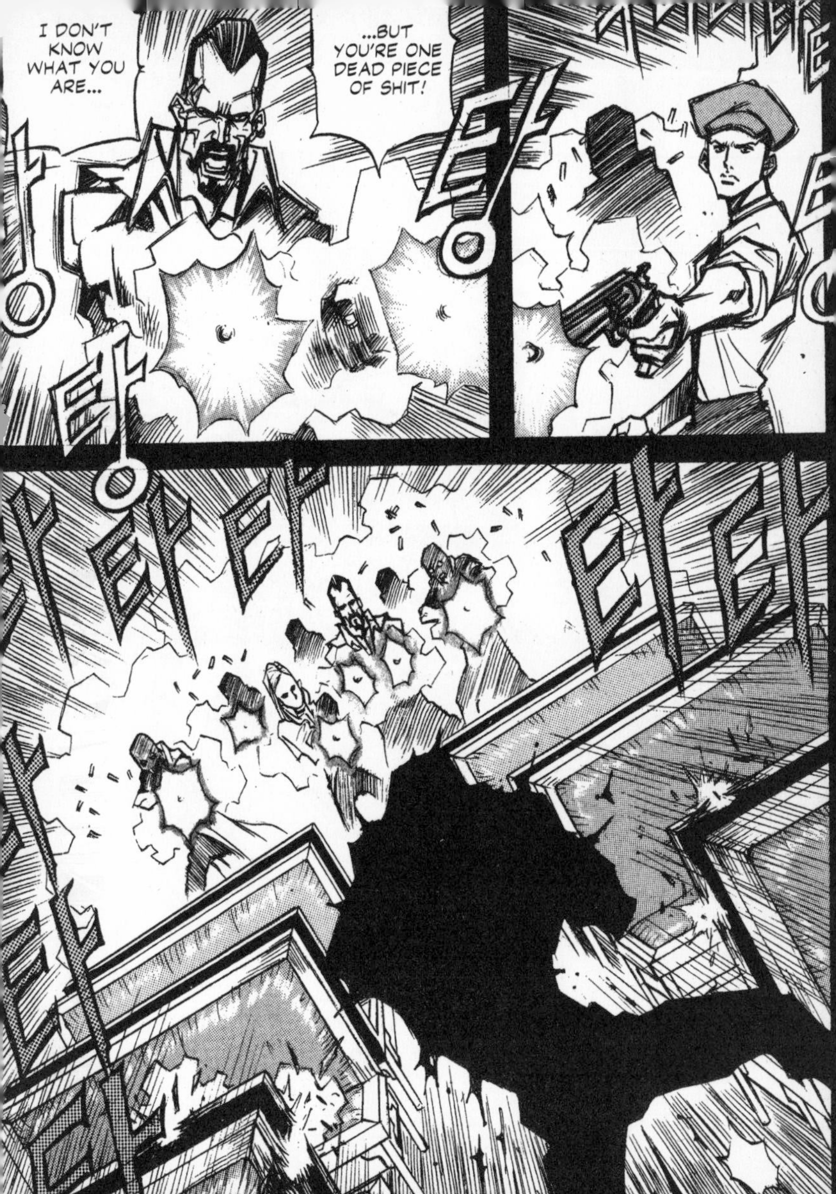
I DON'T KNOW WHAT YOU ARE...
...BUT YOU'RE ONE DEAD PIECE OF SHIT!

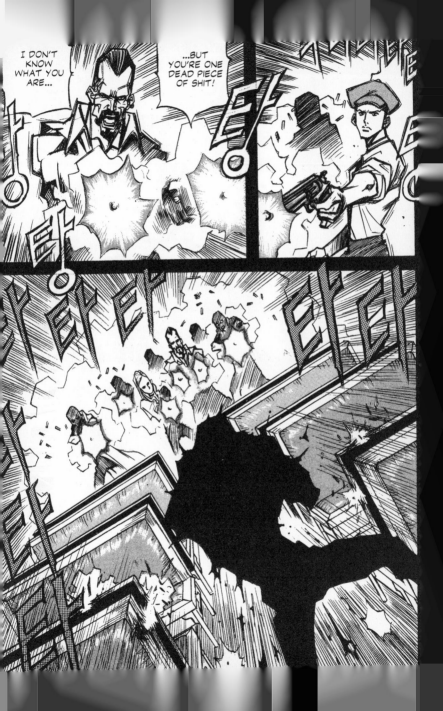

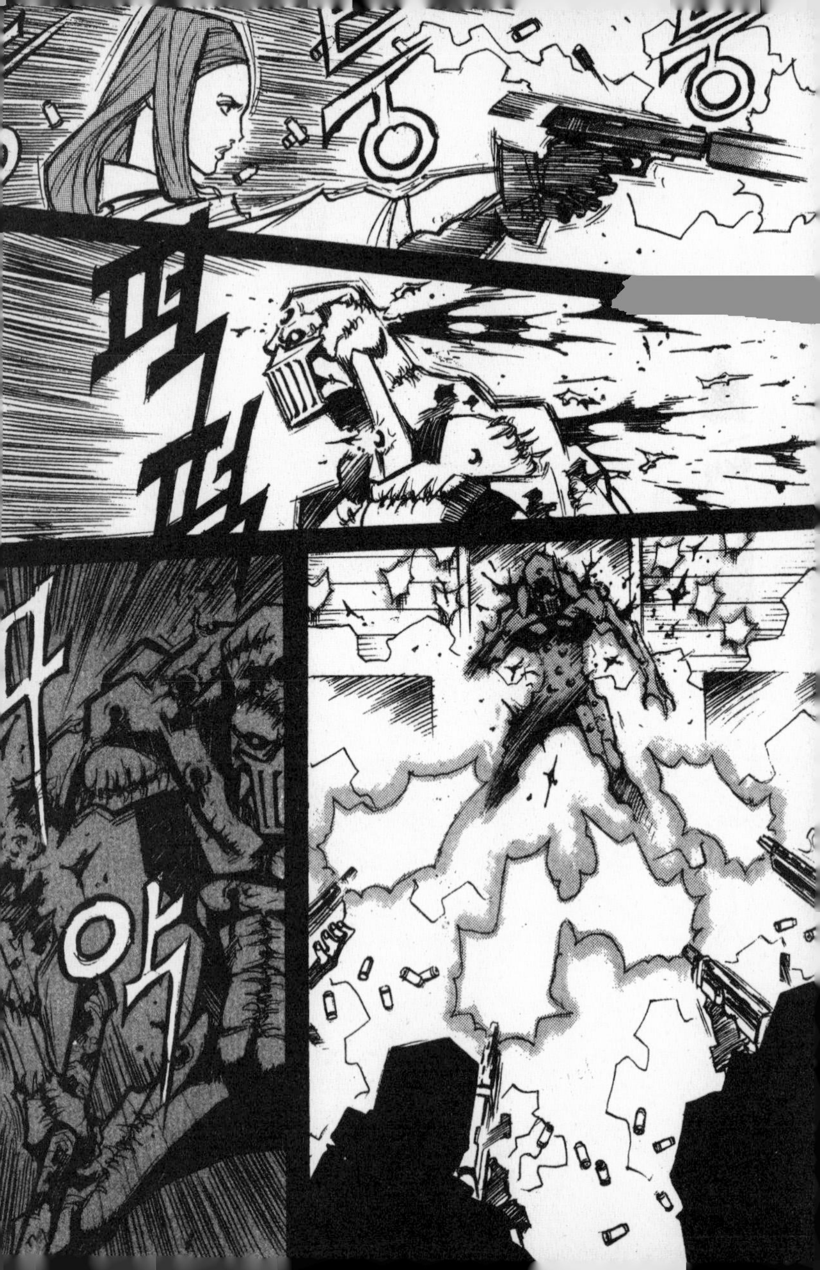
탕
탕
퍽 퍽
크악

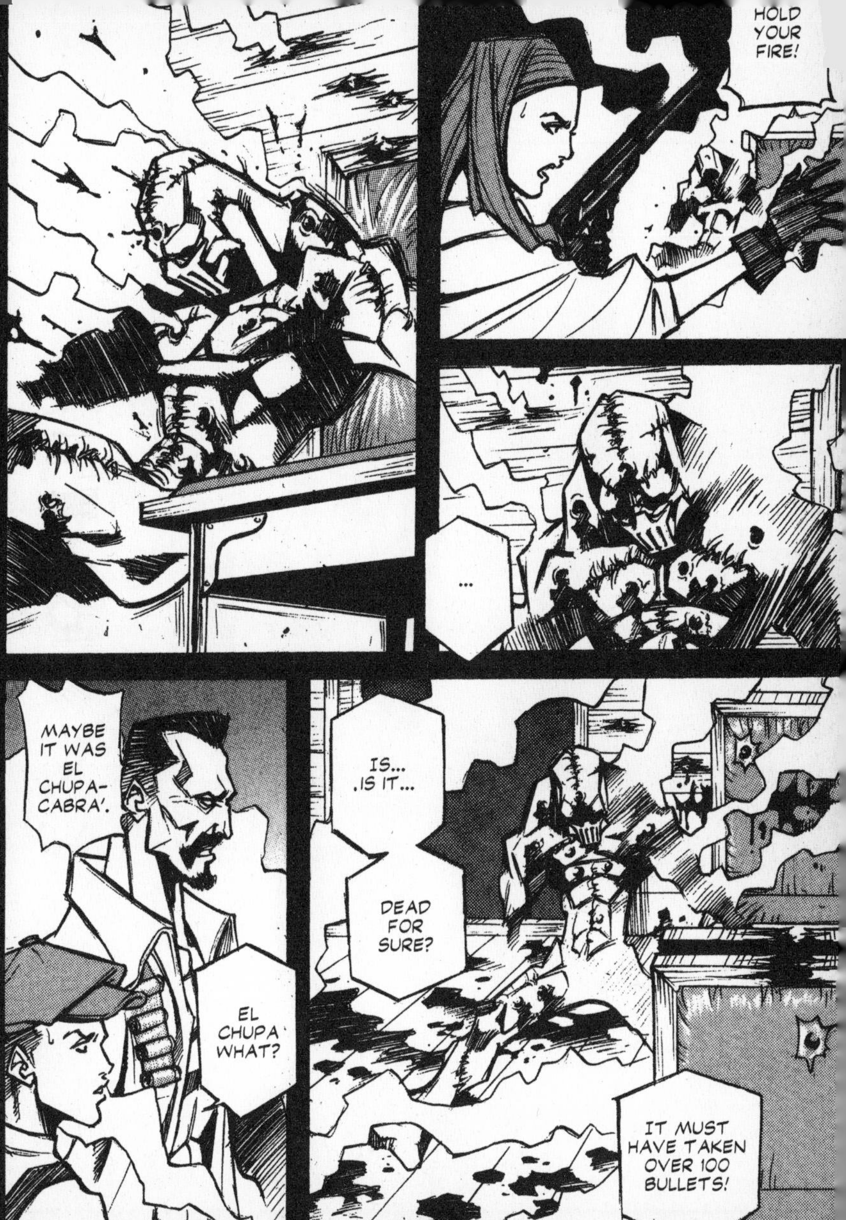
HOLD YOUR FIRE!
...
MAYBE IT WAS EL CHUPA-CABRA'.
EL CHUPA WHAT?
IS... .IS IT...
DEAD FOR SURE?
IT MUST HAVE TAKEN OVER 100 BULLETS!

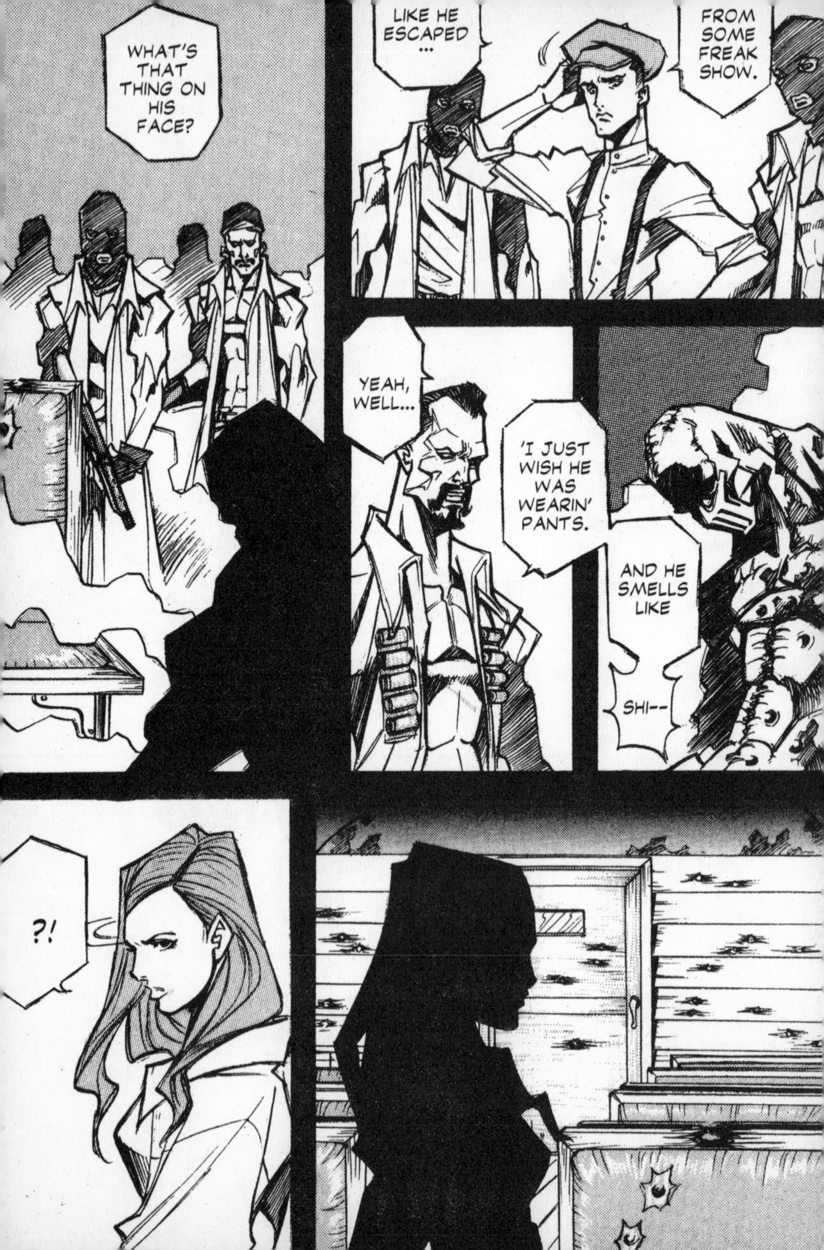
WHAT'S THAT THING ON HIS FACE?
LIKE HE ESCAPED ...
FROM SOME FREAK SHOW.
YEAH, WELL...
'I JUST WISH HE WAS WEARIN' PANTS.
AND HE SMELLS LIKE
SHI--
?!

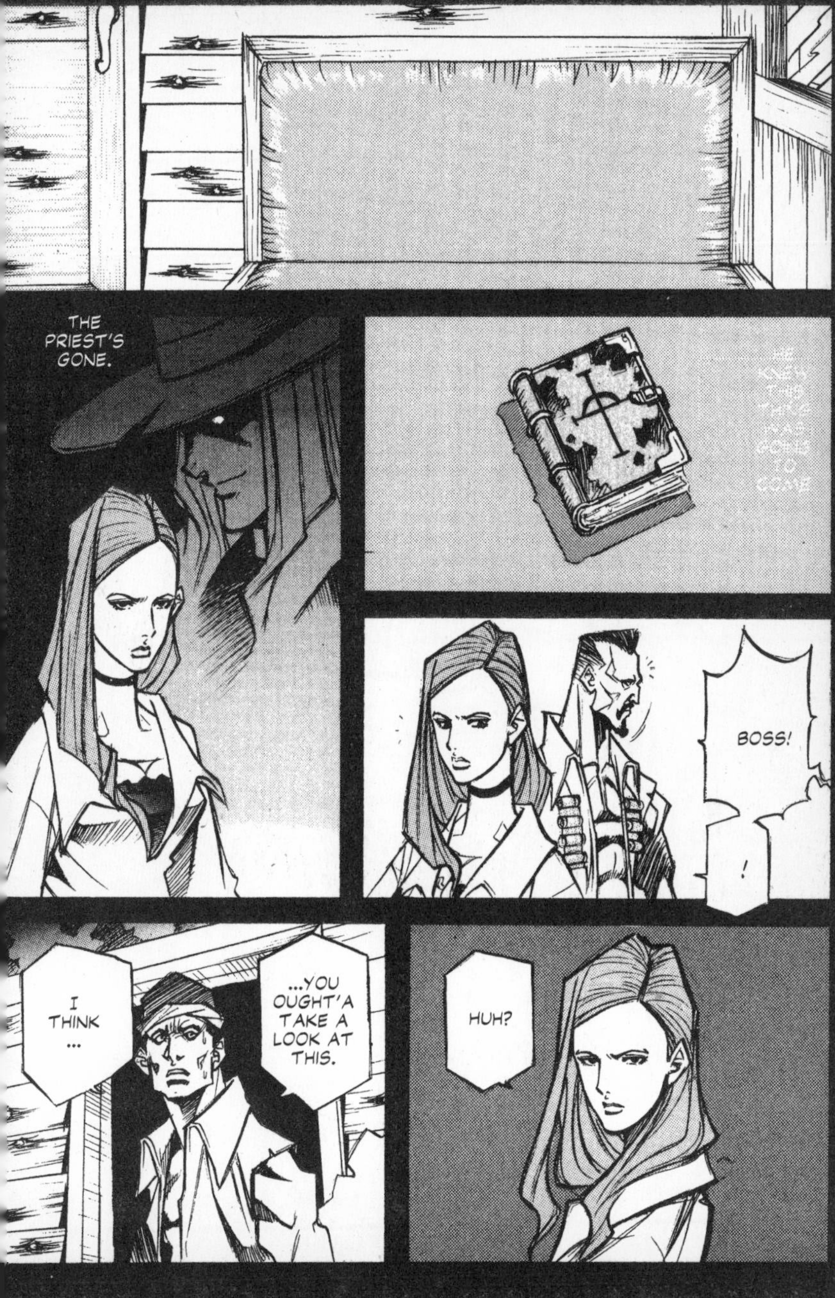
THE PRIEST'S GONE.
HE KNEW THIS THUG WAS GOING TO COME
BOSS!
!
HUH?
I THINK ...
...YOU OUGHT'A TAKE A LOOK AT THIS.

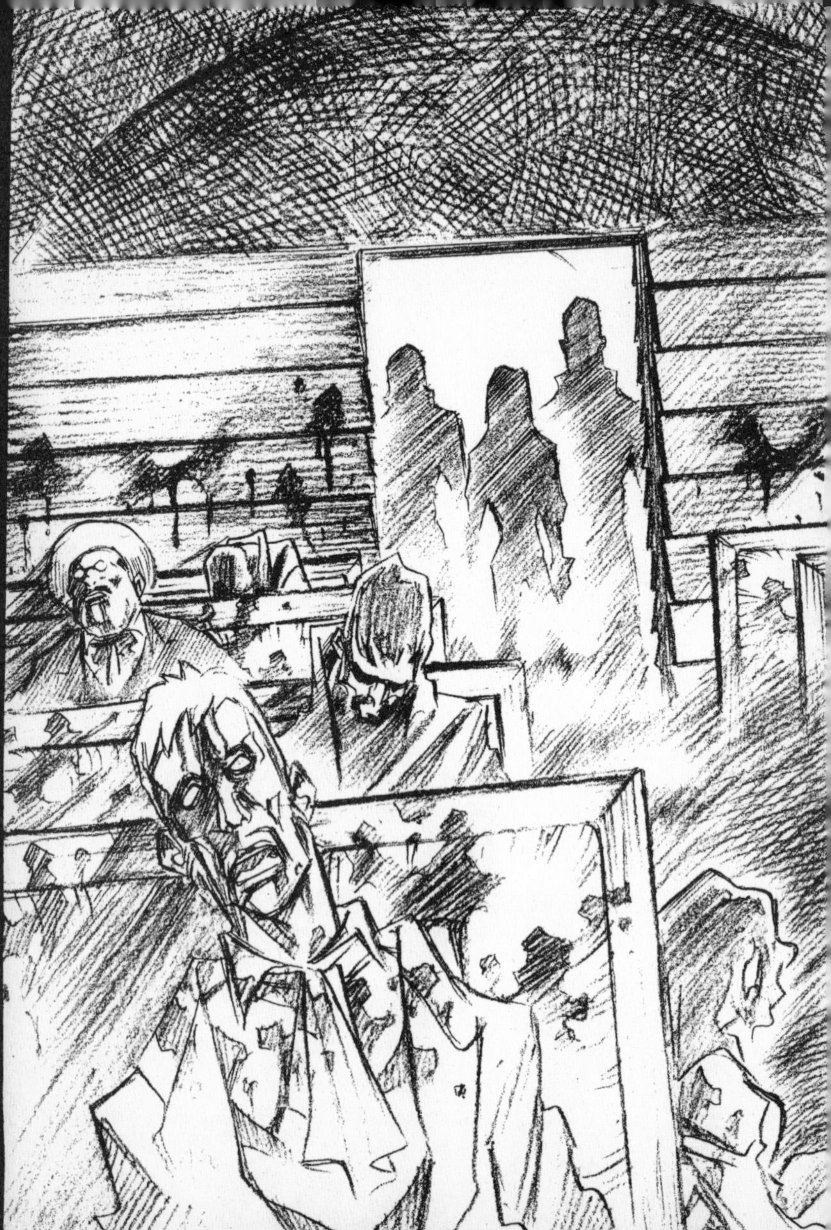

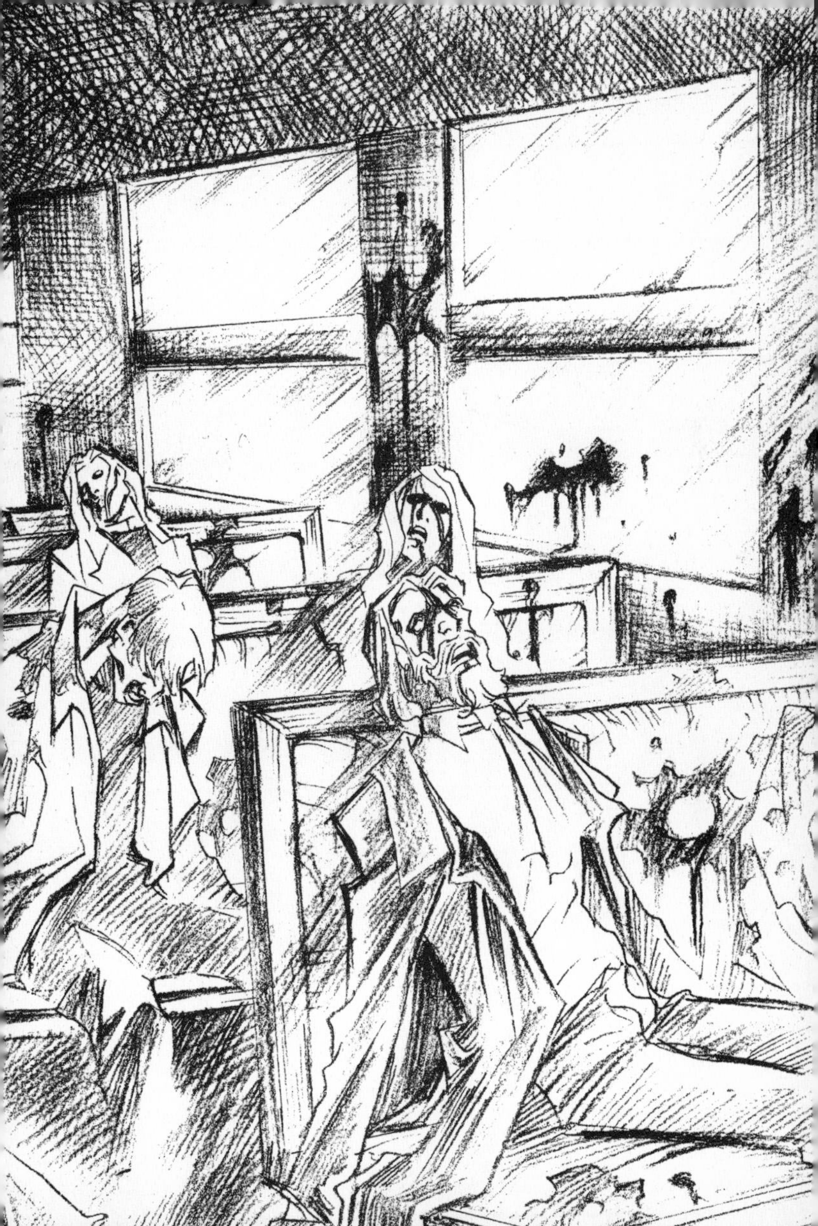

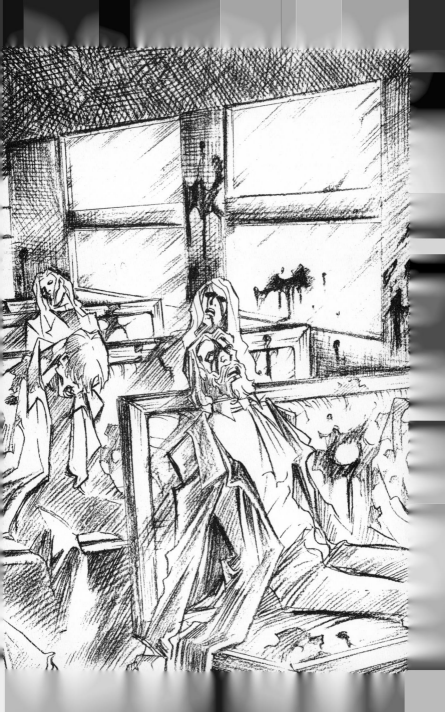

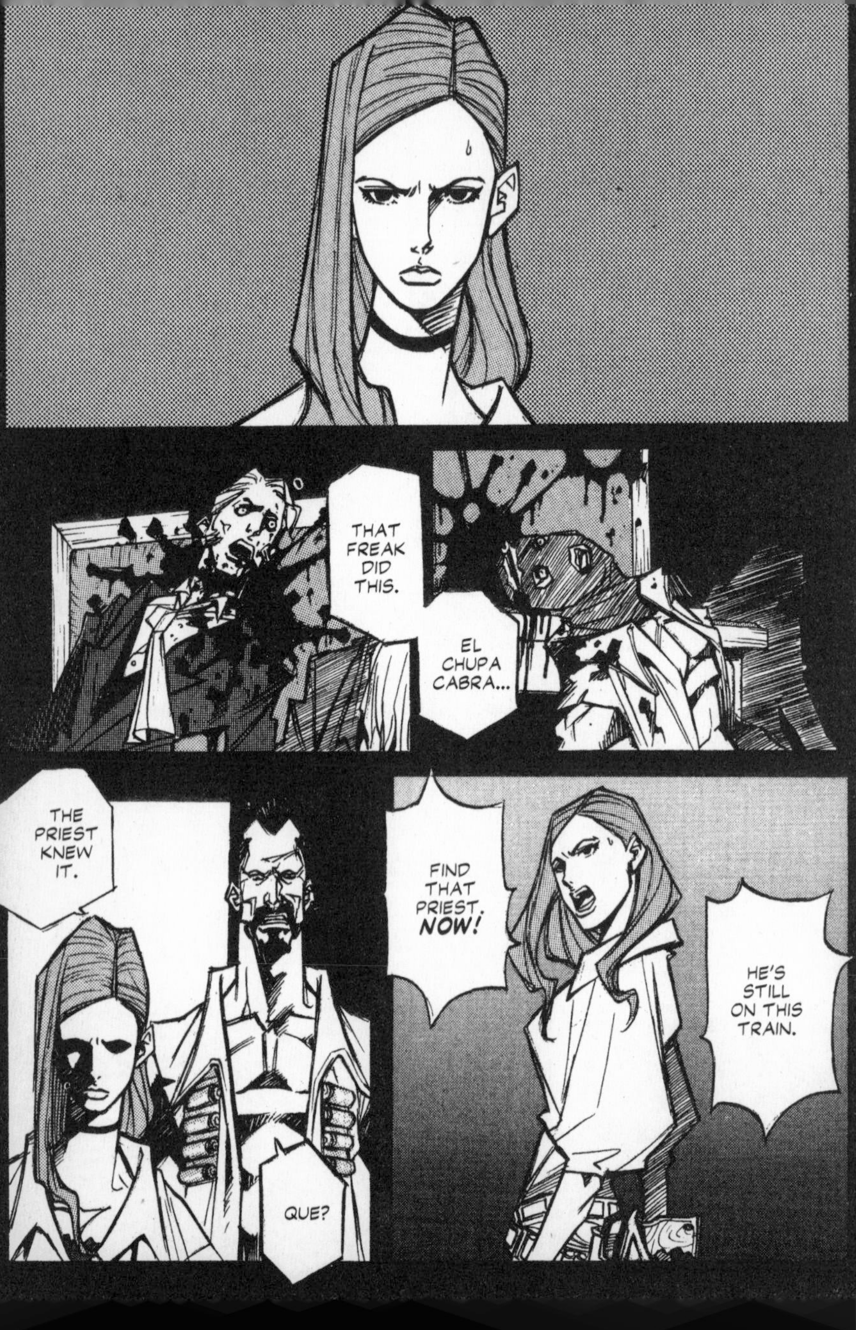
THAT FREAK DID THIS.
EL CHUPA CABRA...
THE PRIEST KNEW IT.
QUE?
FIND THAT PRIEST. **NOW!**
HE'S STILL ON THIS TRAIN.

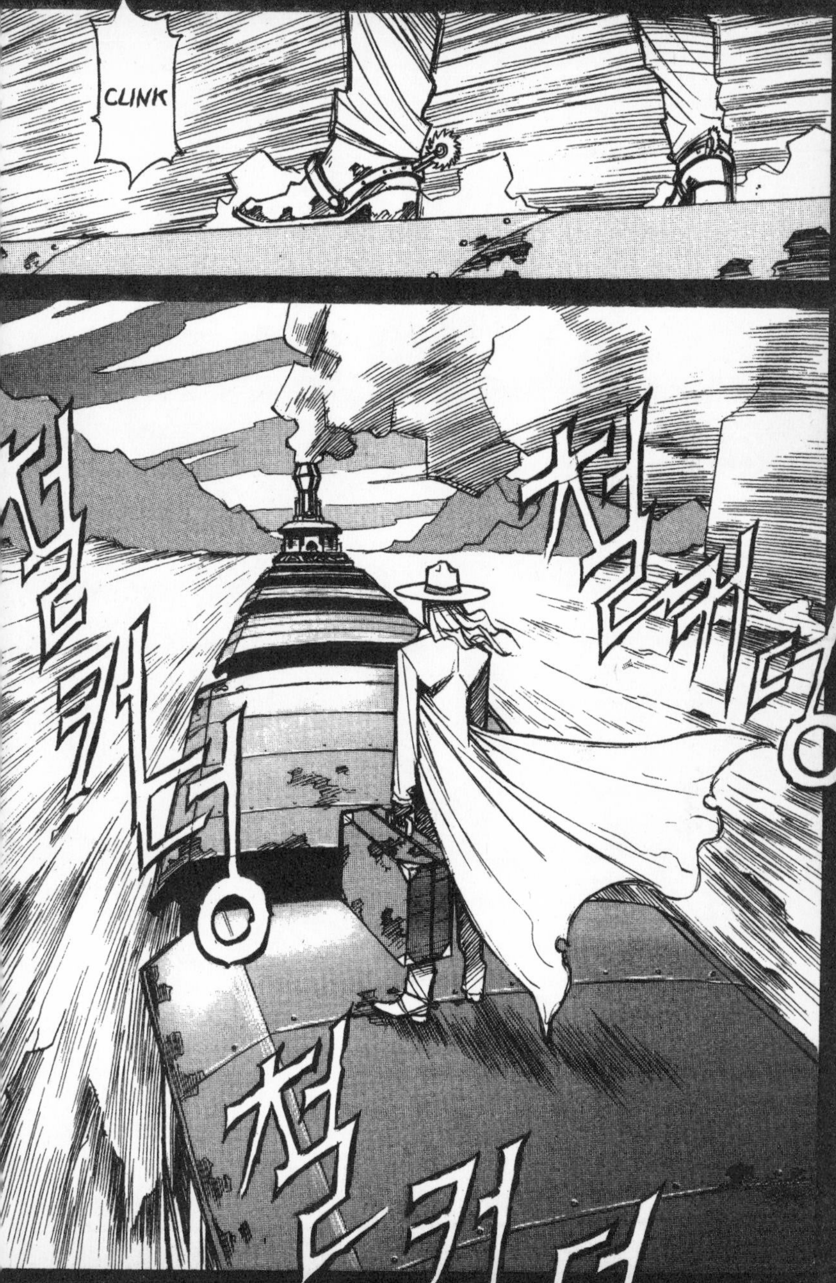
CLINK
덜컹덩
철컹덩
철컹더

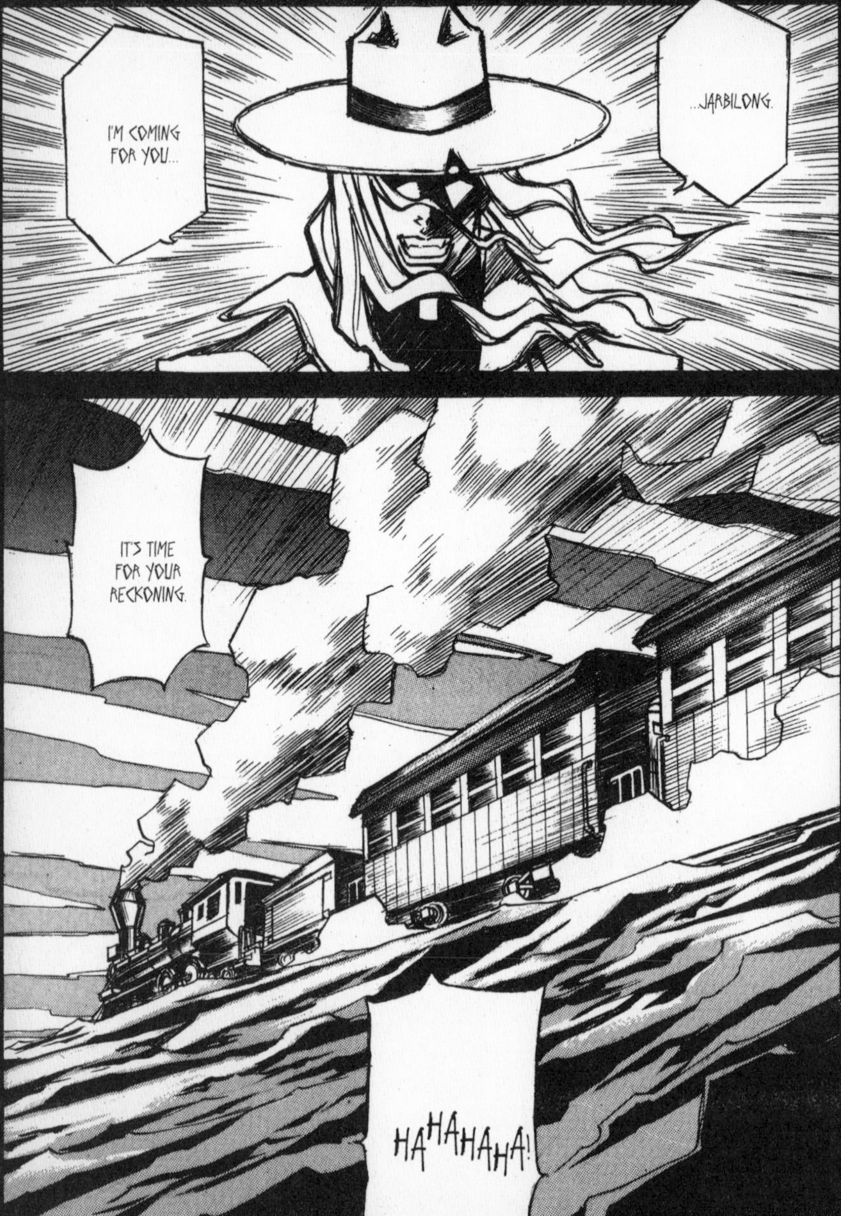
I'M COMING FOR YOU...
...JARBILONG.
IT'S TIME FOR YOUR RECKONING.
HAHAHAHAHA!

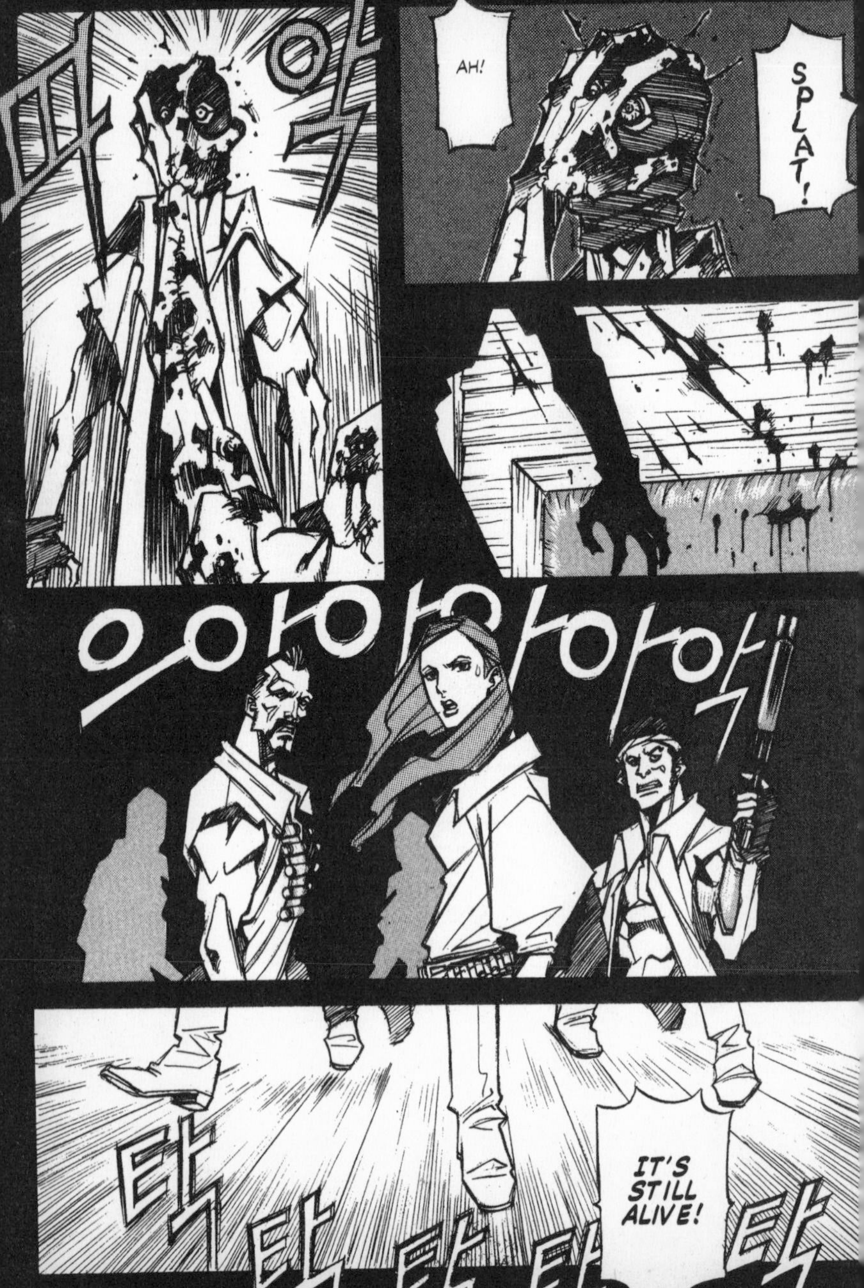
AH!
SPLAT!
IT'S STILL ALIVE!

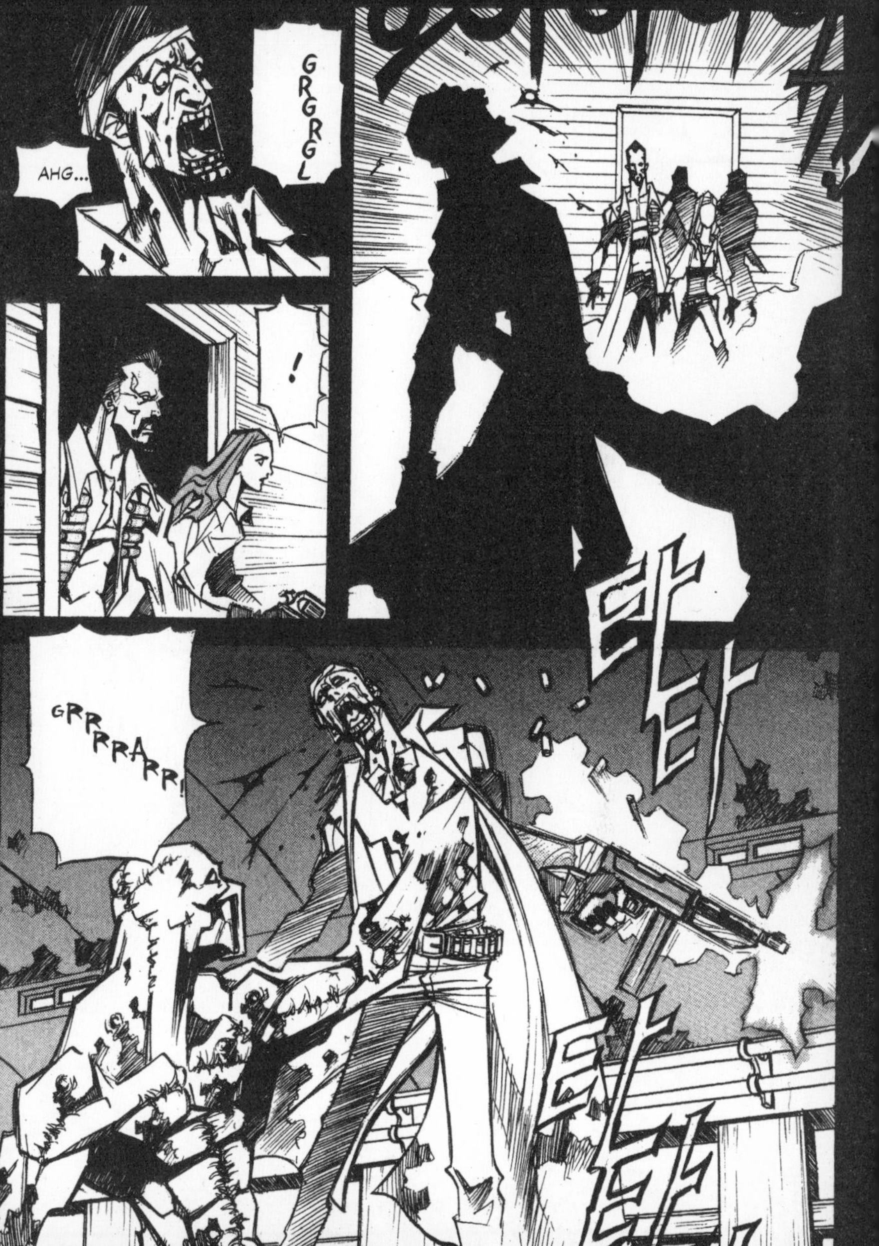
AHG...
GRGRGL
!
GRRRRRARR!

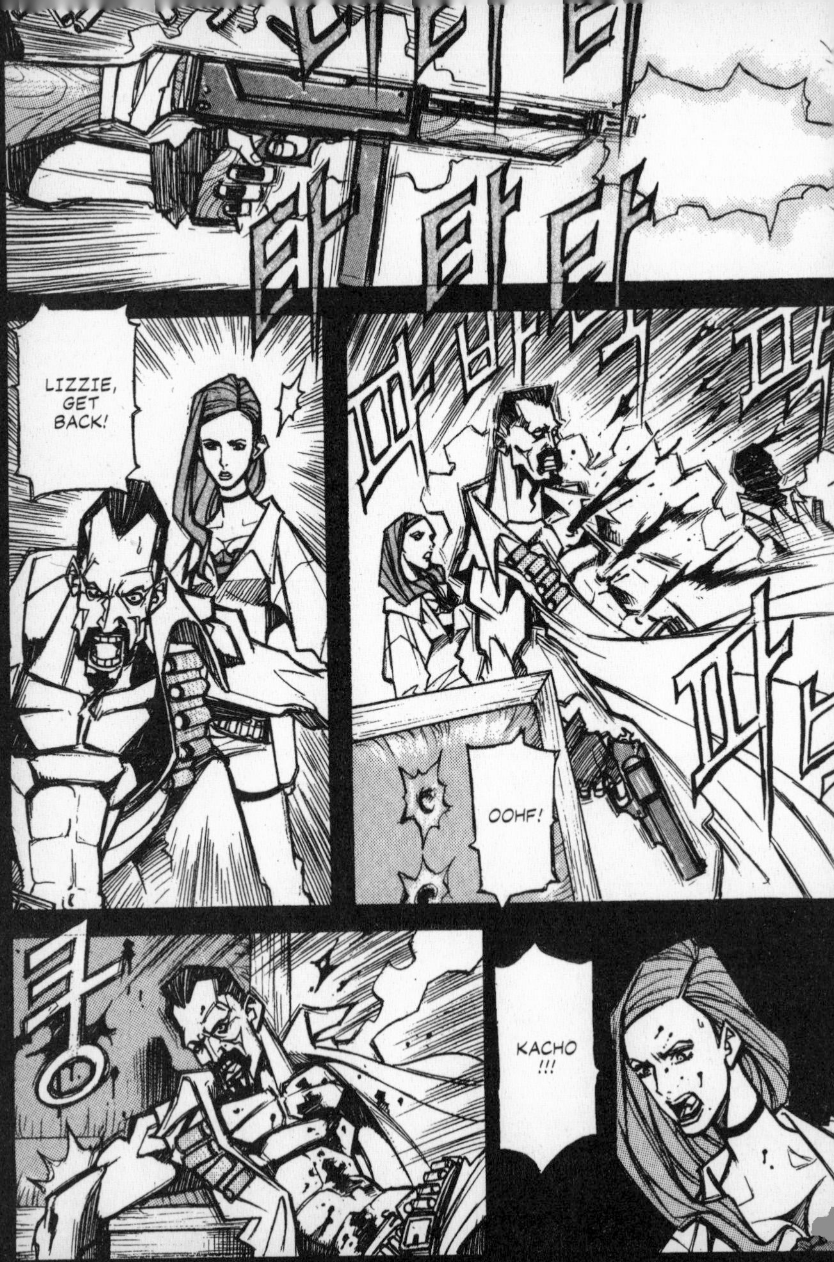
LIZZIE, GET BACK!
OOHF!
KACHO !!!

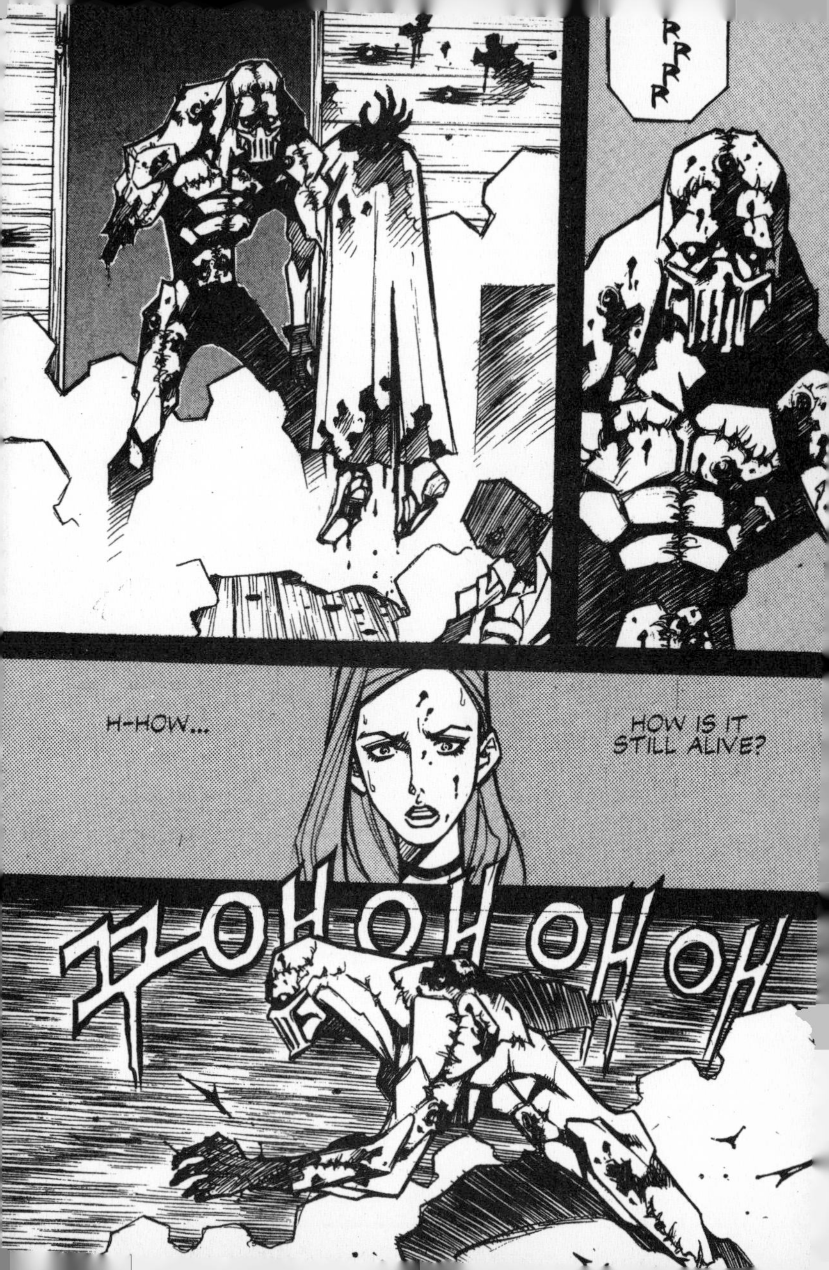
RRRR
H-HOW...
HOW IS IT STILL ALIVE?
ZOHOHOHOHOH

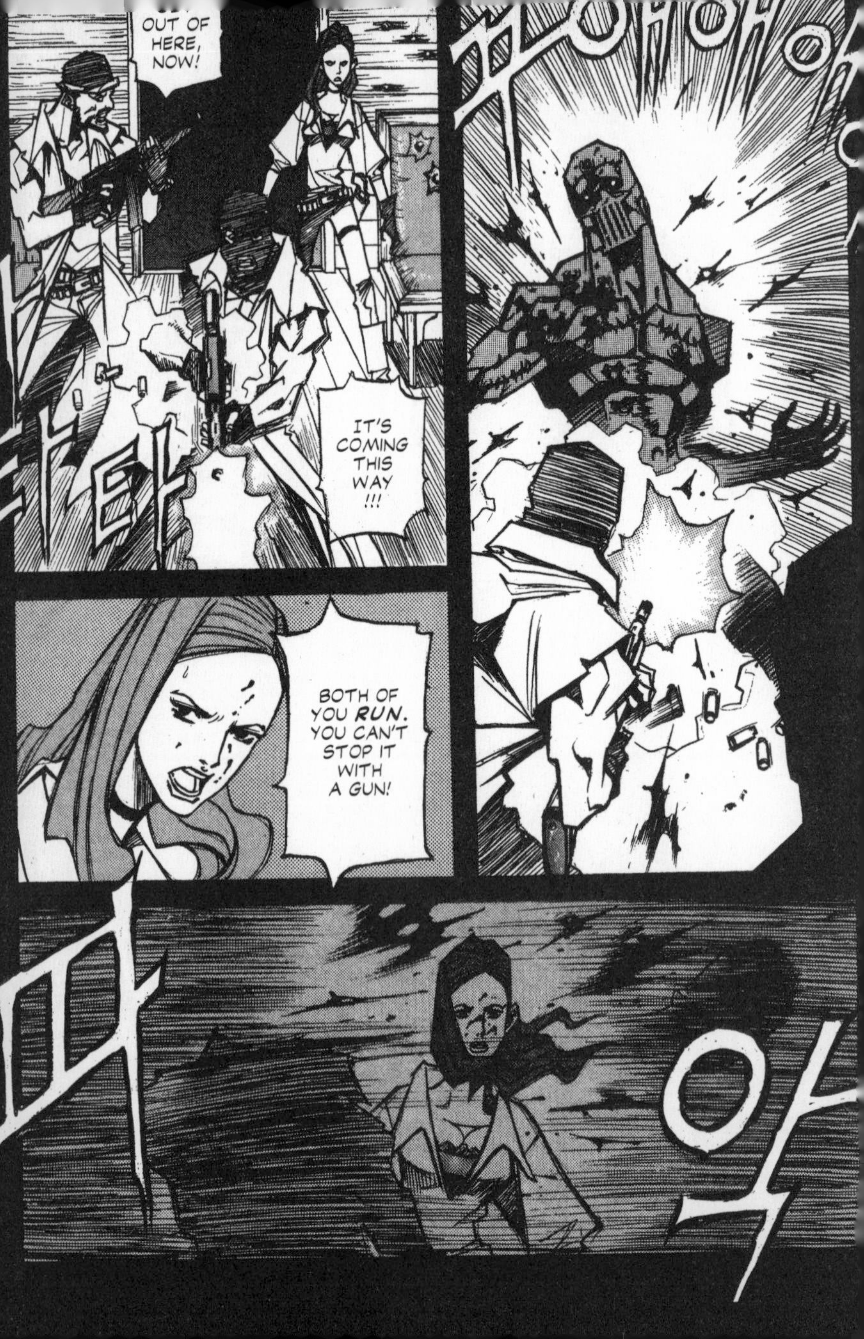
OUT OF HERE, NOW!
IT'S COMING THIS WAY !!!
BOTH OF YOU **RUN**. YOU CAN'T STOP IT WITH A GUN!

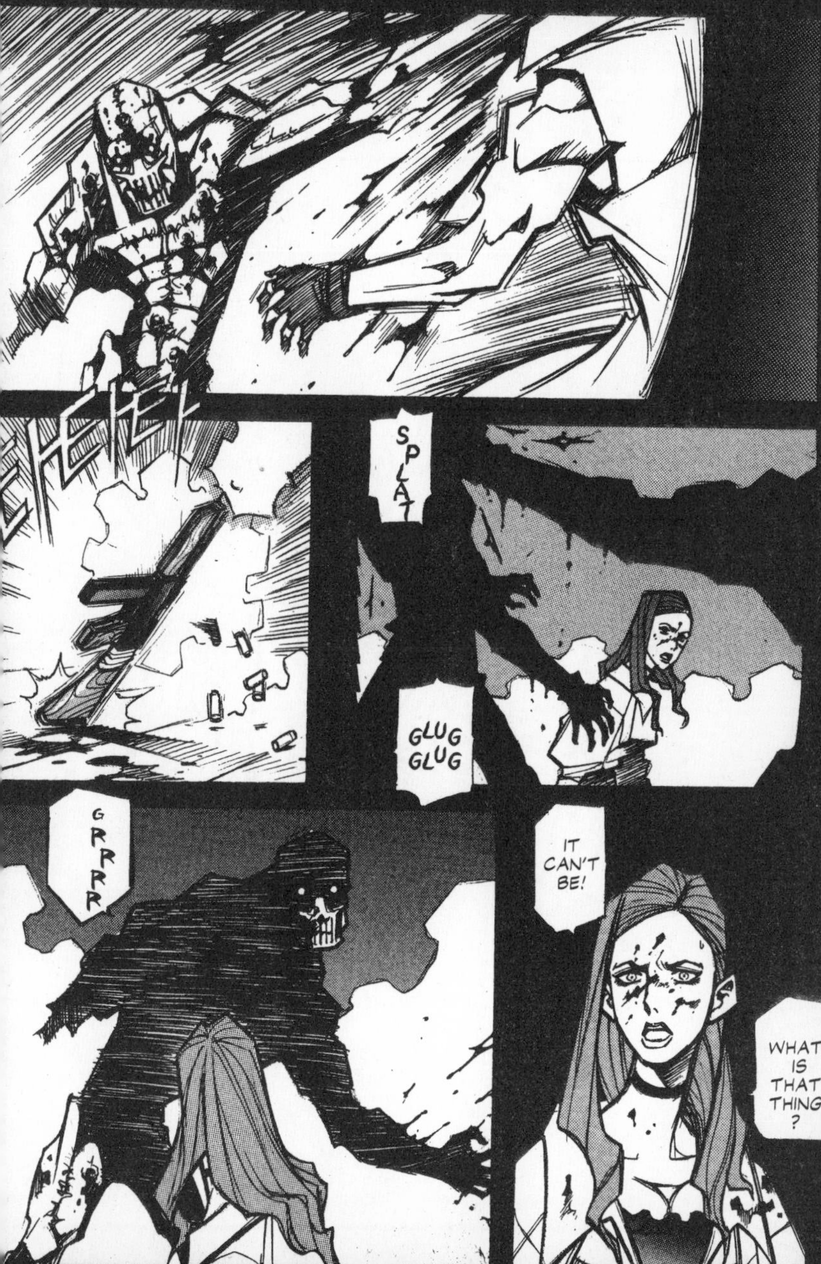
SPLAT
GLUG GLUG
GRRRR
IT CAN'T BE!
WHAT IS THAT THING?

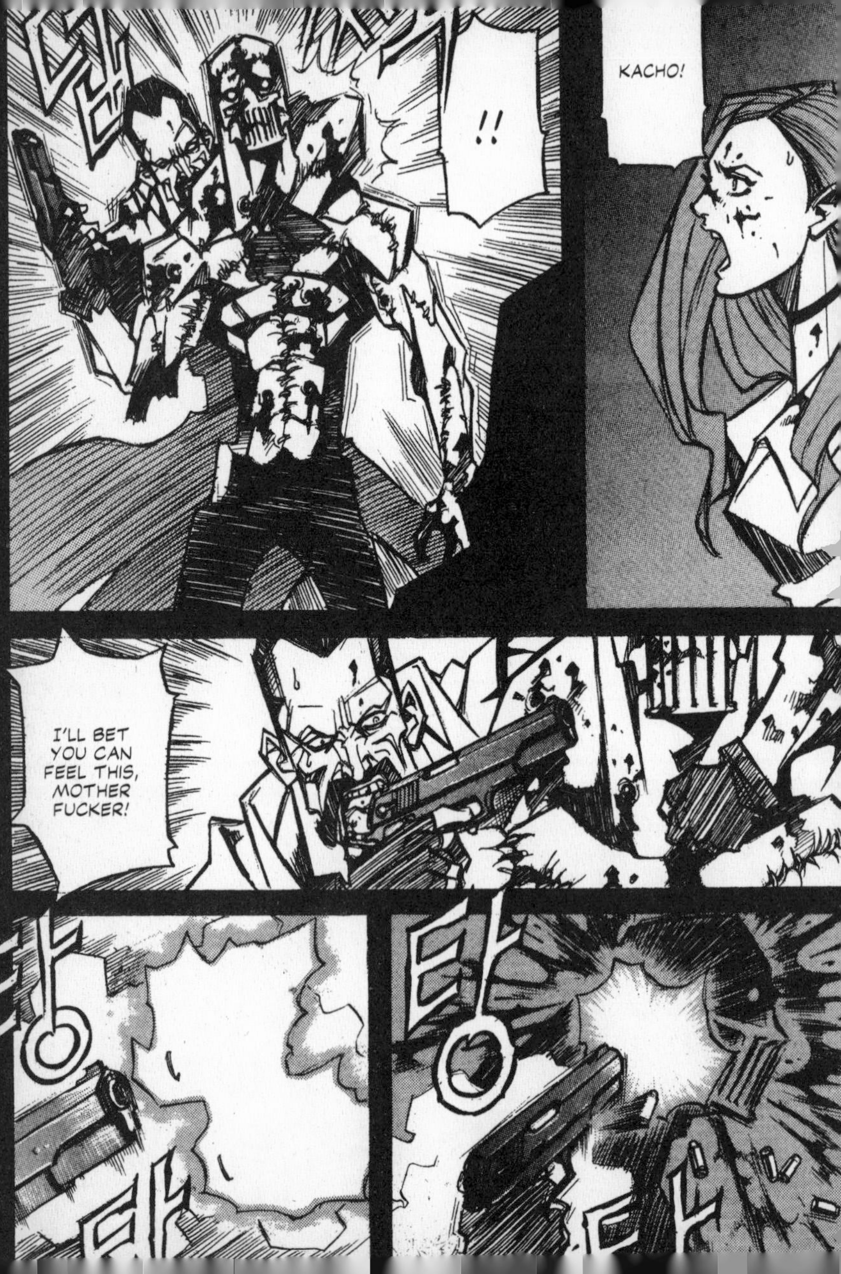
KACHO!
!!
I'LL BET YOU CAN FEEL THIS, MOTHER FUCKER!

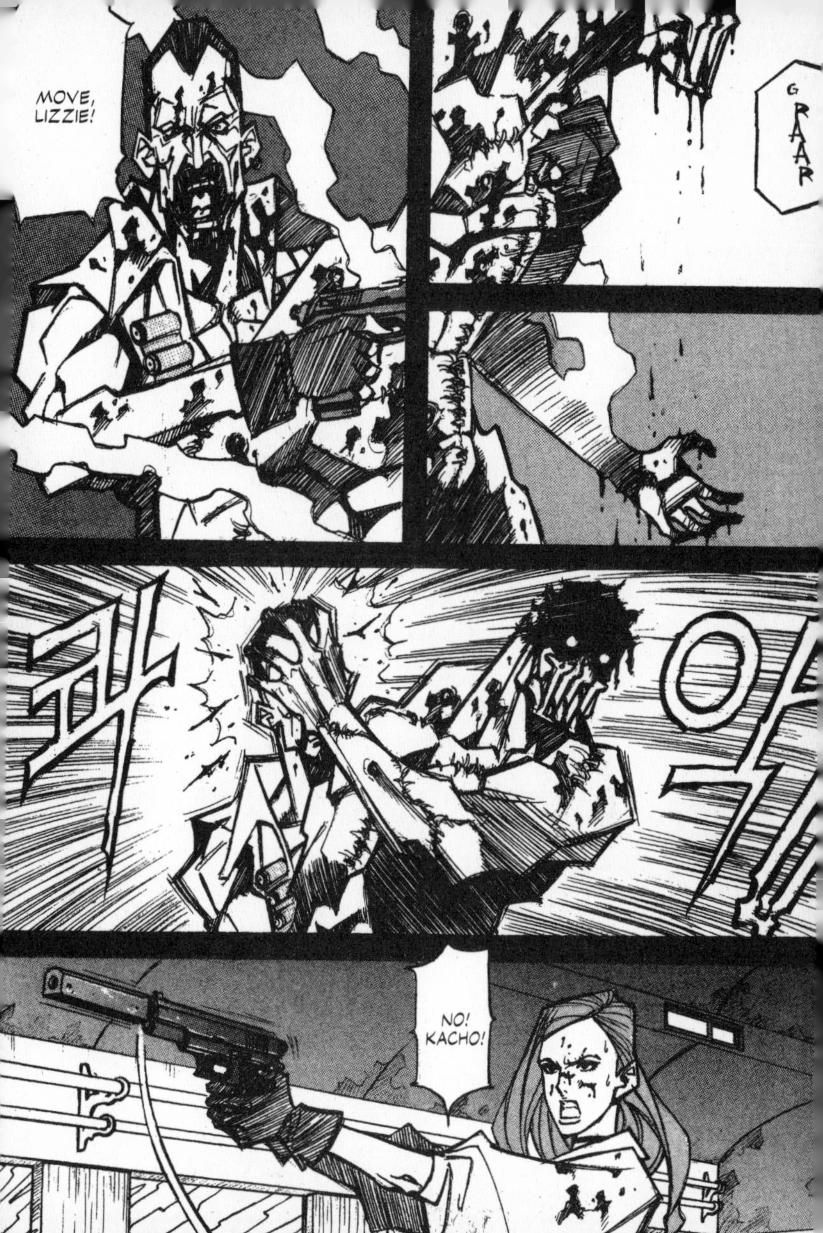
MOVE, LIZZIE!
GRAAR
NO! KACHO!

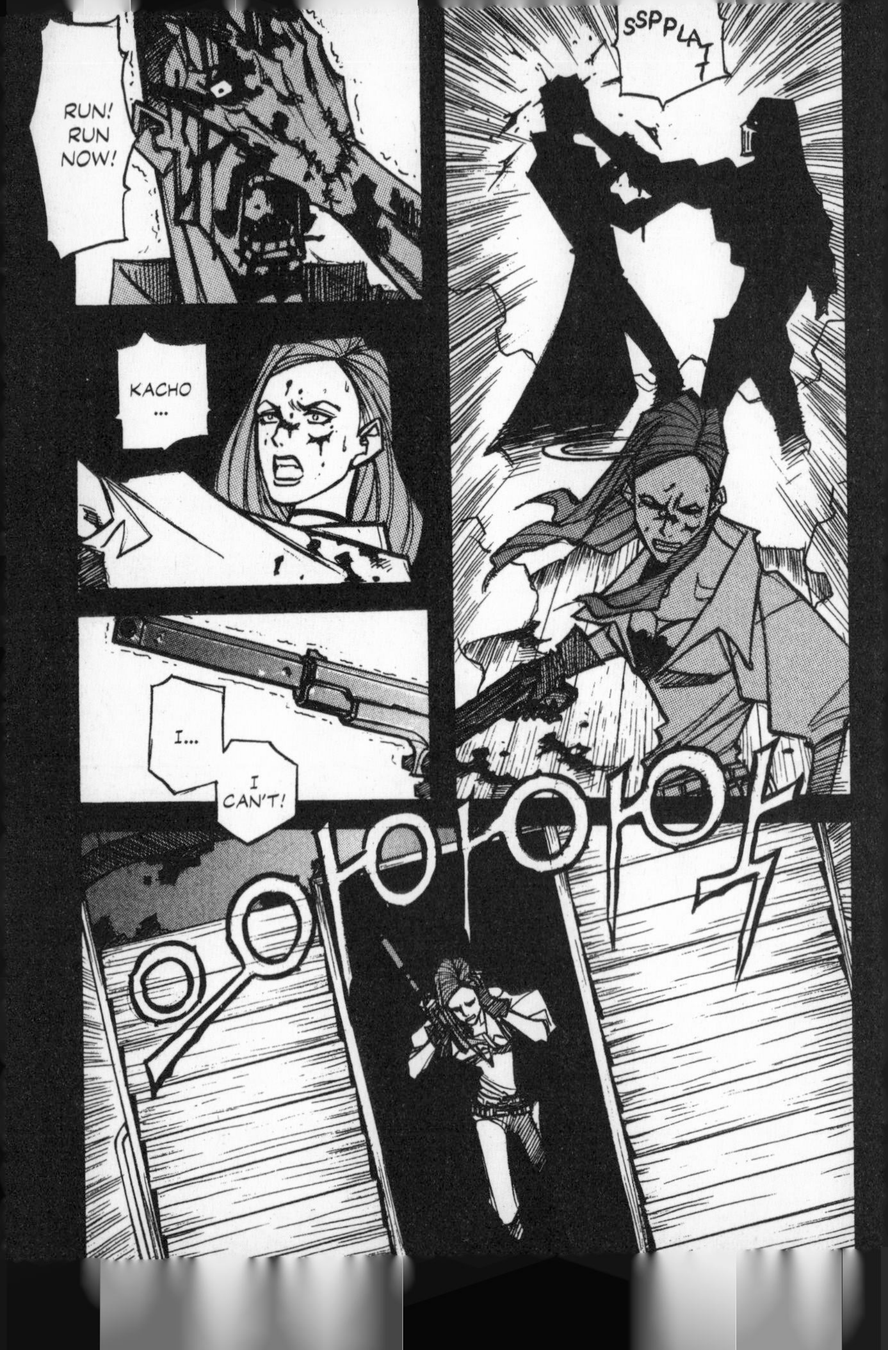
RUN! RUN NOW!
KACHO ...
I...
I CAN'T!
SSPPLAT

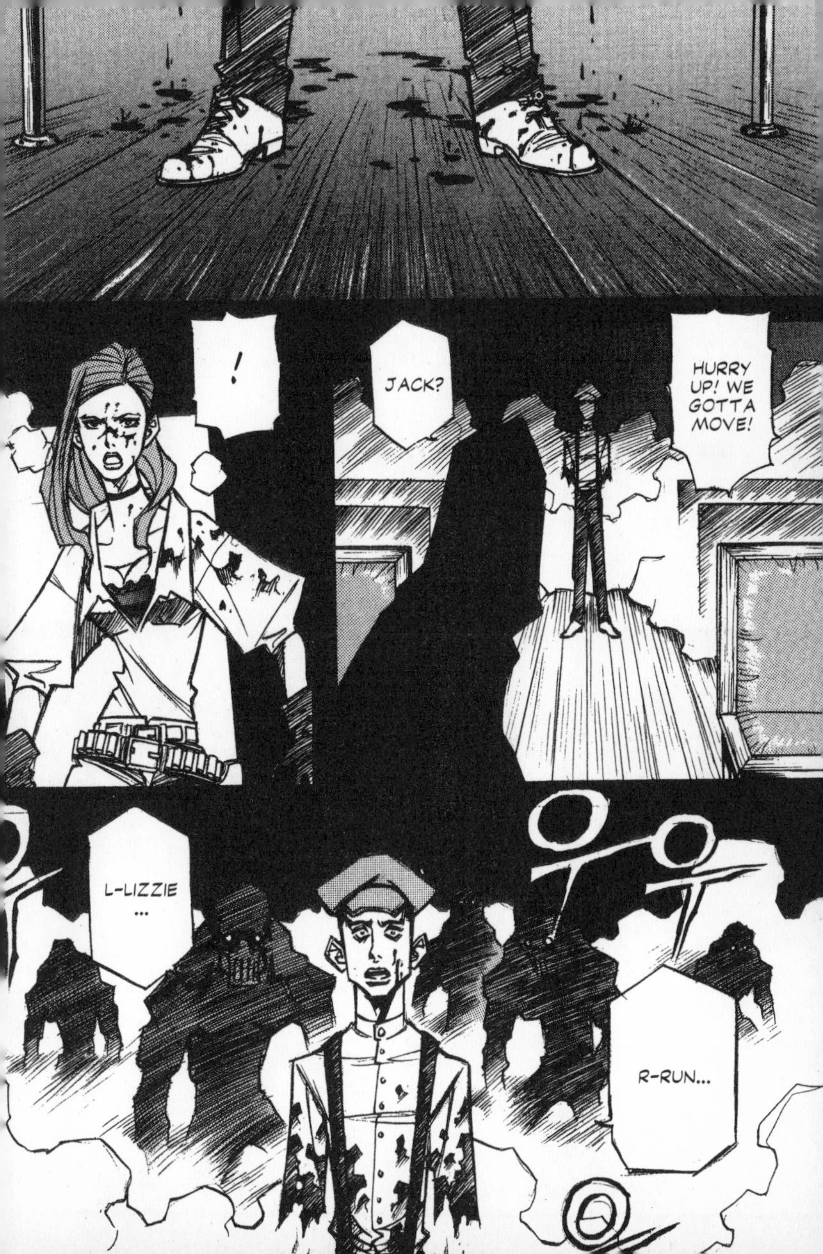
!
JACK?
HURRY UP! WE GOTTA MOVE!
L-LIZZIE ...
R-RUN...

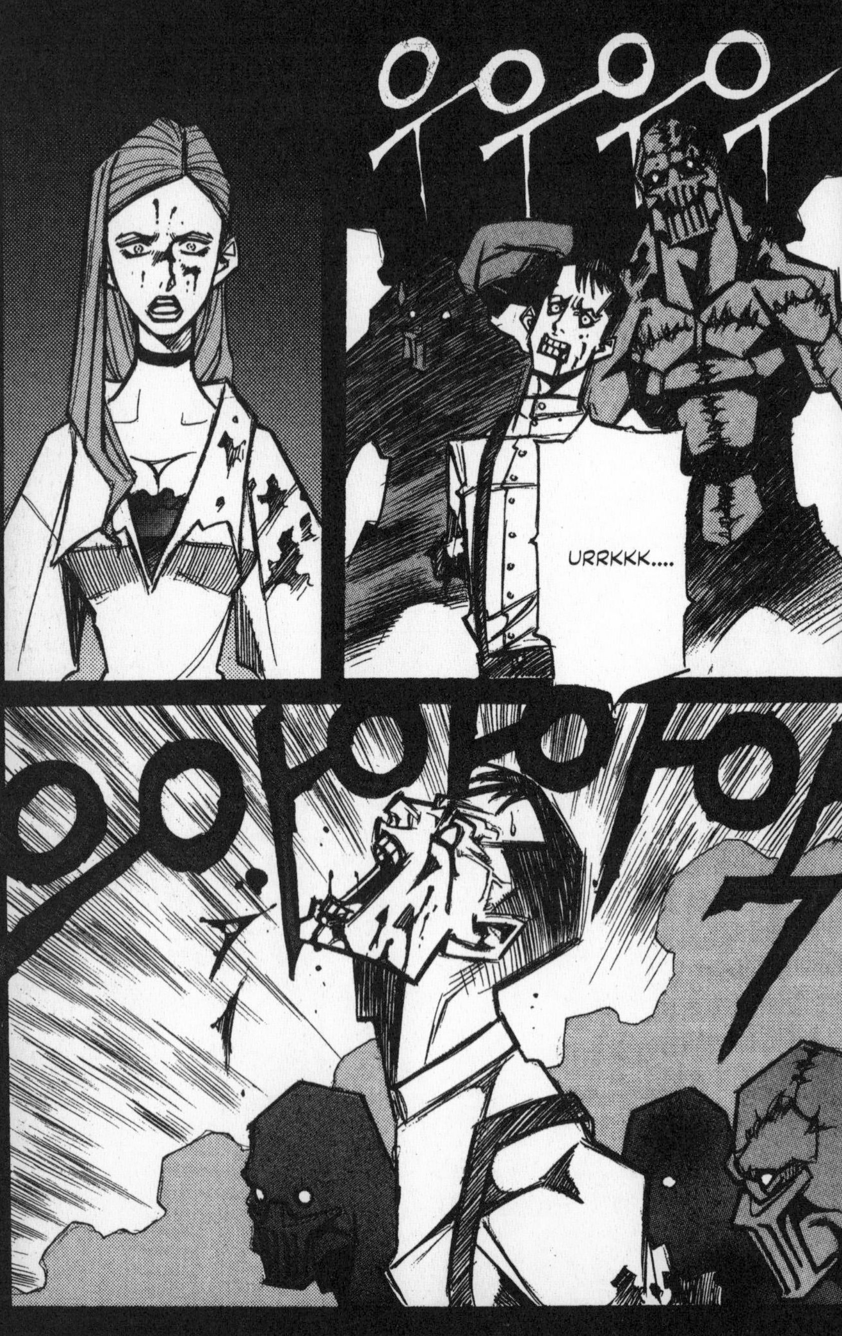
URRKKK....

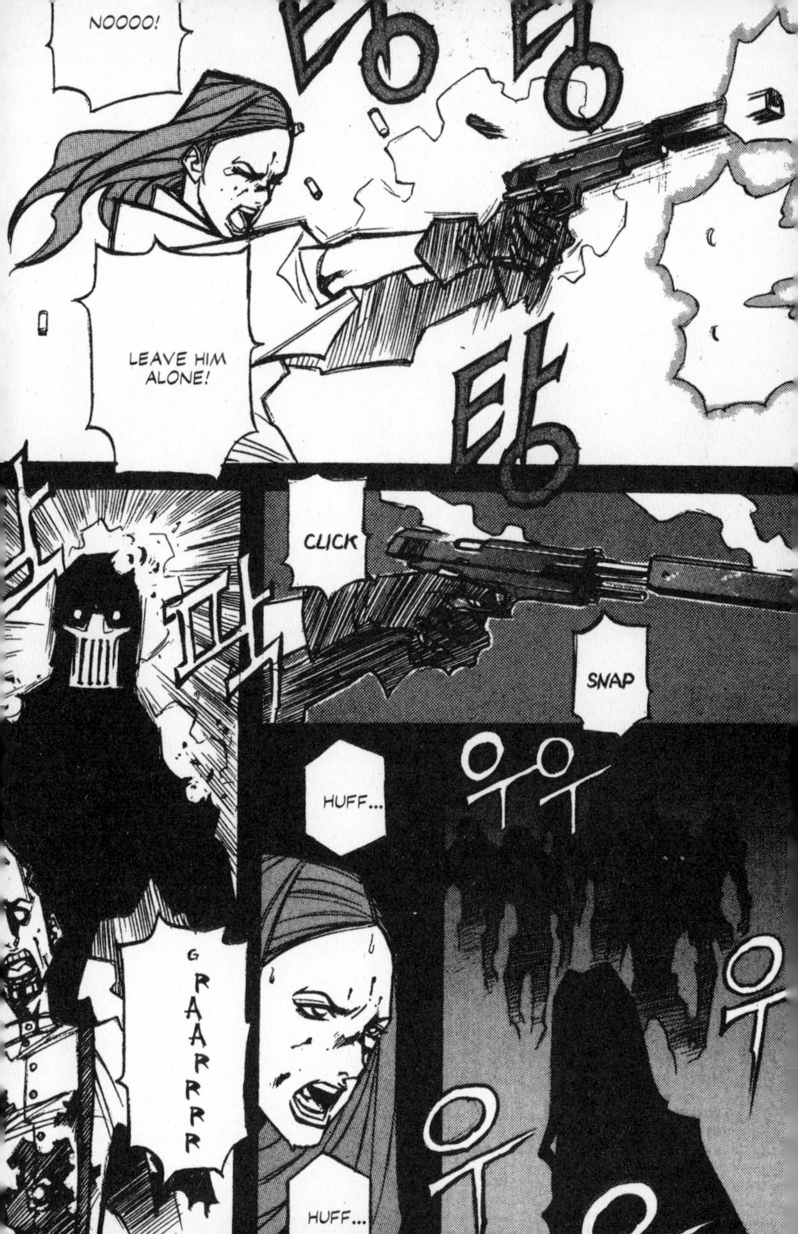
NOOOO!
탕
탕
LEAVE HIM ALONE!
탕
퍽
GRAARRRR
CLICK
SNAP
HUFF...
우우
우
우
우
HUFF...

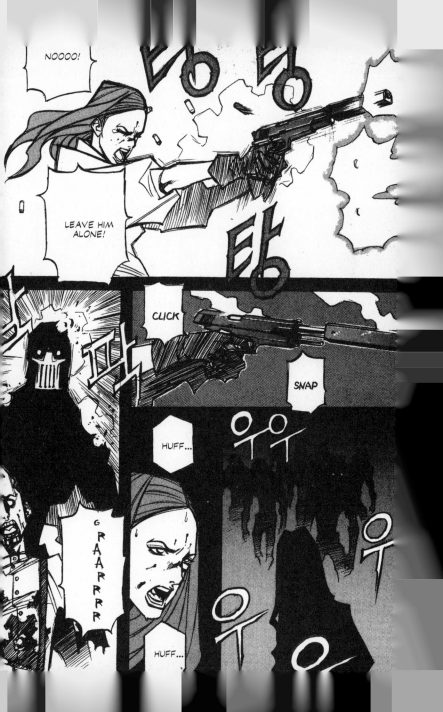

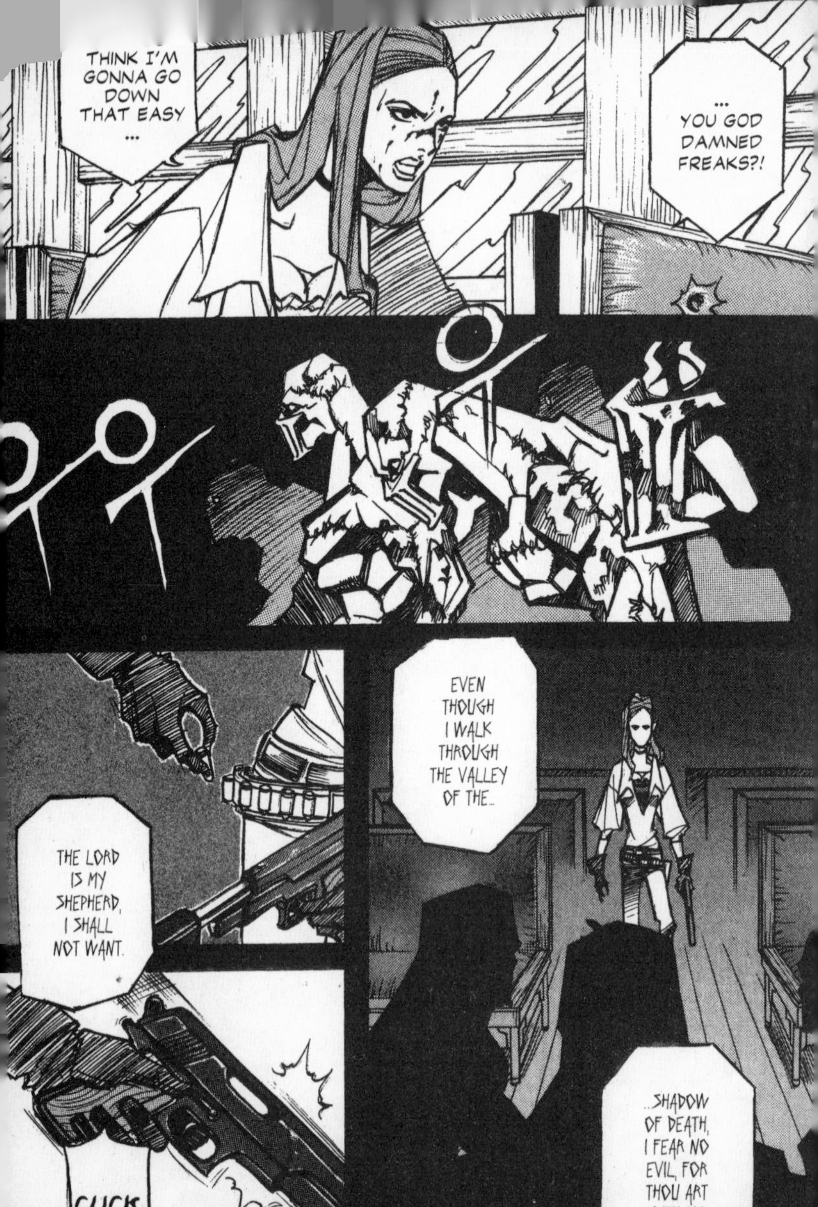
THINK I'M GONNA GO DOWN THAT EASY ...
... YOU GOD DAMNED FREAKS?!
THE LORD IS MY SHEPHERD, I SHALL NOT WANT.
CLICK
EVEN THOUGH I WALK THROUGH THE VALLEY OF THE...
...SHADOW OF DEATH, I FEAR NO EVIL, FOR THOU ART WITH ME.

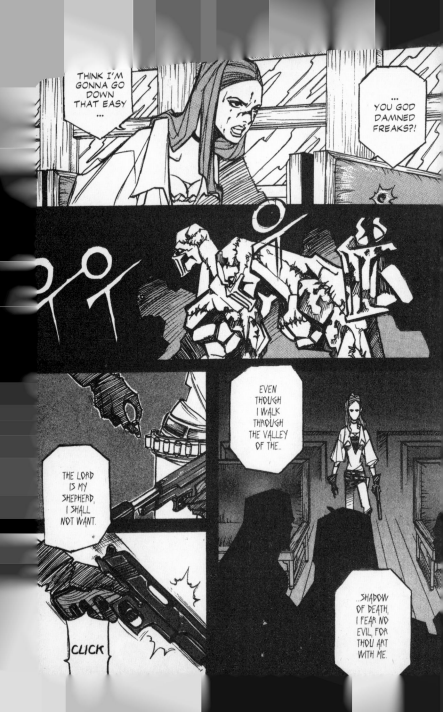

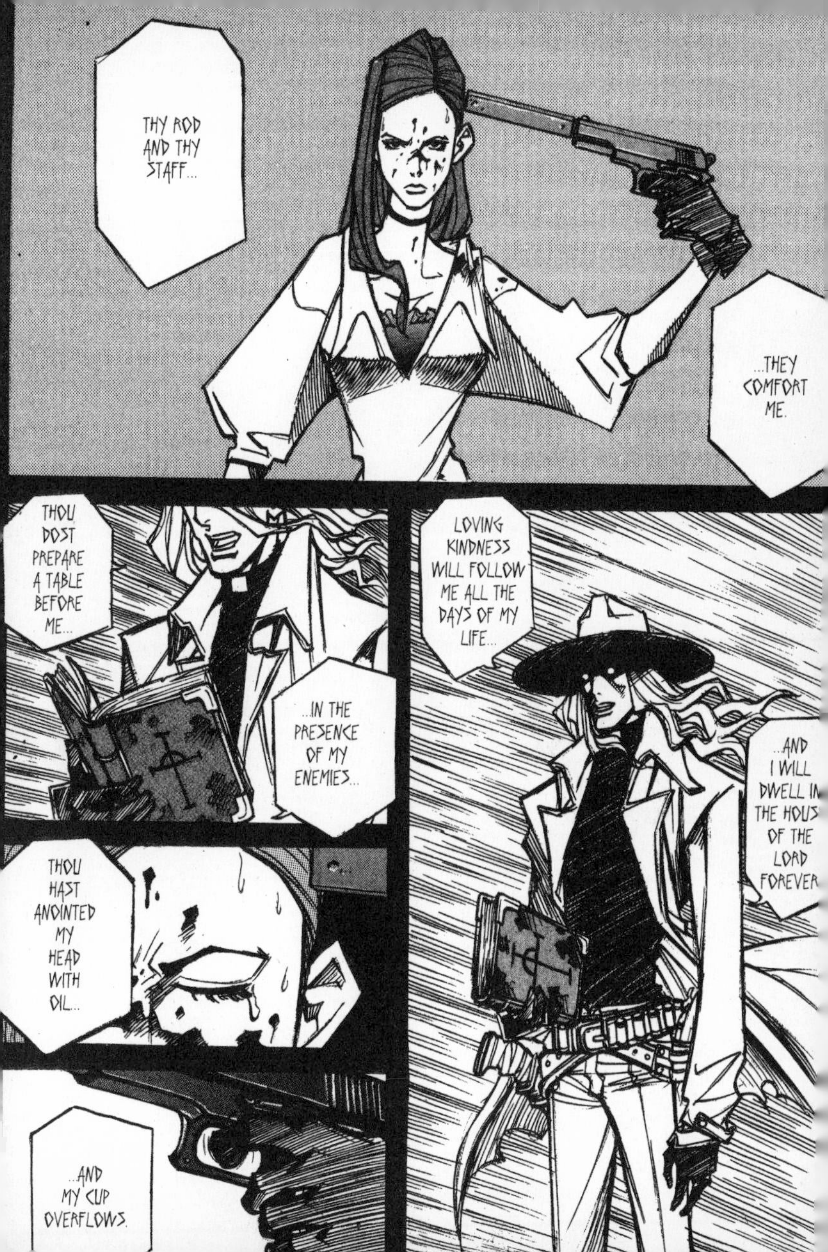
THY ROD AND THY STAFF...
...THEY COMFORT ME.
THOU DOST PREPARE A TABLE BEFORE ME...
...IN THE PRESENCE OF MY ENEMIES...
THOU HAST ANOINTED MY HEAD WITH OIL...
...AND MY CUP OVERFLOWS.
LOVING KINDNESS WILL FOLLOW ME ALL THE DAYS OF MY LIFE...
...AND I WILL DWELL IN THE HOUS OF THE LORD FOREVER

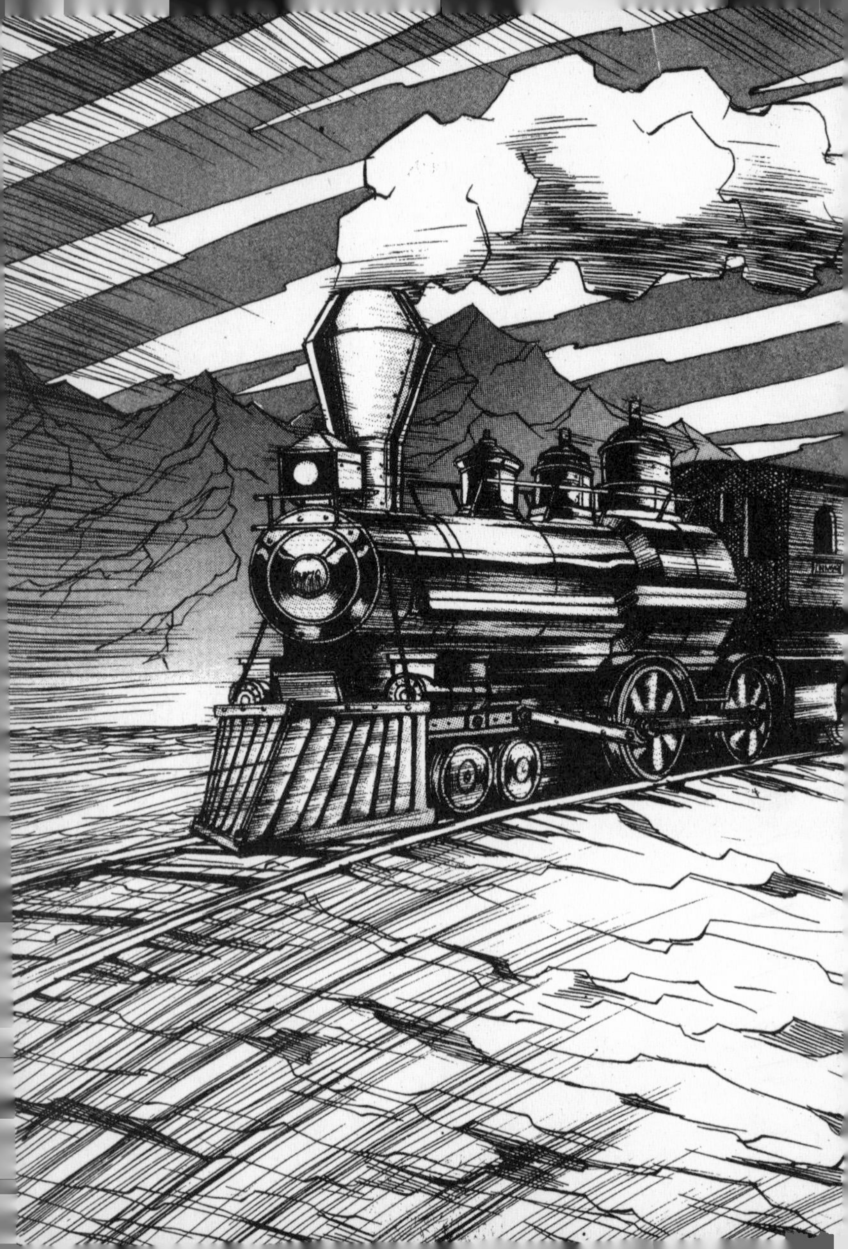

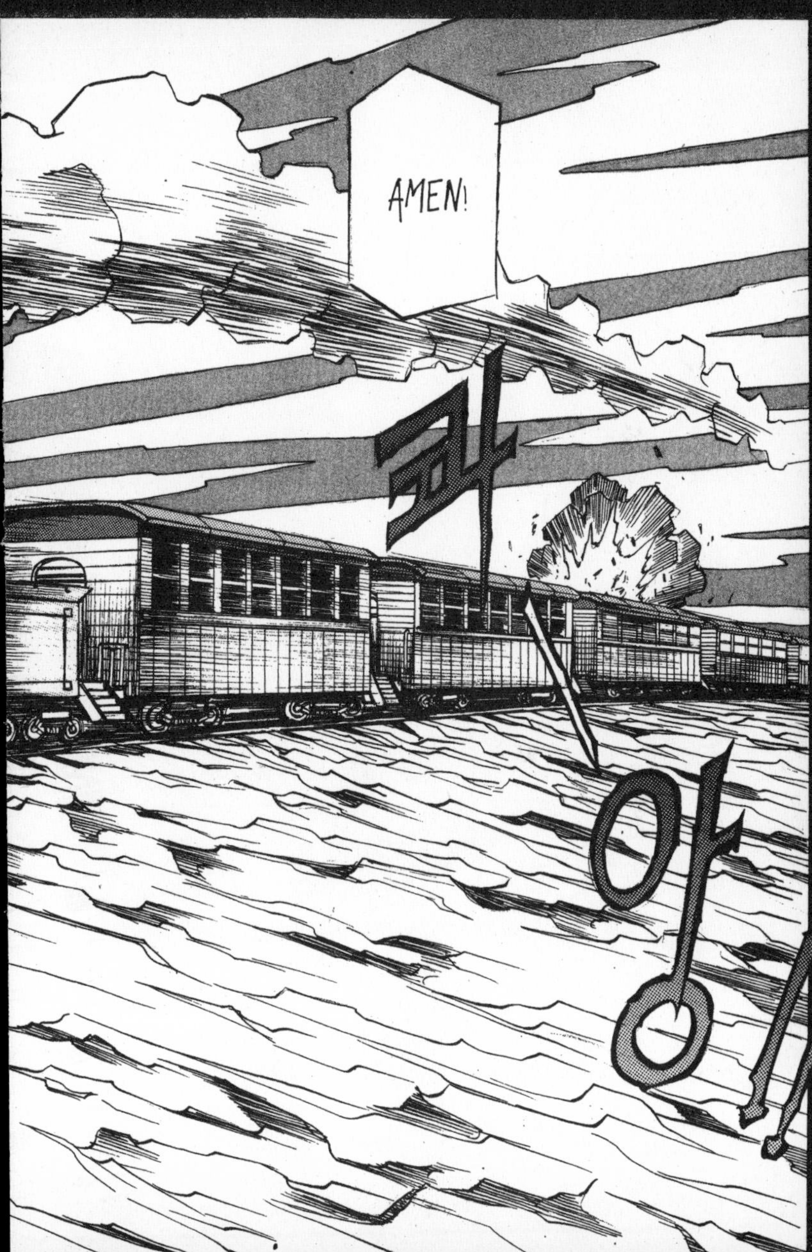
AMEN!
콰앙!!

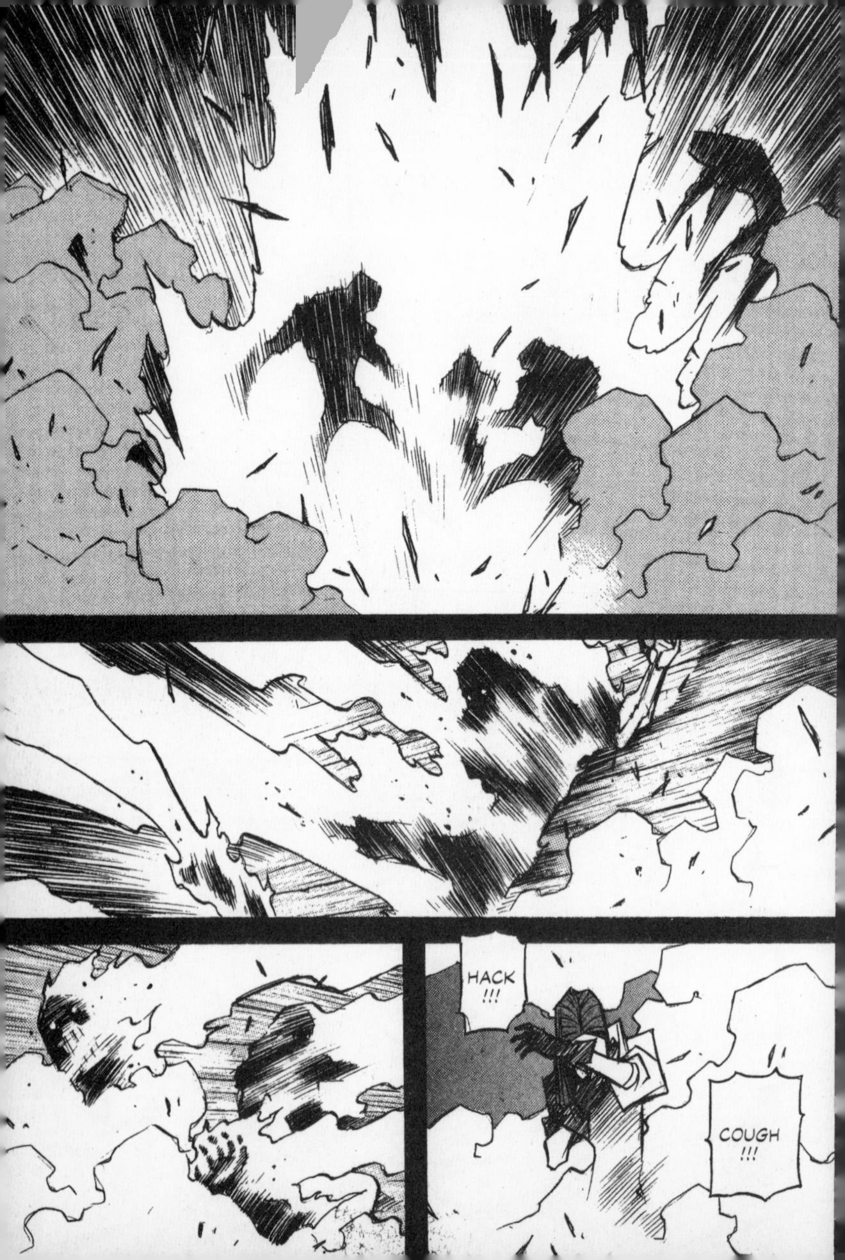
HACK !!!
COUGH !!!

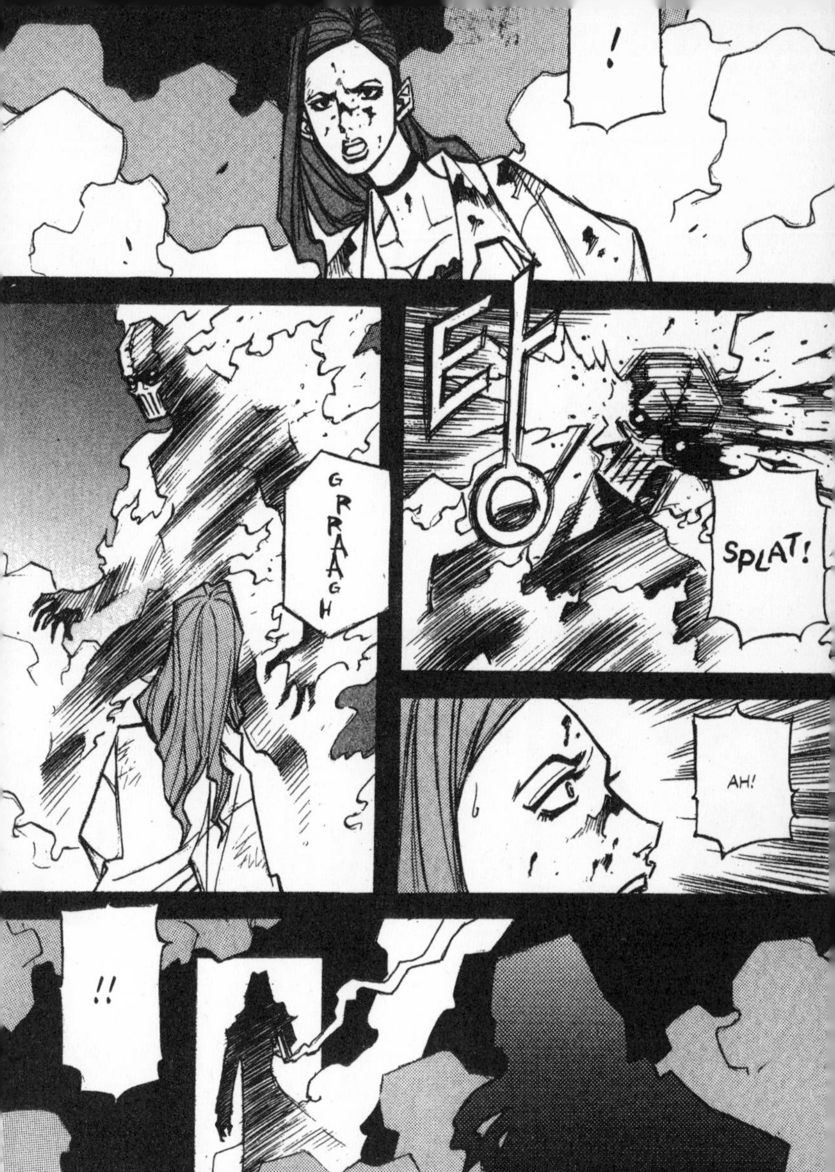
!
GRRAAGH
SPLAT!
AH!
!!

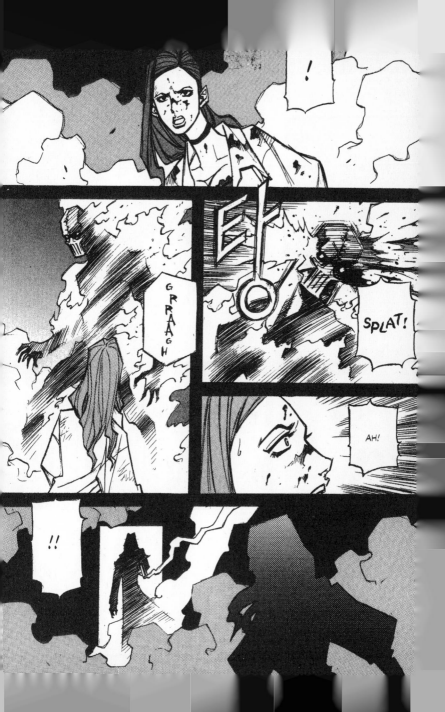

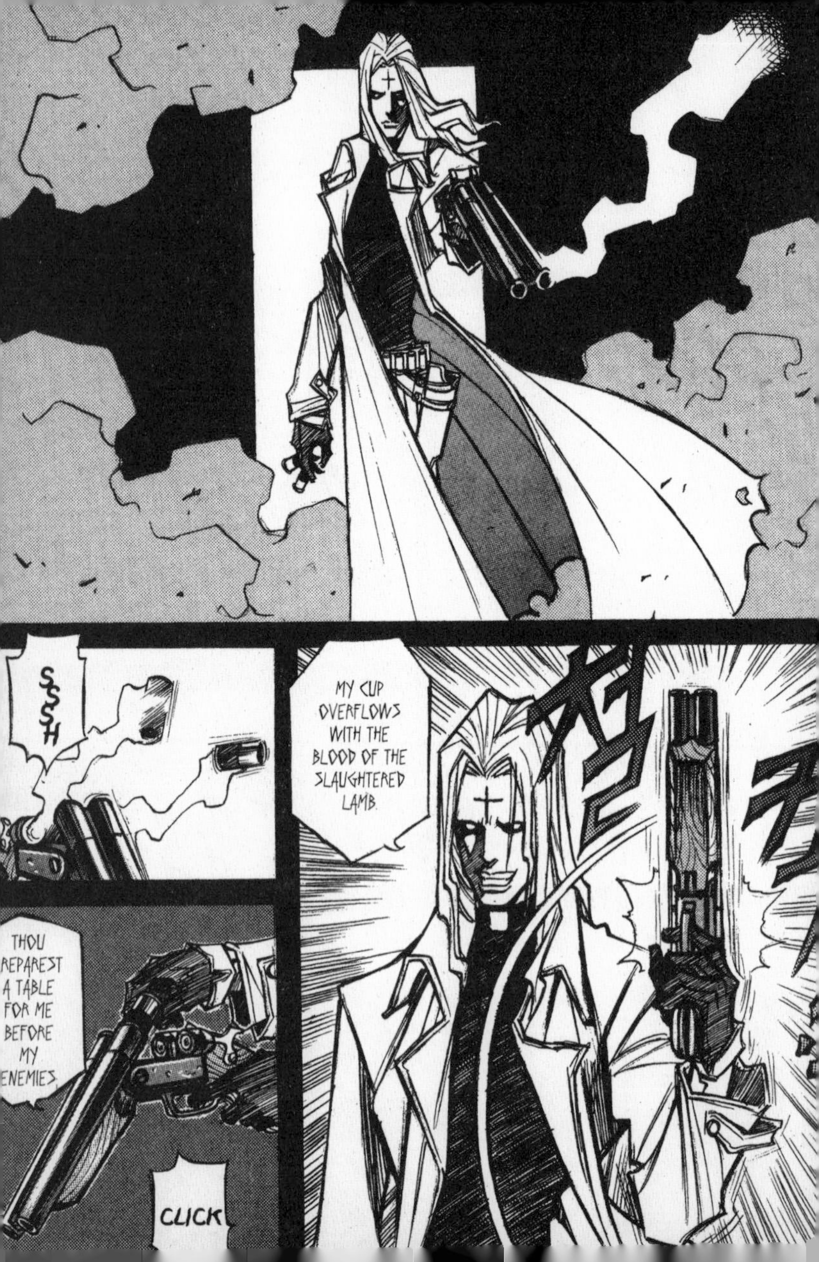
SSSH
THOU REPAREST A TABLE FOR ME BEFORE MY ENEMIES.
CLICK
MY CUP OVERFLOWS WITH THE BLOOD OF THE SLAUGHTERED LAMB.

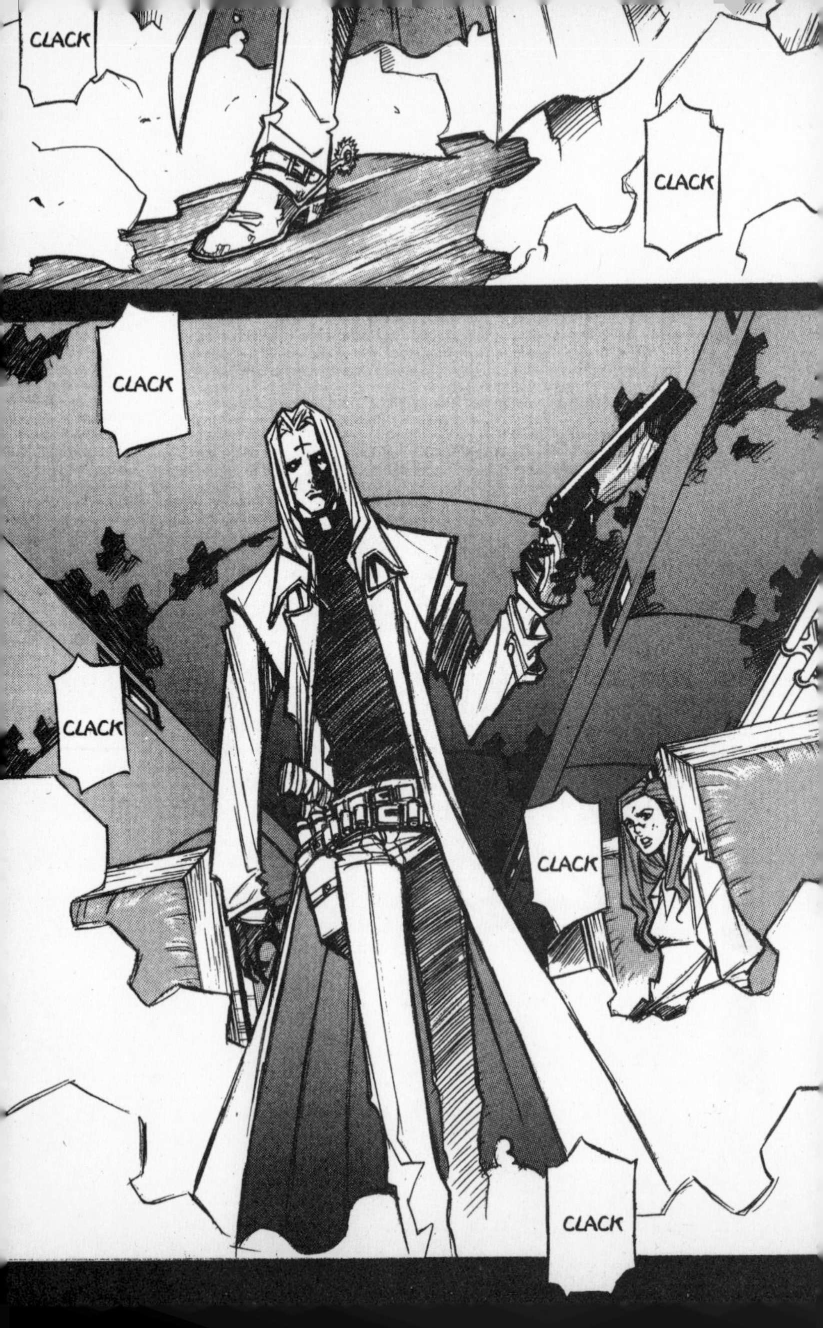
CLACK
CLACK
CLACK
CLACK
CLACK
CLACK

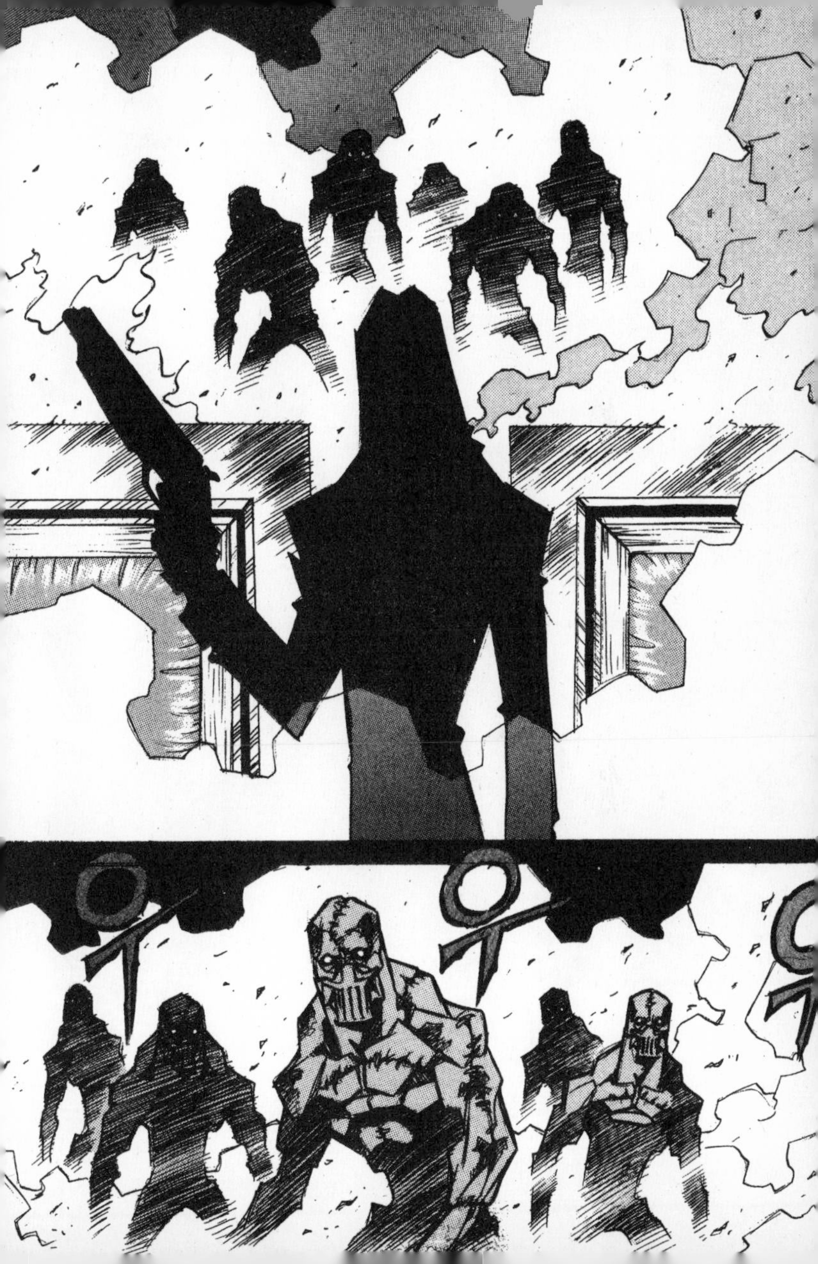

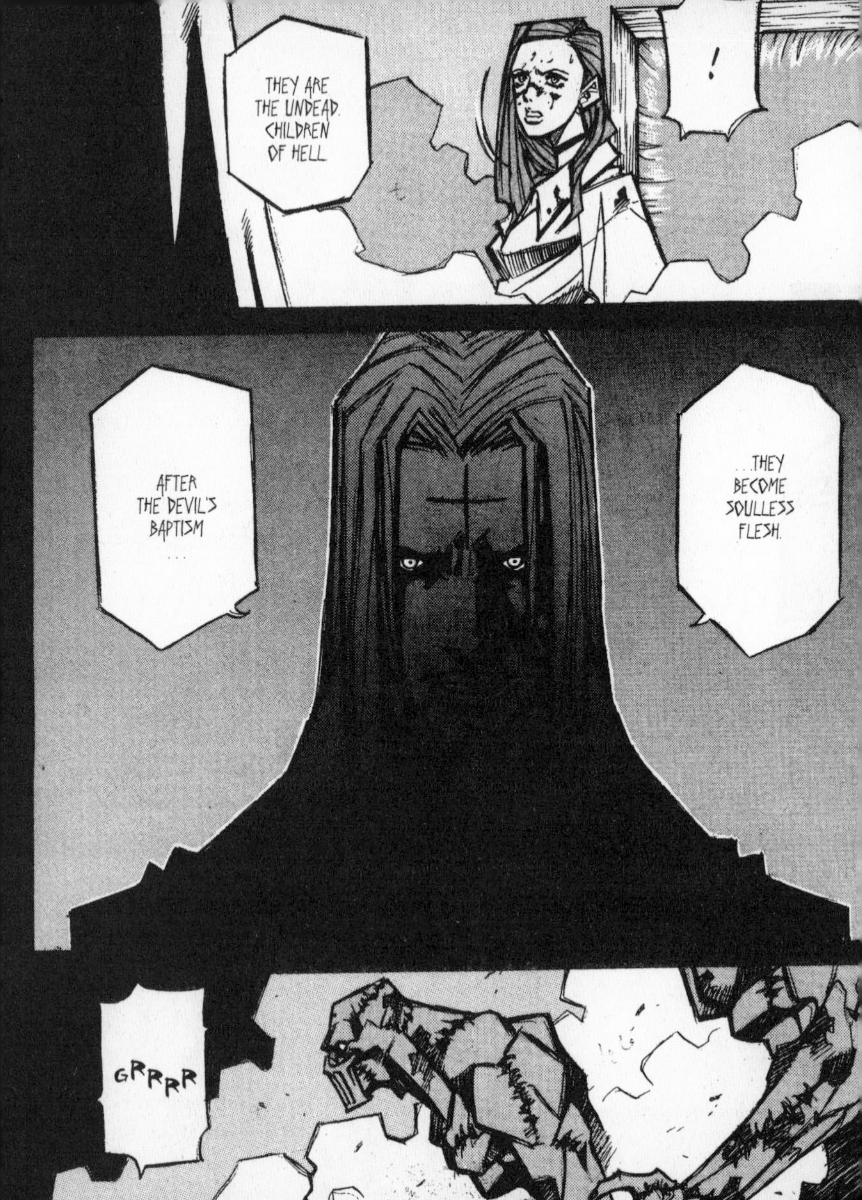
THEY ARE THE UNDEAD. CHILDREN OF HELL.
!
AFTER THE DEVIL'S BAPTISM ...
...THEY BECOME SOULLESS FLESH.
GRRRR

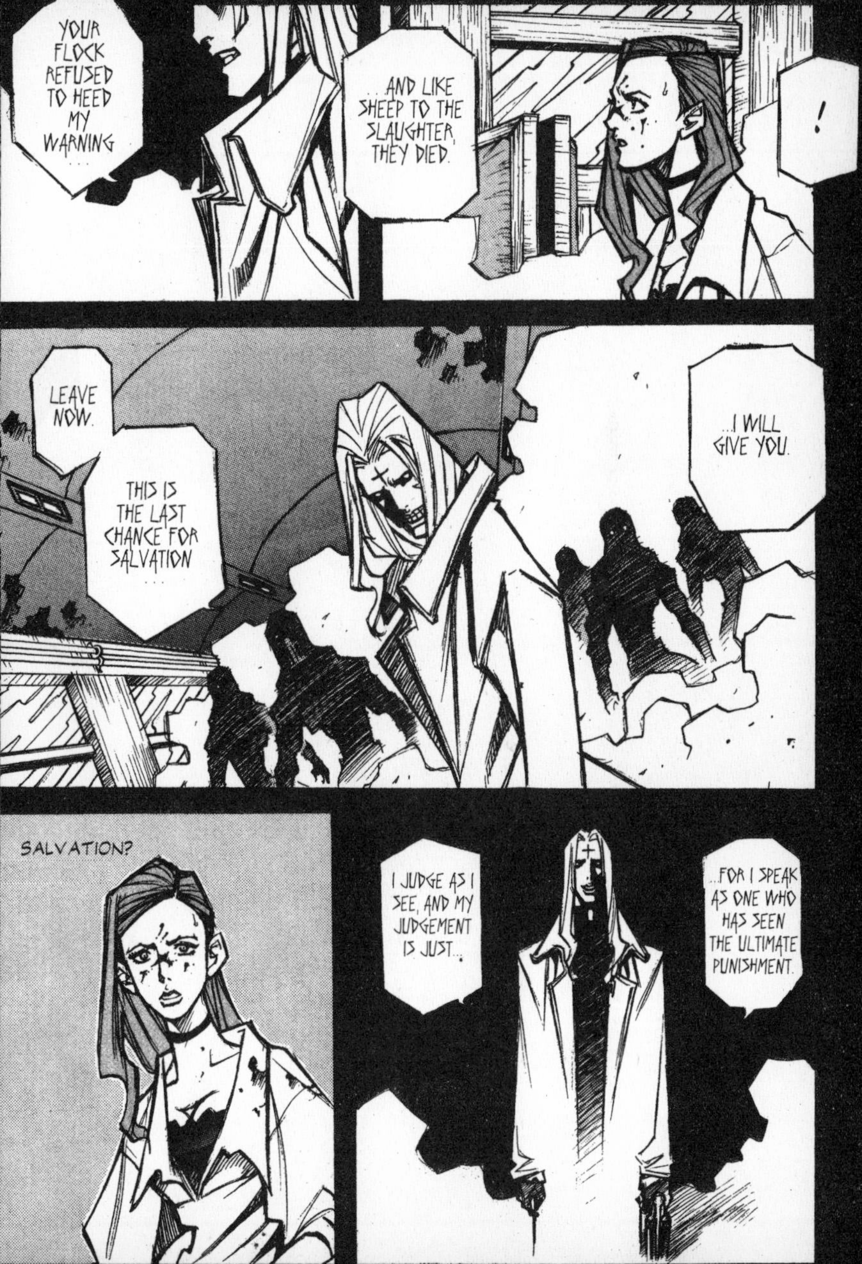
YOUR FLOCK REFUSED TO HEED MY WARNING . . .
. . . AND LIKE SHEEP TO THE SLAUGHTER, THEY DIED.
!
LEAVE NOW.
THIS IS THE LAST CHANCE FOR SALVATION . . .
...I WILL GIVE YOU.
SALVATION?
I JUDGE AS I SEE, AND MY JUDGEMENT IS JUST...
...FOR I SPEAK AS ONE WHO HAS SEEN THE ULTIMATE PUNISHMENT.

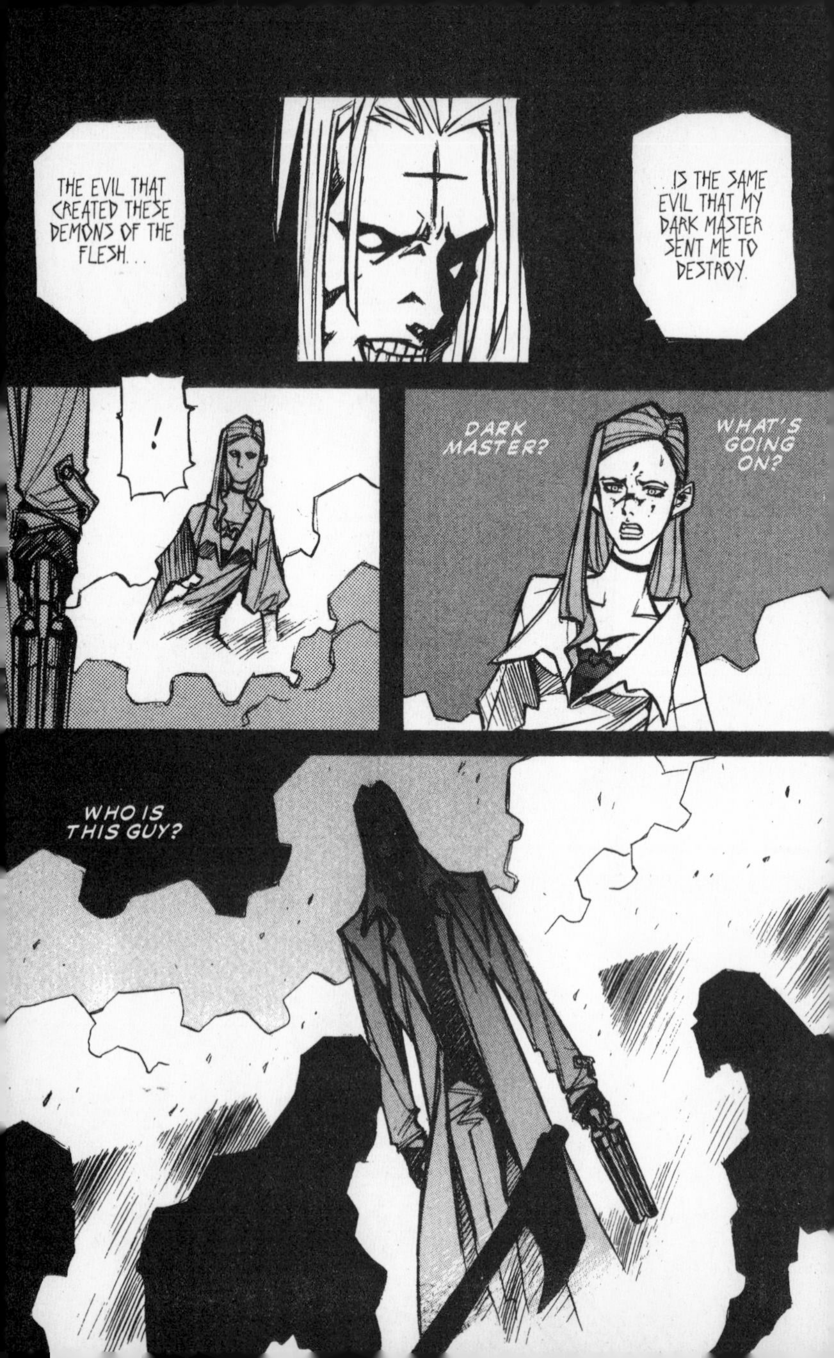
THE EVIL THAT CREATED THESE DEMONS OF THE FLESH...
...IS THE SAME EVIL THAT MY DARK MASTER SENT ME TO DESTROY.
!
DARK MASTER?
WHAT'S GOING ON?
WHO IS THIS GUY?

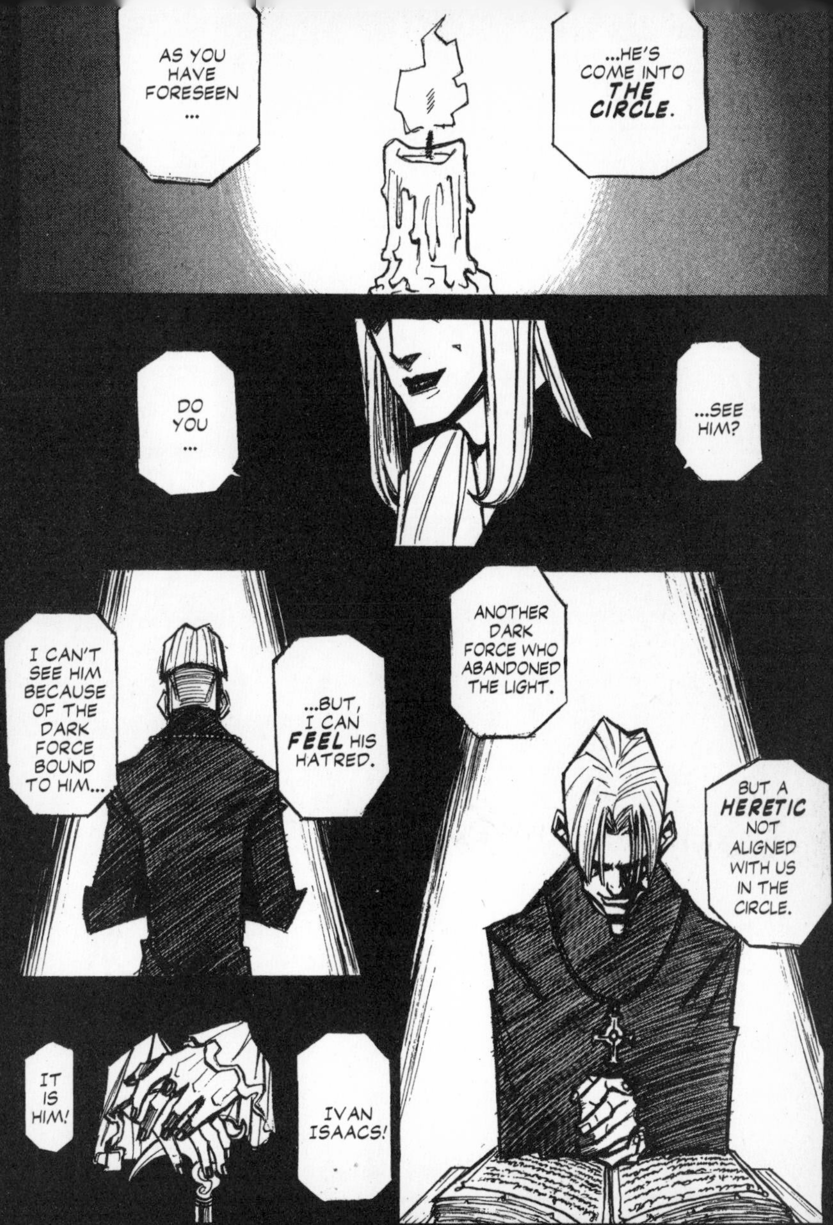
AS YOU HAVE FORESEEN ...
...HE'S COME INTO THE CIRCLE.
DO YOU ...
...SEE HIM?
I CAN'T SEE HIM BECAUSE OF THE DARK FORCE BOUND TO HIM...
...BUT, I CAN FEEL HIS HATRED.
ANOTHER DARK FORCE WHO ABANDONED THE LIGHT.
BUT A HERETIC NOT ALIGNED WITH US IN THE CIRCLE.
IT IS HIM!
IVAN ISAACS!

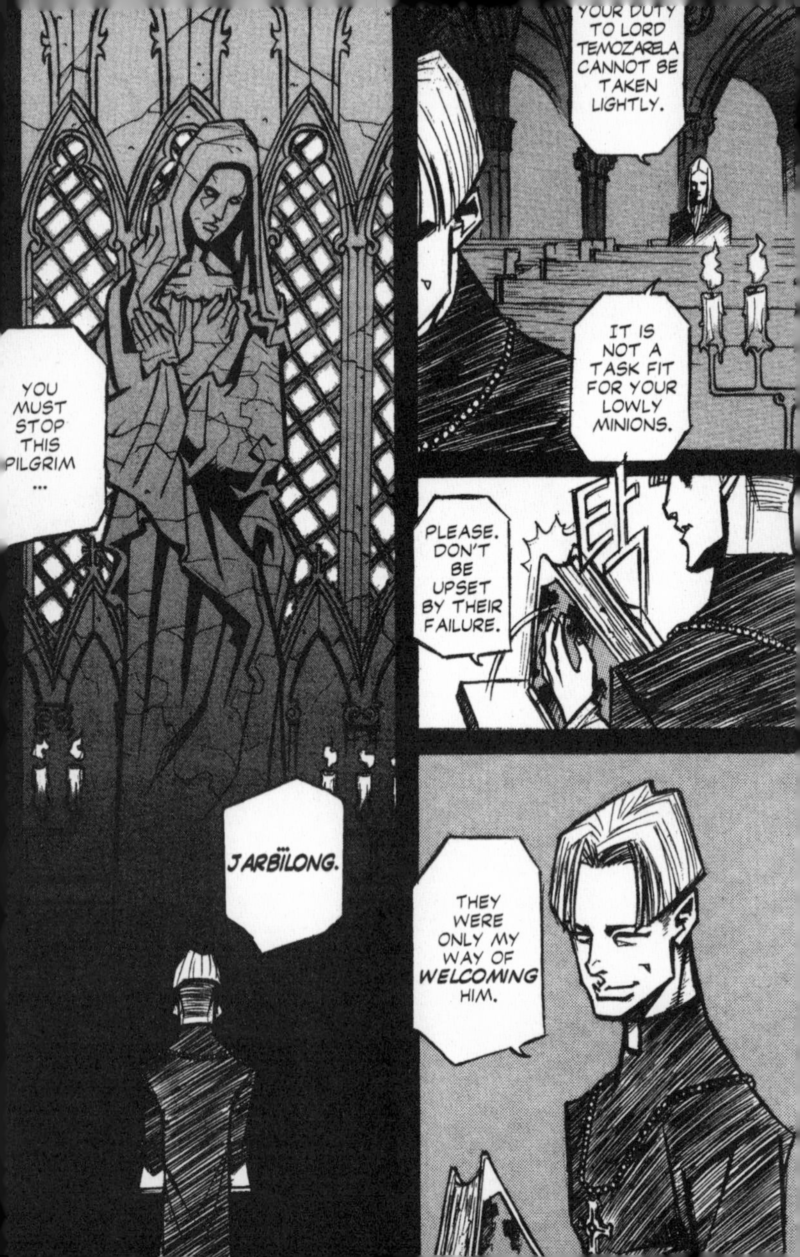
YOU MUST STOP THIS PILGRIM ...
... JARBILONG.
YOUR DUTY TO LORD TEMOZARELA CANNOT BE TAKEN LIGHTLY.
IT IS NOT A TASK FIT FOR YOUR LOWLY MINIONS.
PLEASE. DON'T BE UPSET BY THEIR FAILURE.
THEY WERE ONLY MY WAY OF WELCOMING HIM.

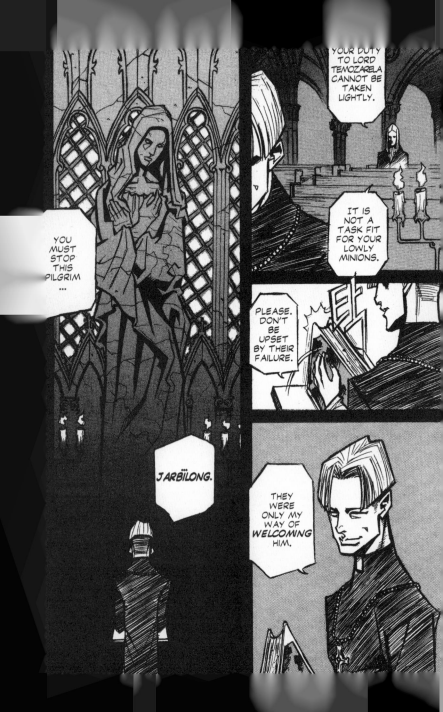

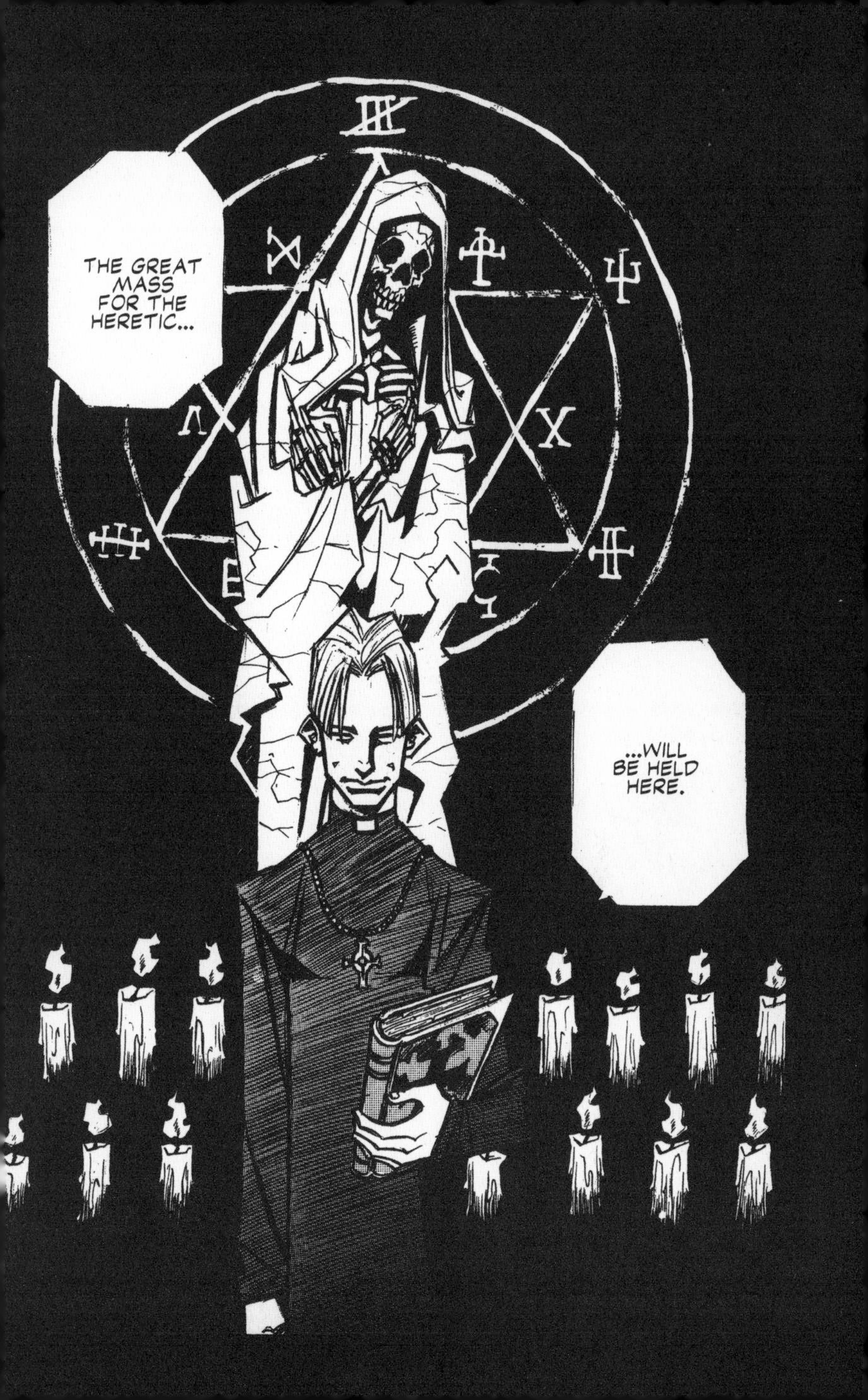
THE GREAT MASS FOR THE HERETIC...
...WILL BE HELD HERE.

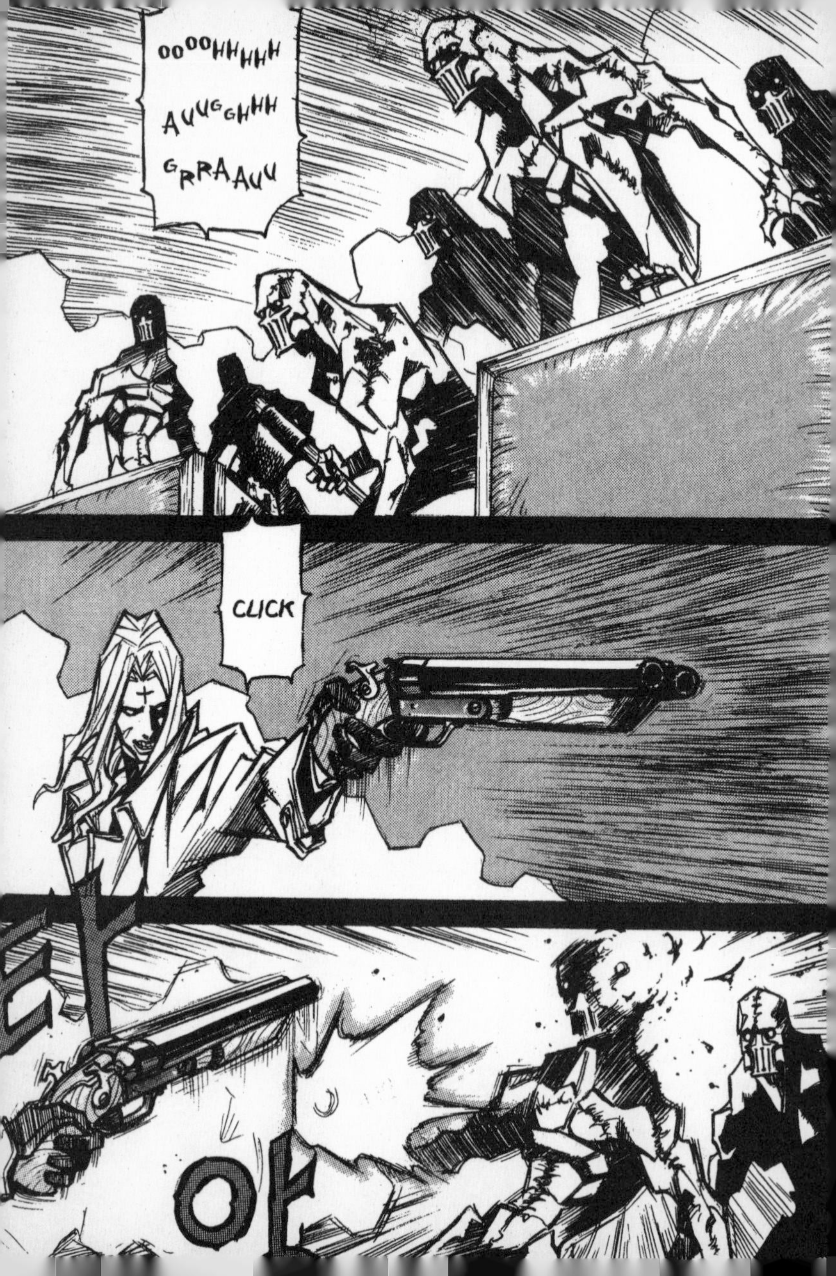
OOOOHHHHH
AUUGGHHH
GRRAAUU
CLICK
OP

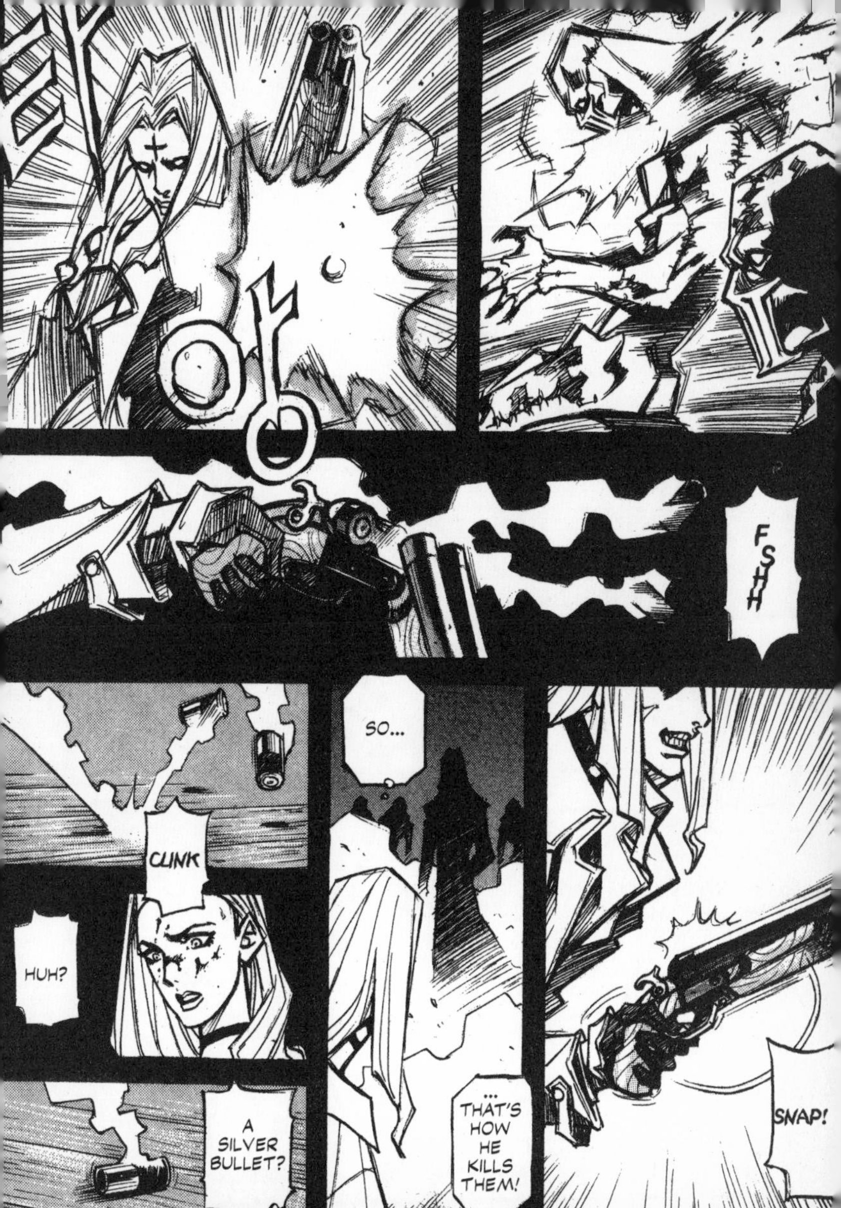
FSHH
CLINK
HUH?
A SILVER BULLET?
SO...
...THAT'S HOW HE KILLS THEM!
SNAP!

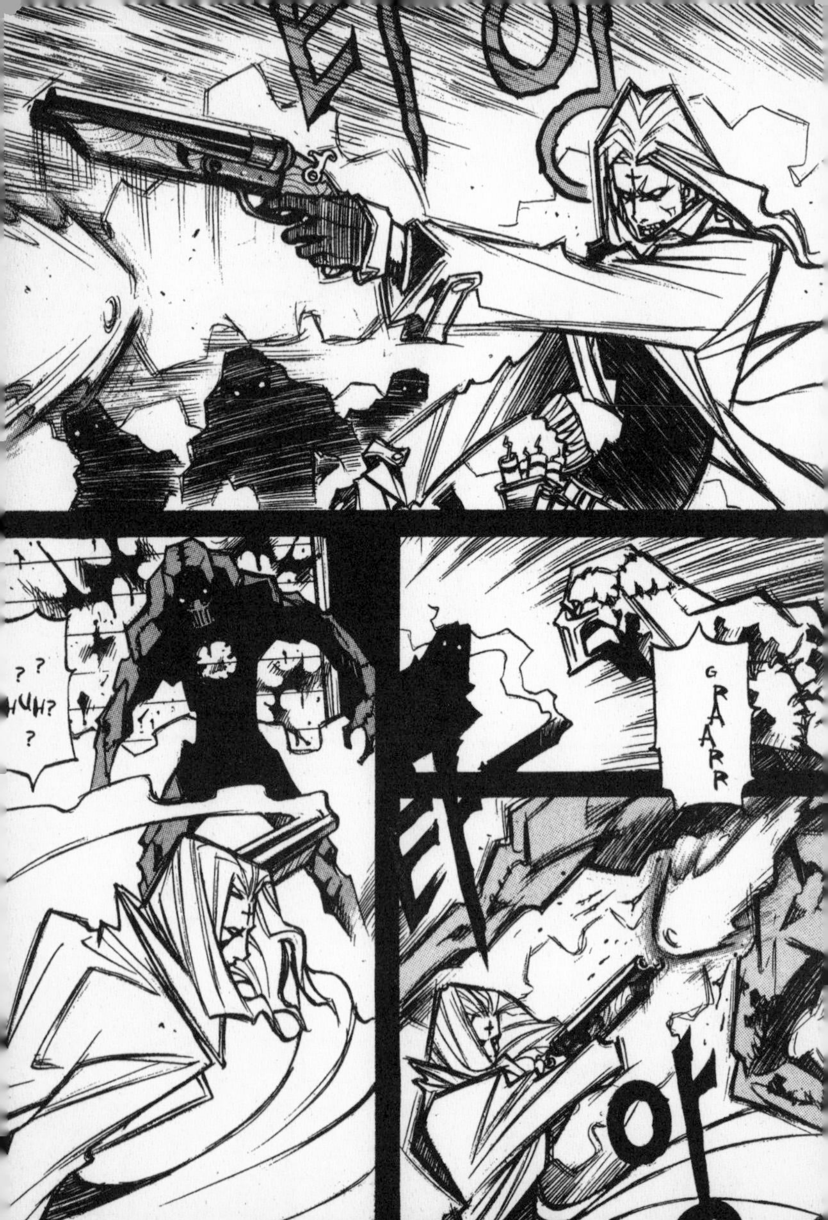
? ? HUH? ?
GRARR

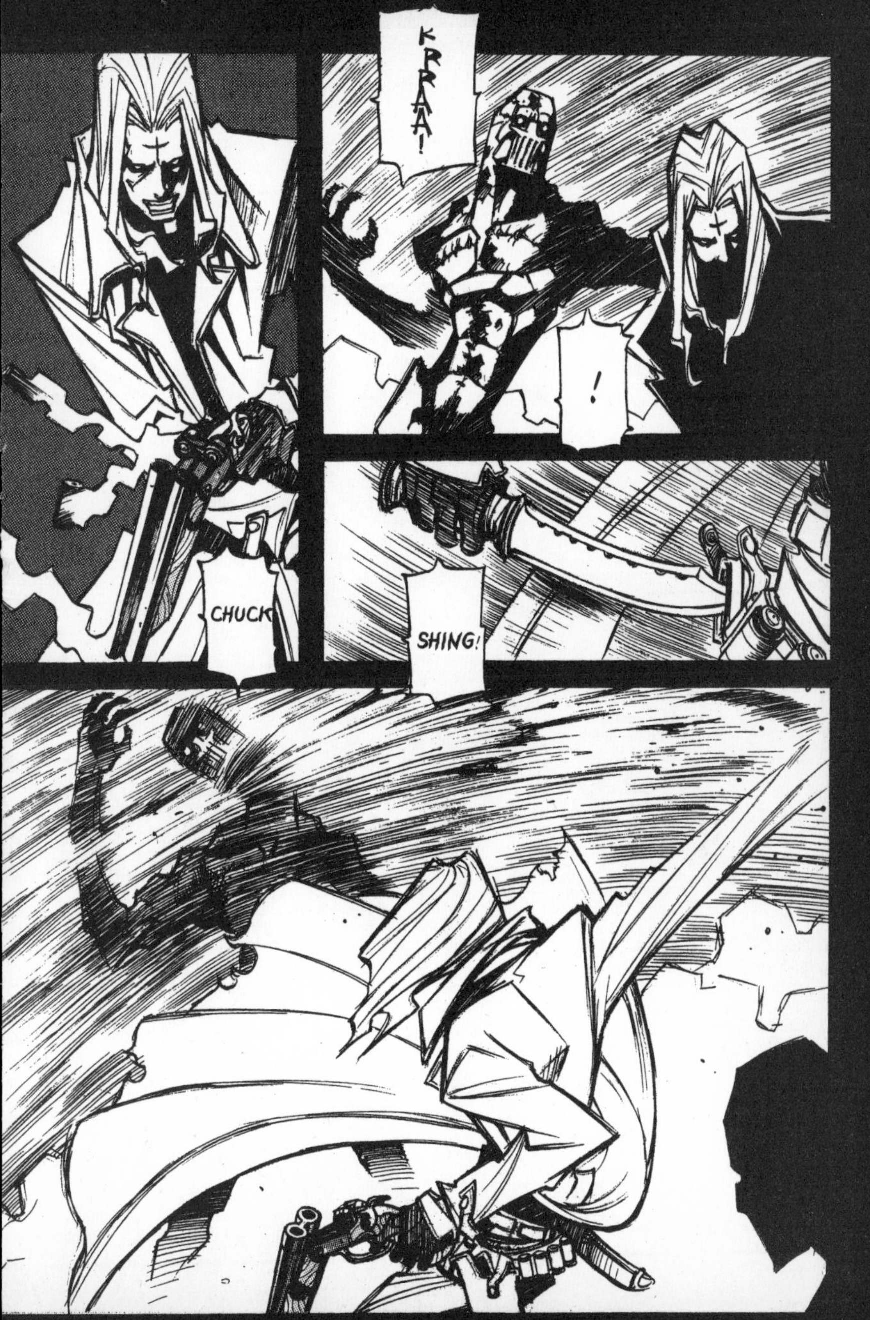
KRRAAA!
!
SHING!
CHUCK

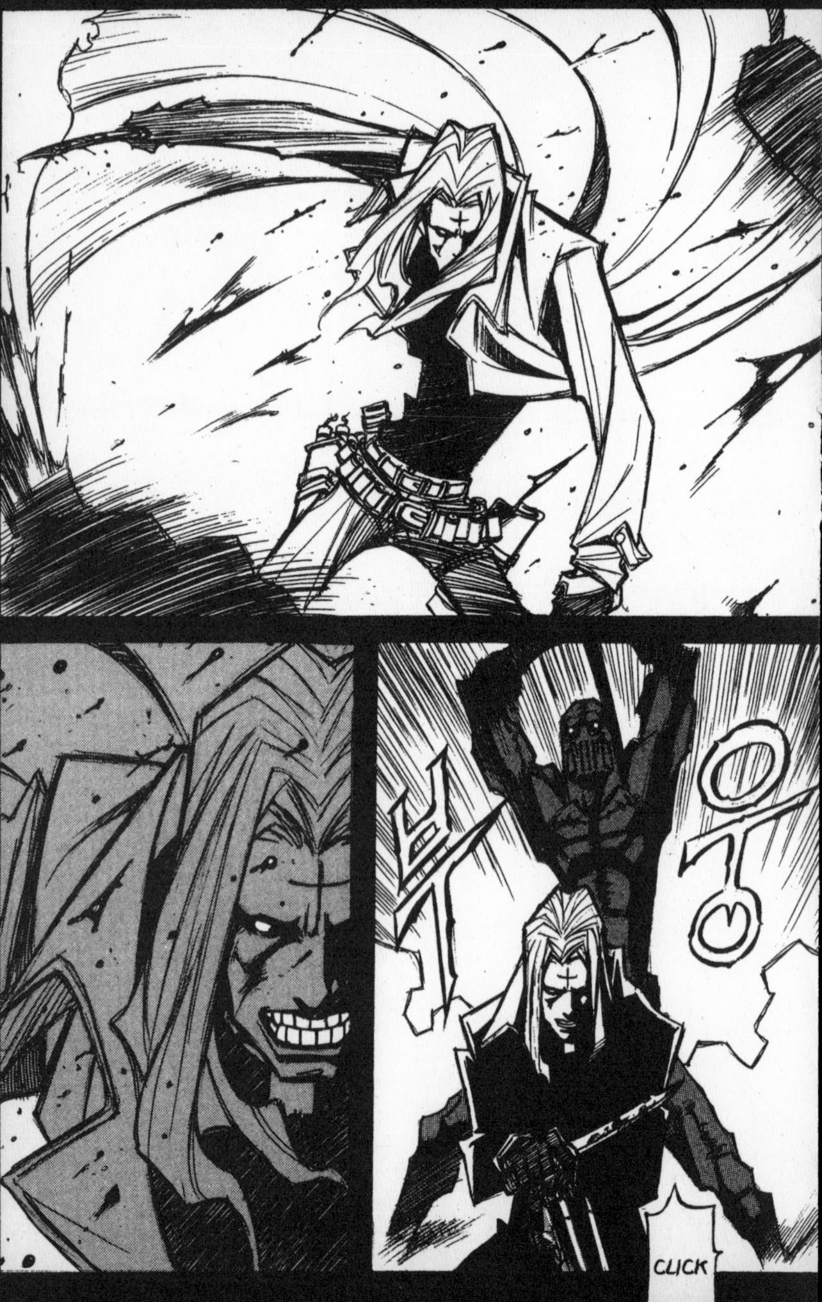
CLICK

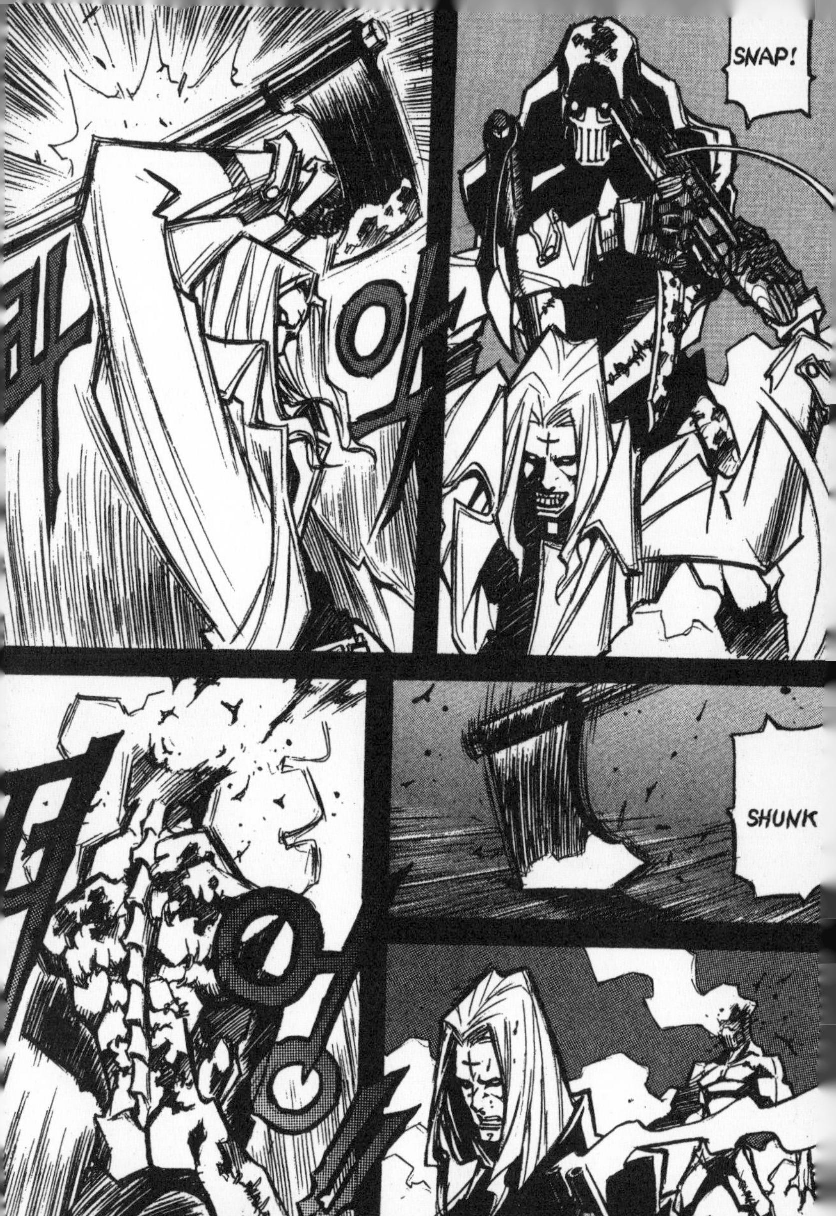
SNAP!
SHUNK

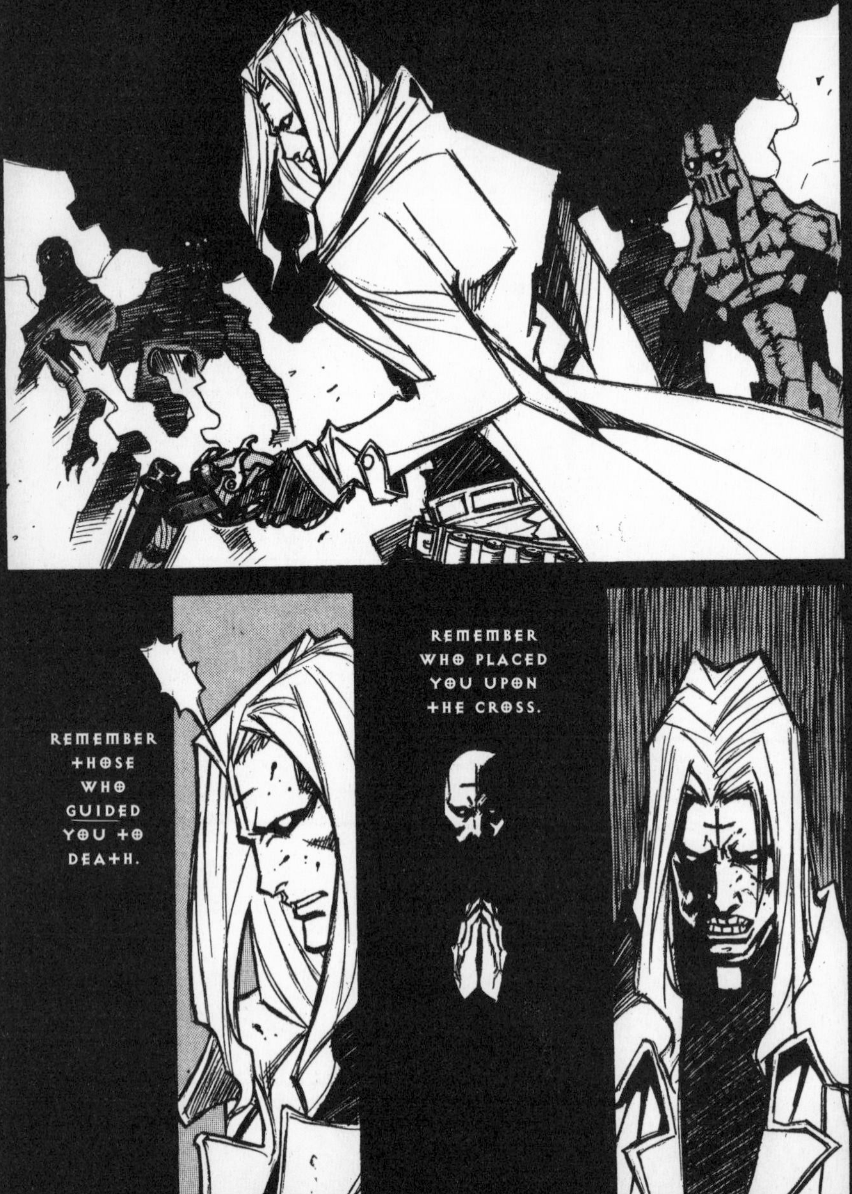
REMEMBER THOSE WHO GUIDED YOU TO DEATH.
REMEMBER WHO PLACED YOU UPON THE CROSS.

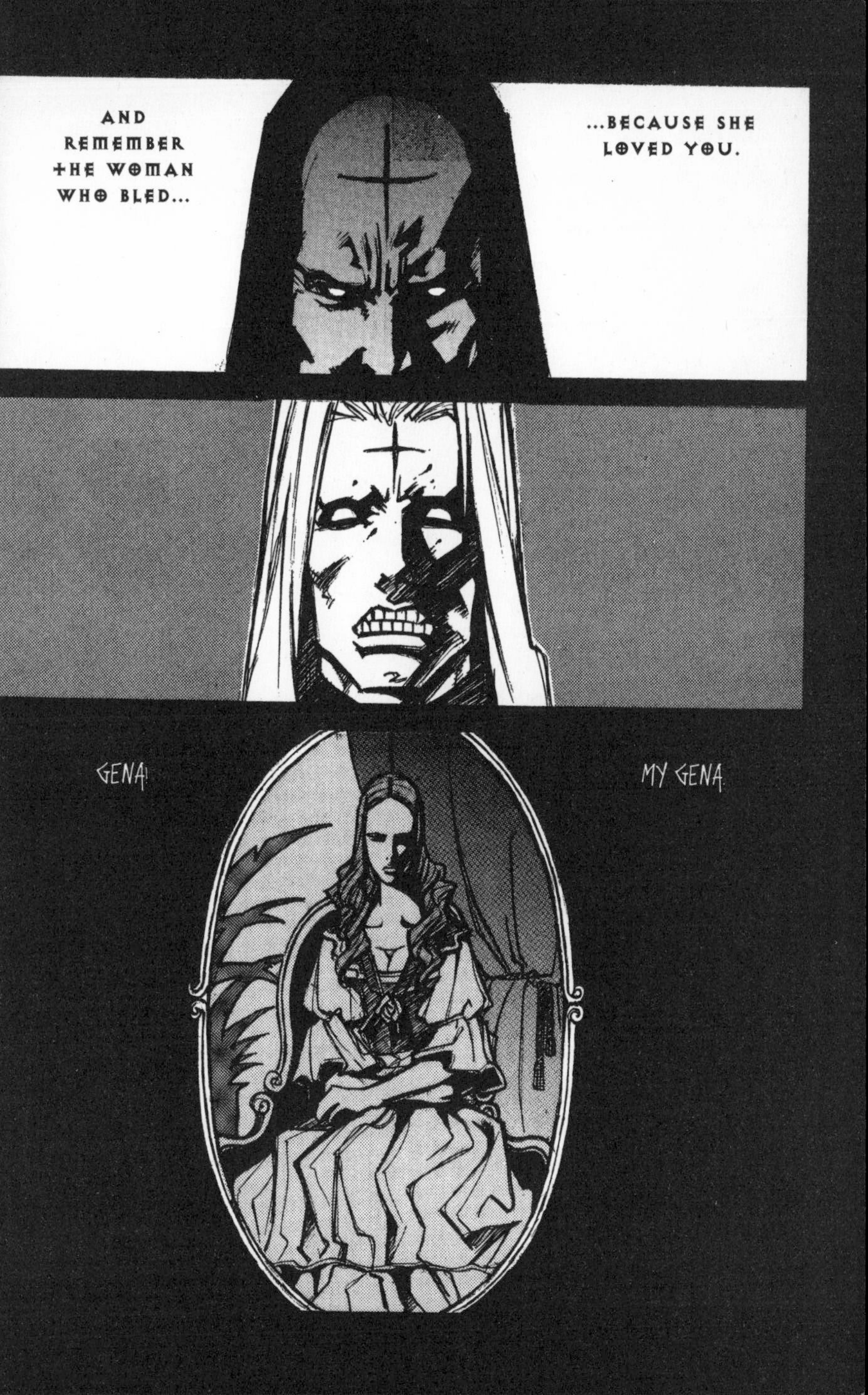
AND REMEMBER THE WOMAN WHO BLED...
...BECAUSE SHE LOVED YOU.
GENA!
MY GENA.

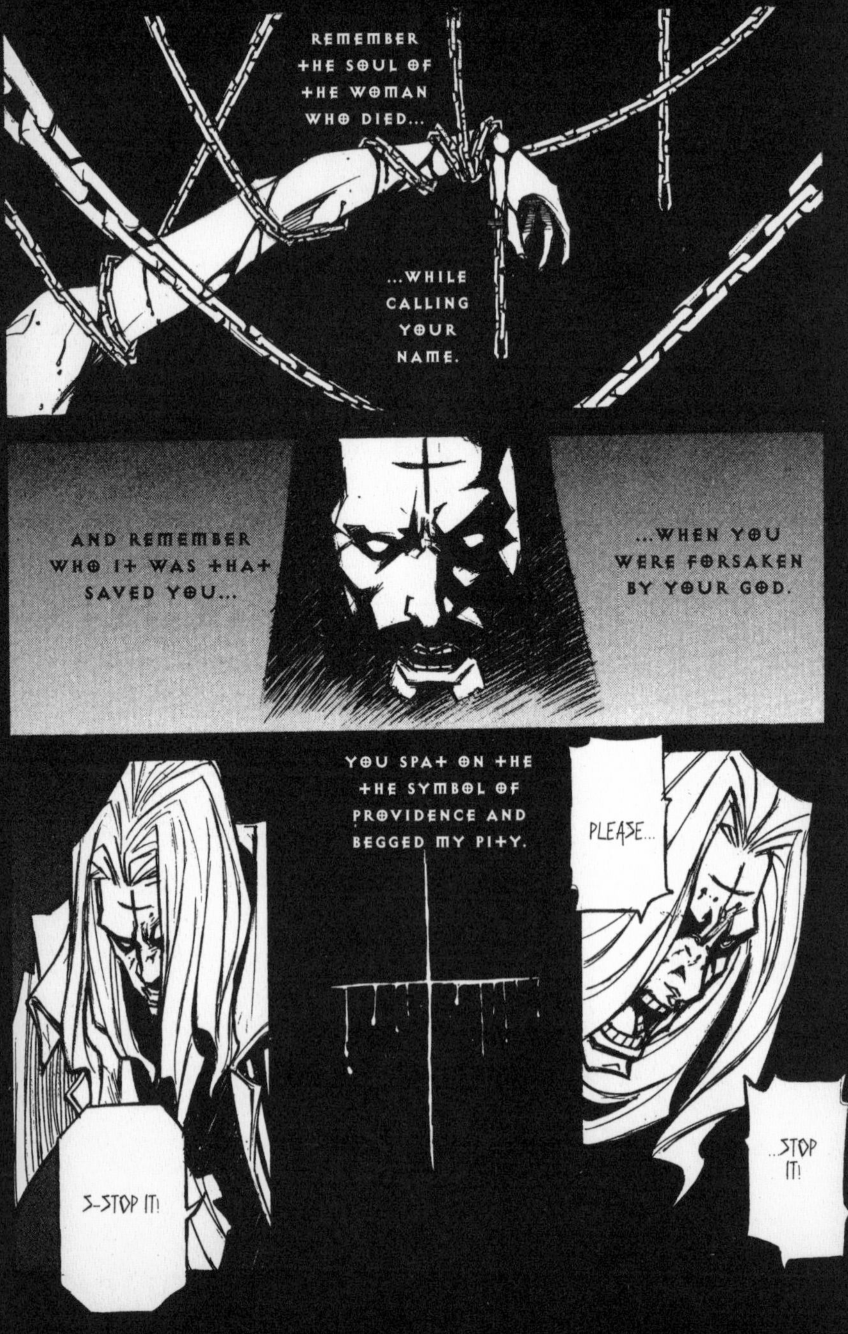
REMEMBER THE SOUL OF THE WOMAN WHO DIED...
...WHILE CALLING YOUR NAME.
AND REMEMBER WHO IT WAS THAT SAVED YOU...
...WHEN YOU WERE FORSAKEN BY YOUR GOD.
S-STOP IT!
YOU SPAT ON THE THE SYMBOL OF PROVIDENCE AND BEGGED MY PITY.
PLEASE...
...STOP IT!

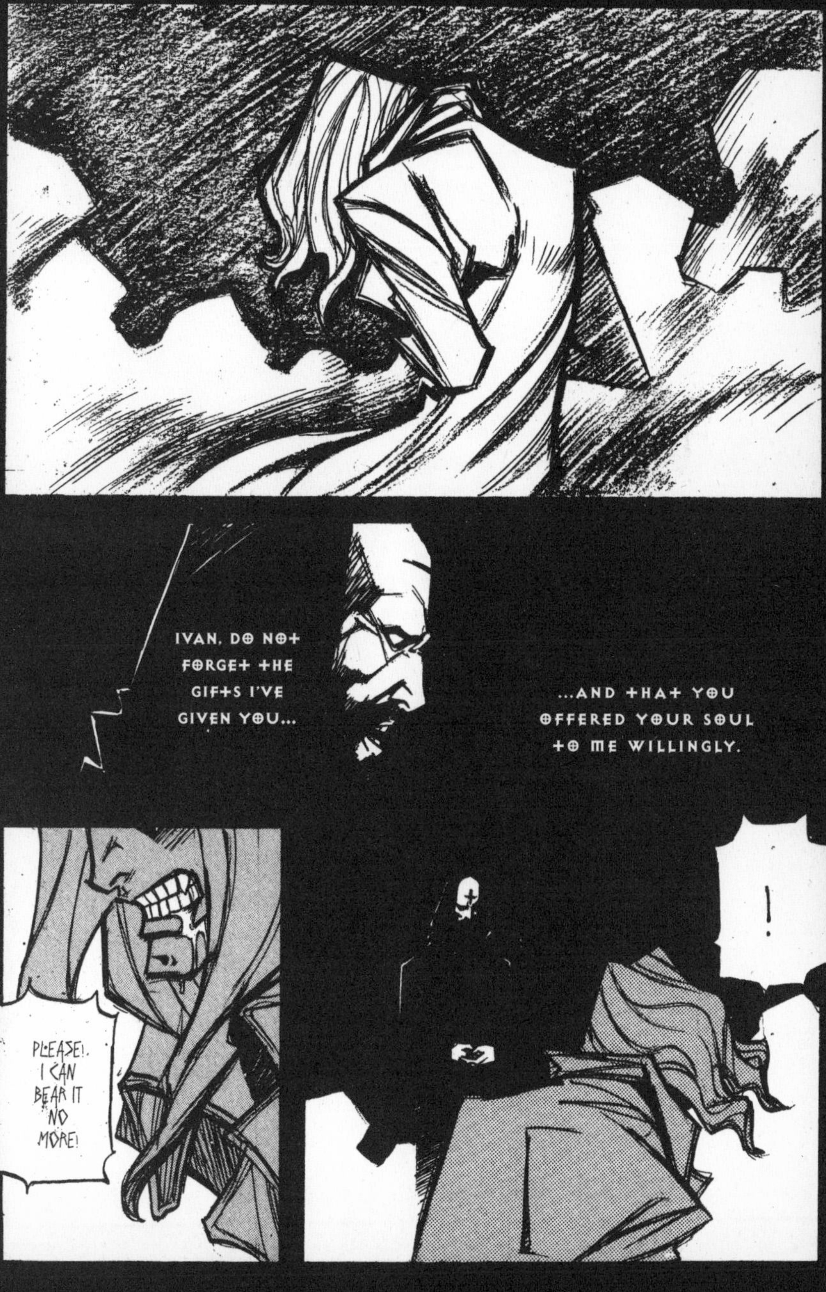
IVAN, DO NOT FORGET THE GIFTS I'VE GIVEN YOU...
...AND THAT YOU OFFERED YOUR SOUL TO ME WILLINGLY.
PLEASE!. I CAN BEAR IT NO MORE!
!

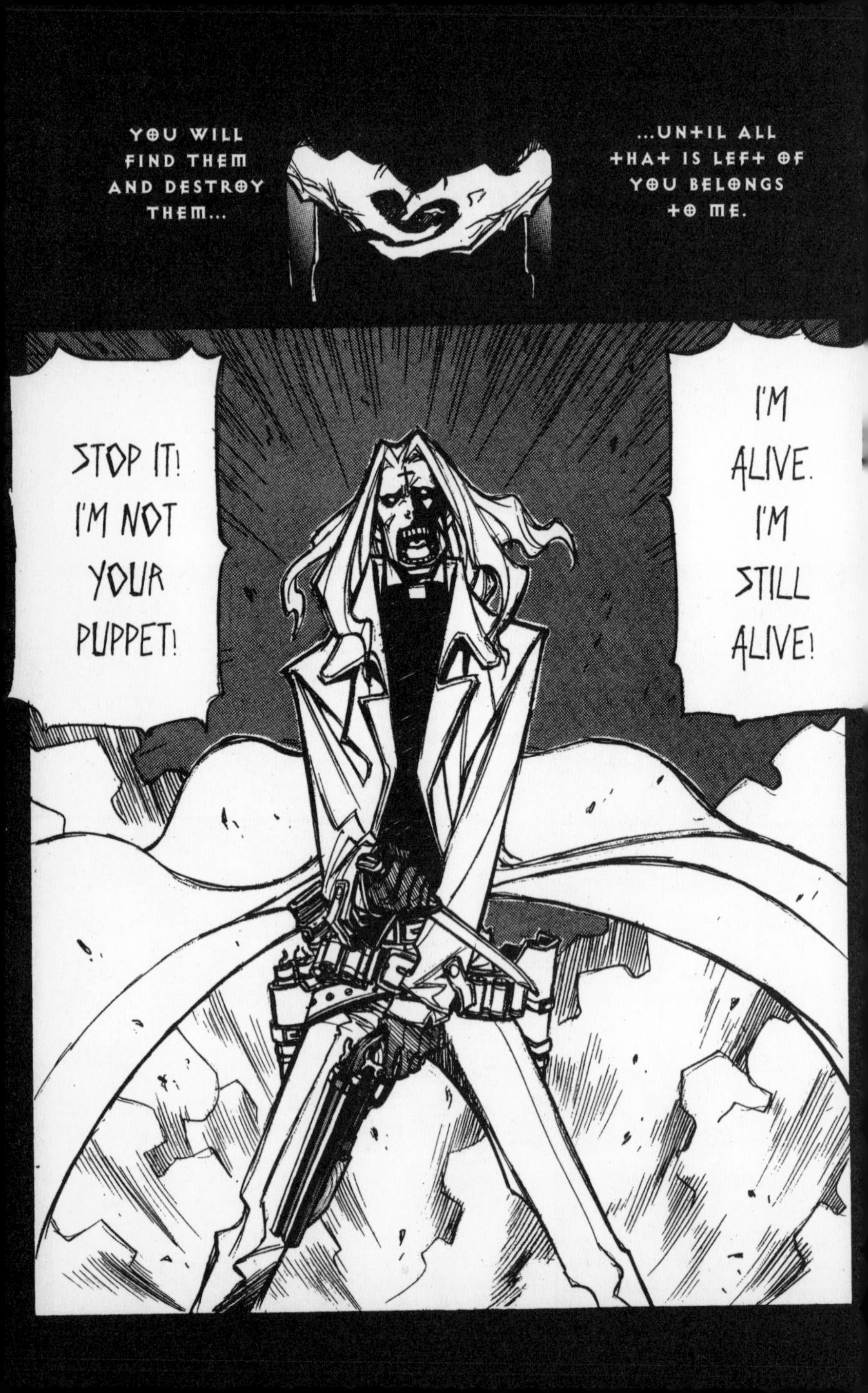
YOU WILL FIND THEM AND DESTROY THEM...
...UNTIL ALL THAT IS LEFT OF YOU BELONGS TO ME.
STOP IT! I'M NOT YOUR PUPPET!
I'M ALIVE. I'M STILL ALIVE!

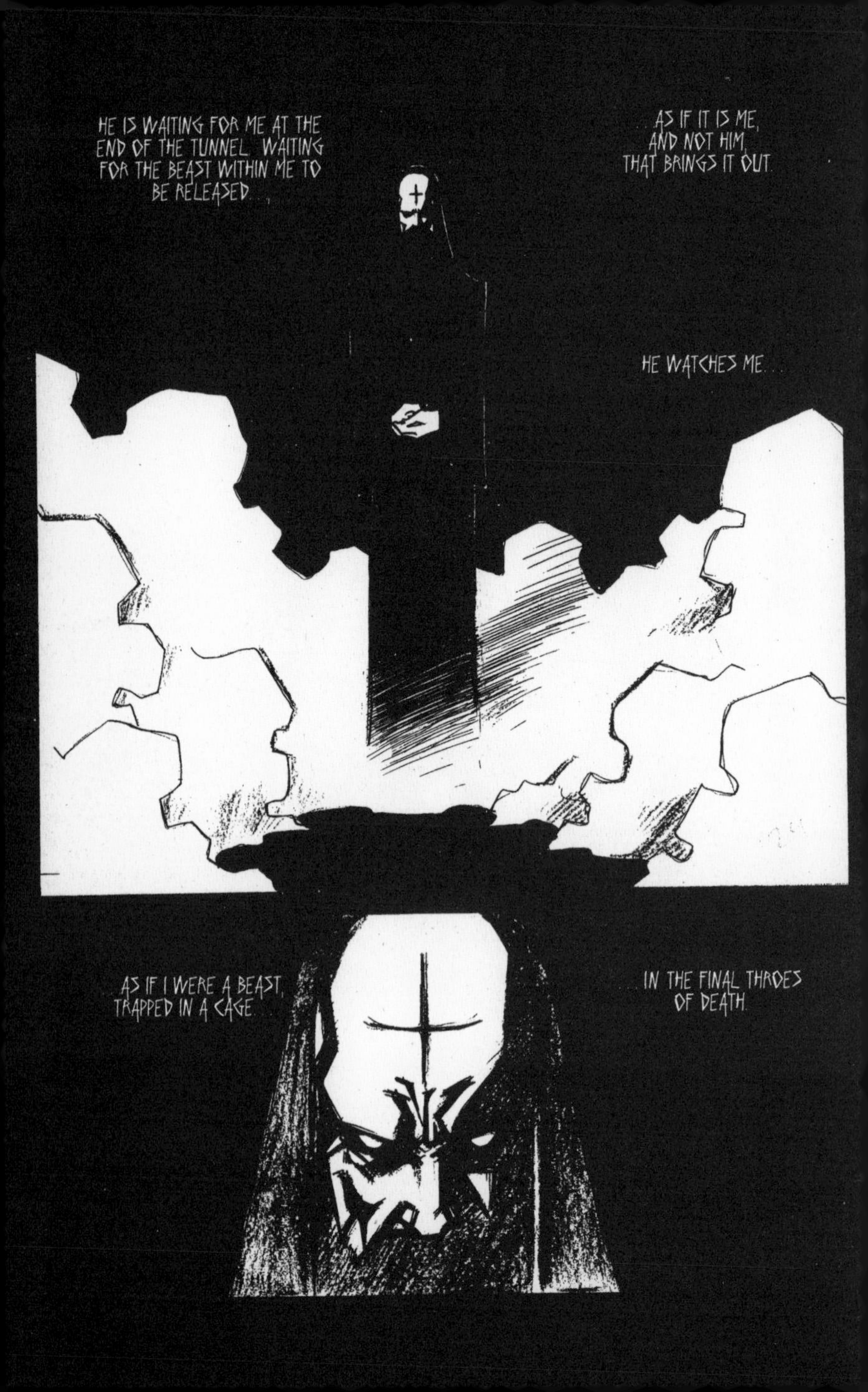

HE IS WAITING FOR ME AT THE END OF THE TUNNEL. WAITING FOR THE BEAST WITHIN ME TO BE RELEASED...
...AS IF IT IS ME, AND NOT HIM, THAT BRINGS IT OUT.
HE WATCHES ME...
...AS IF I WERE A BEAST, TRAPPED IN A CAGE...
...IN THE FINAL THROES OF DEATH.

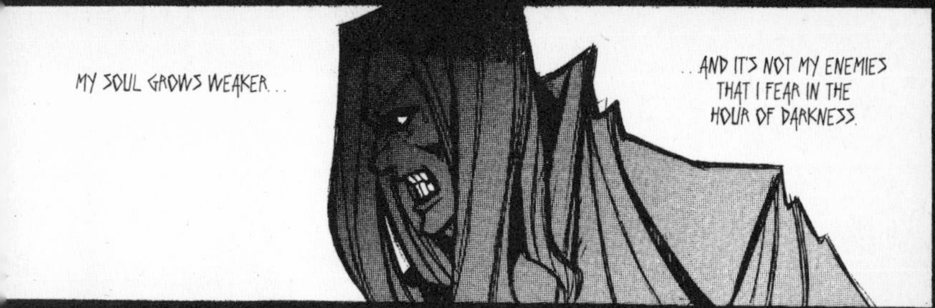
MY SOUL GROWS WEAKER. . .
. . AND IT'S NOT MY ENEMIES THAT I FEAR IN THE HOUR OF DARKNESS.
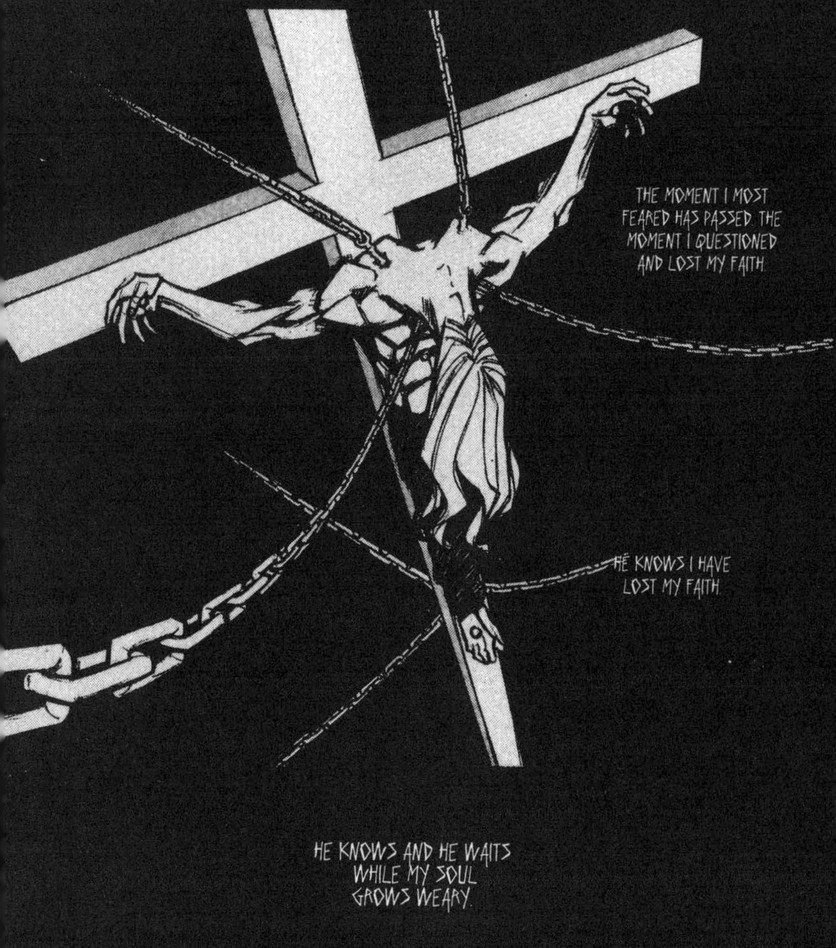
THE MOMENT I MOST FEARED HAS PASSED. THE MOMENT I QUESTIONED AND LOST MY FAITH.
HE KNOWS I HAVE LOST MY FAITH.
HE KNOWS AND HE WAITS WHILE MY SOUL GROWS WEARY.

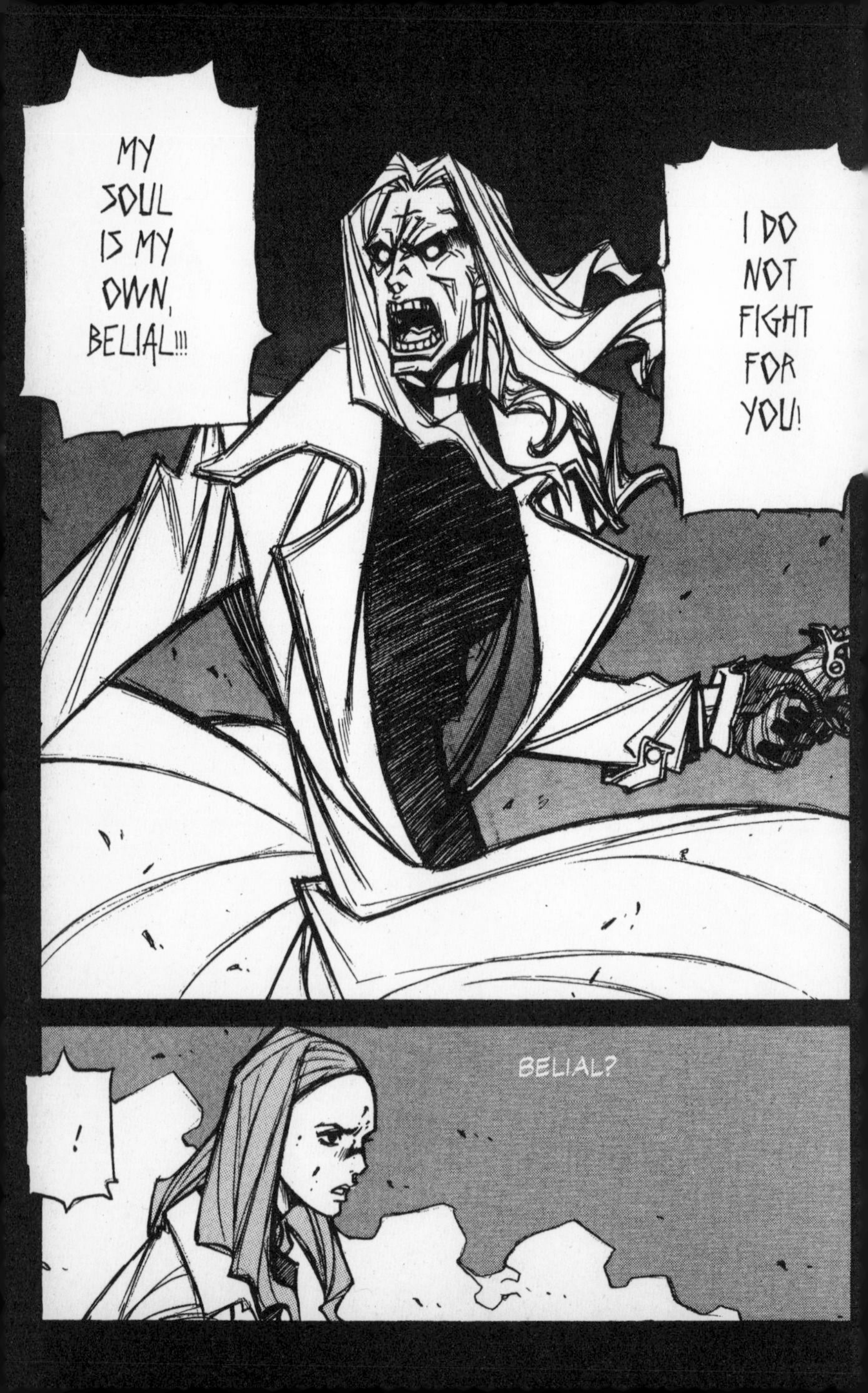
MY SOUL IS MY OWN, BELIAL!!!
I DO NOT FIGHT FOR YOU!
!
BELIAL?

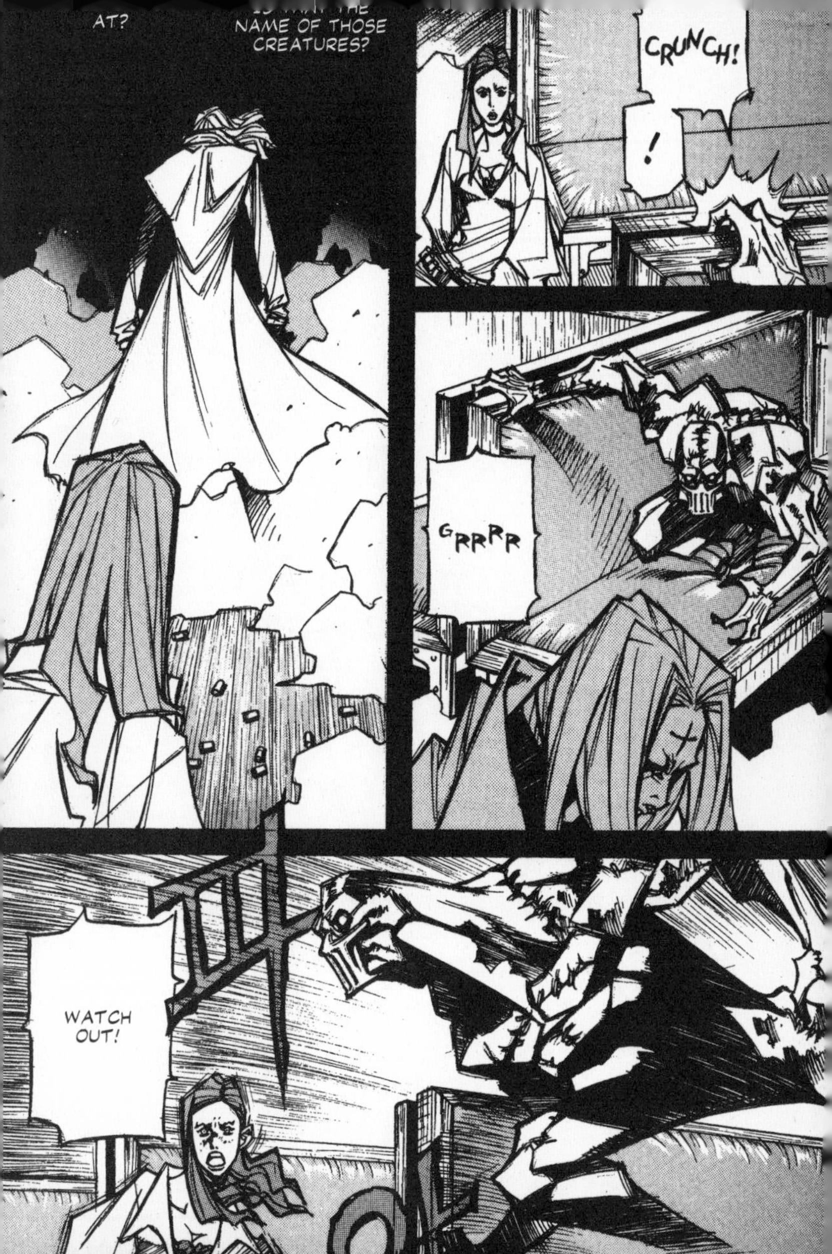
AT?
NAME OF THOSE CREATURES?
CRUNCH!
!
GRRRR
WATCH OUT!

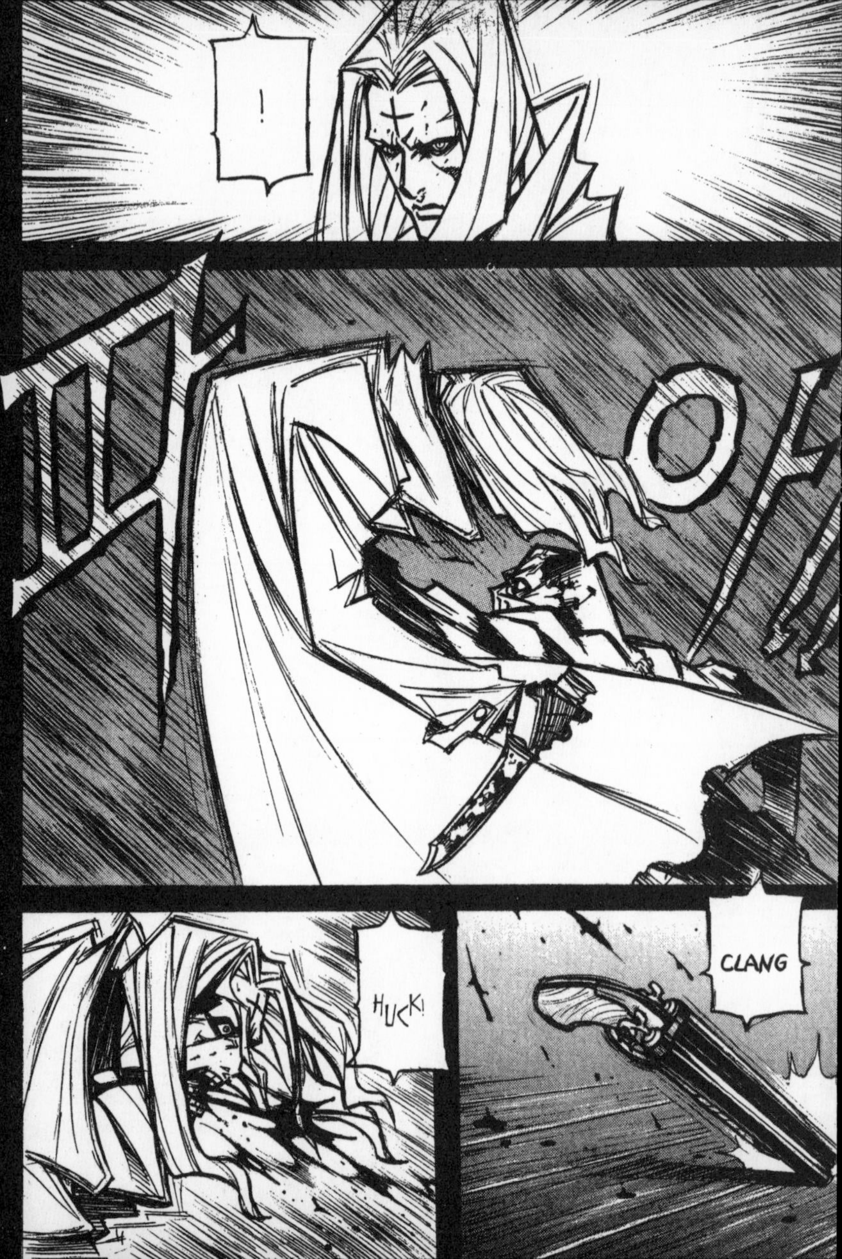
!
HUCK!
CLANG

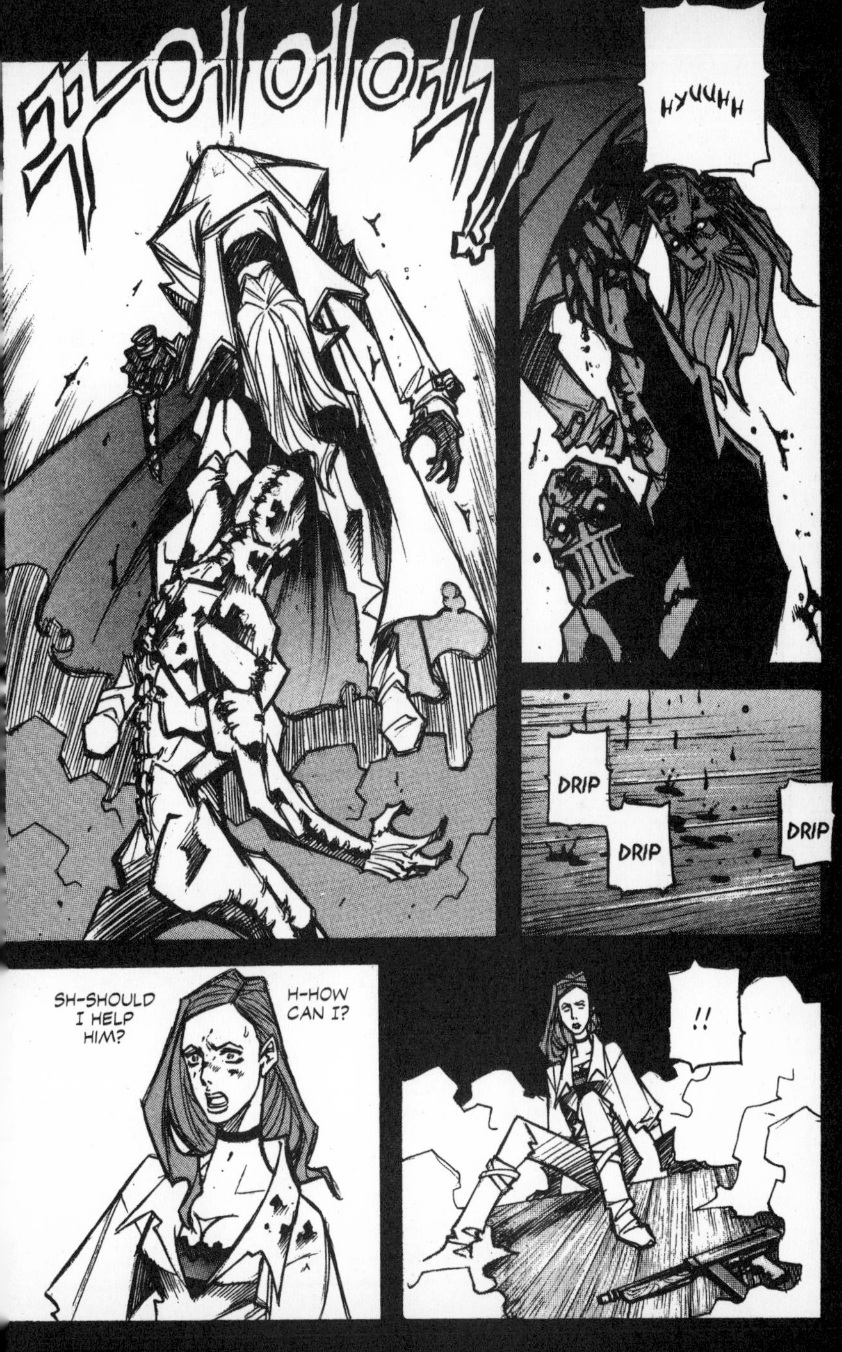
HYUUHH
DRIP
DRIP
DRIP
SH-SHOULD I HELP HIM?
H-HOW CAN I?
!!

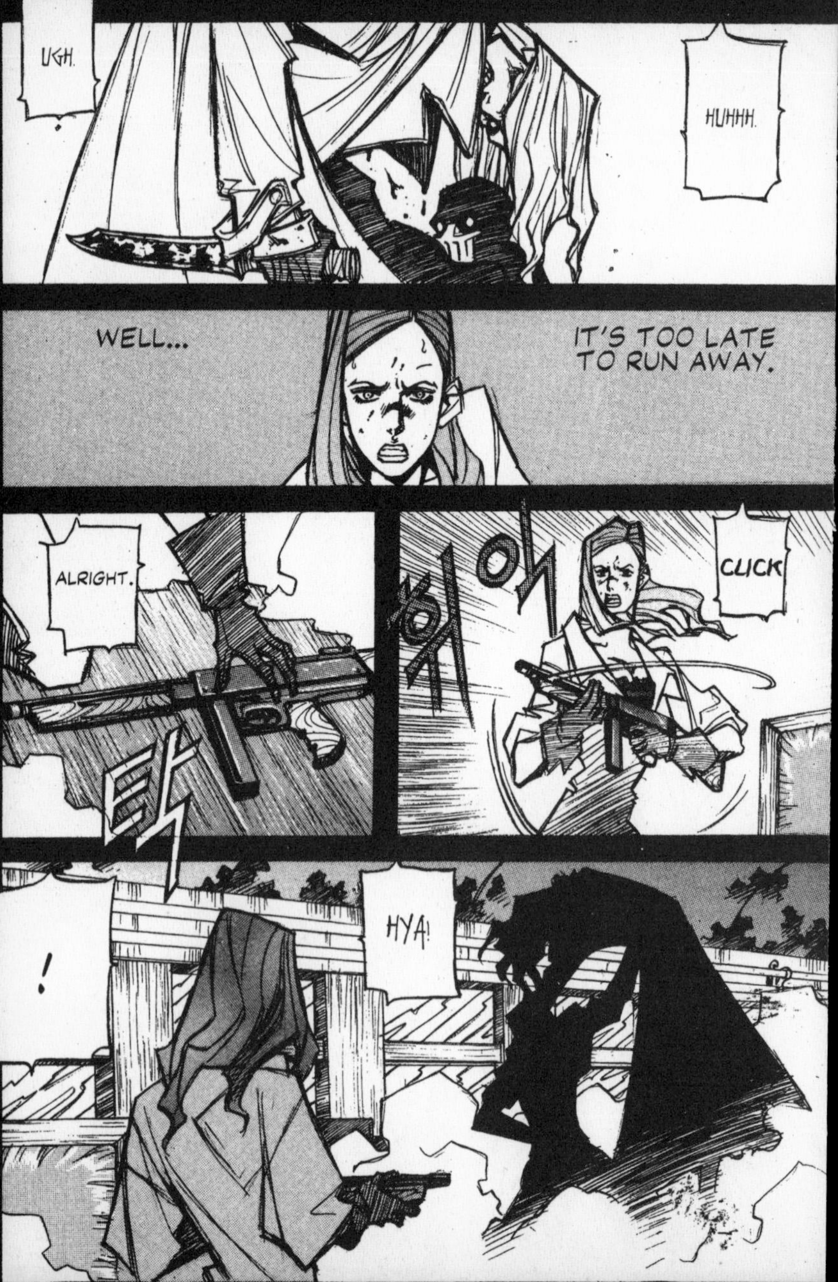
UGH.
HUHHH.
WELL...
IT'S TOO LATE TO RUN AWAY.
ALRIGHT.
탁
CLICK
!
HYA!

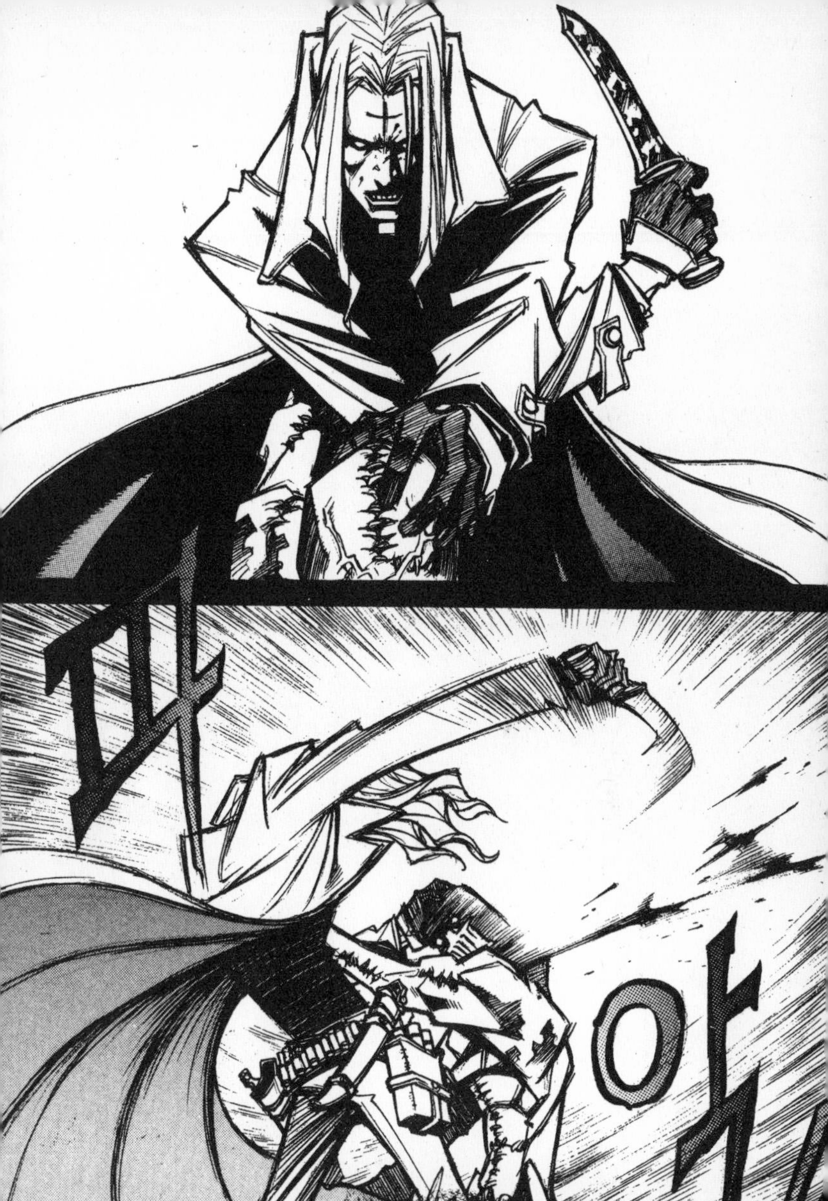

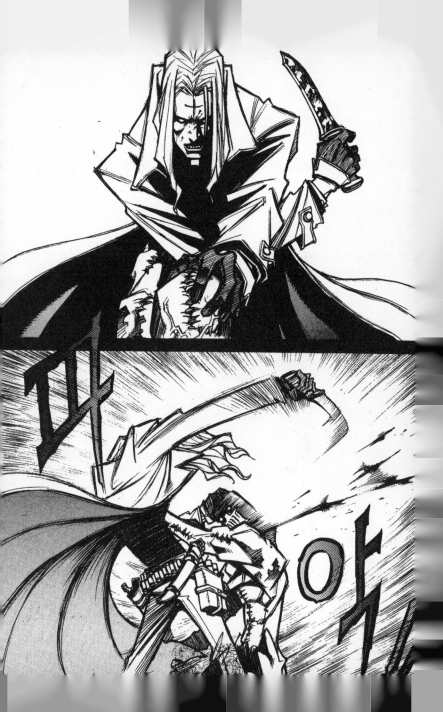

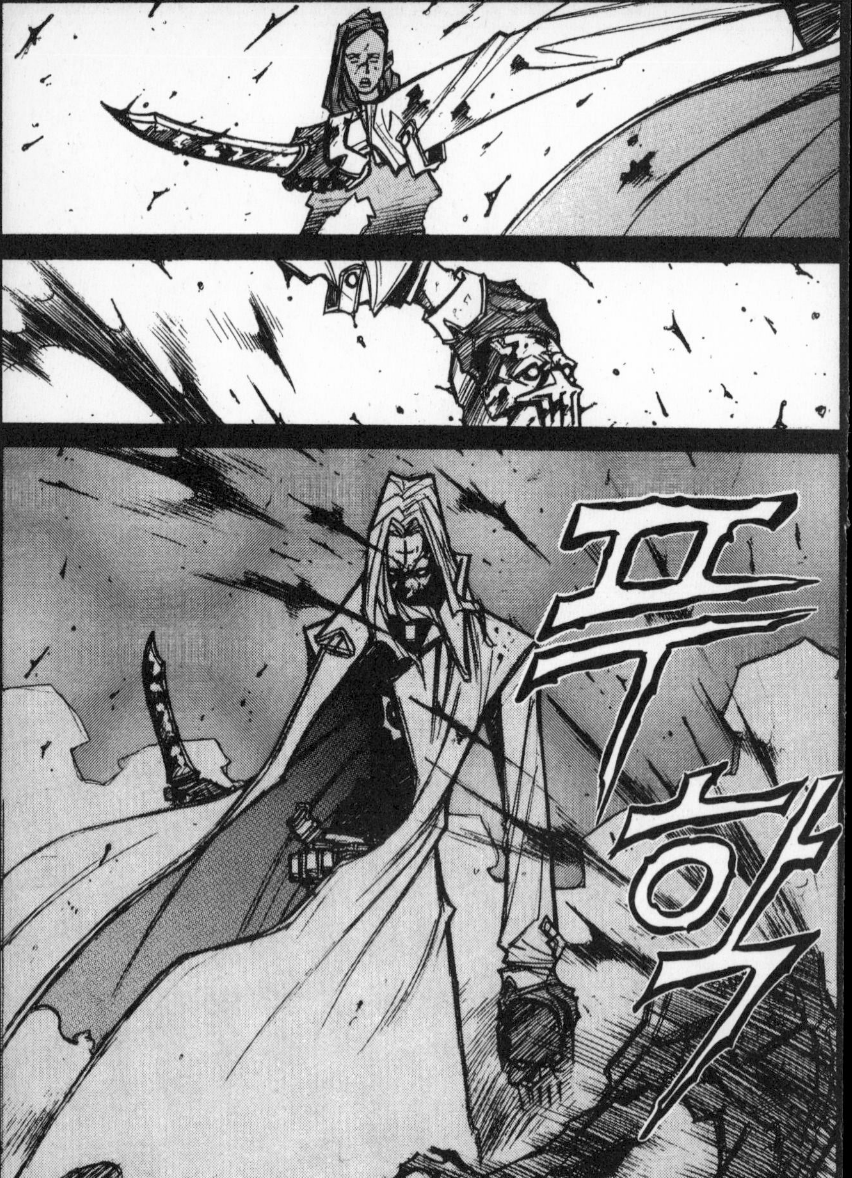
푸학

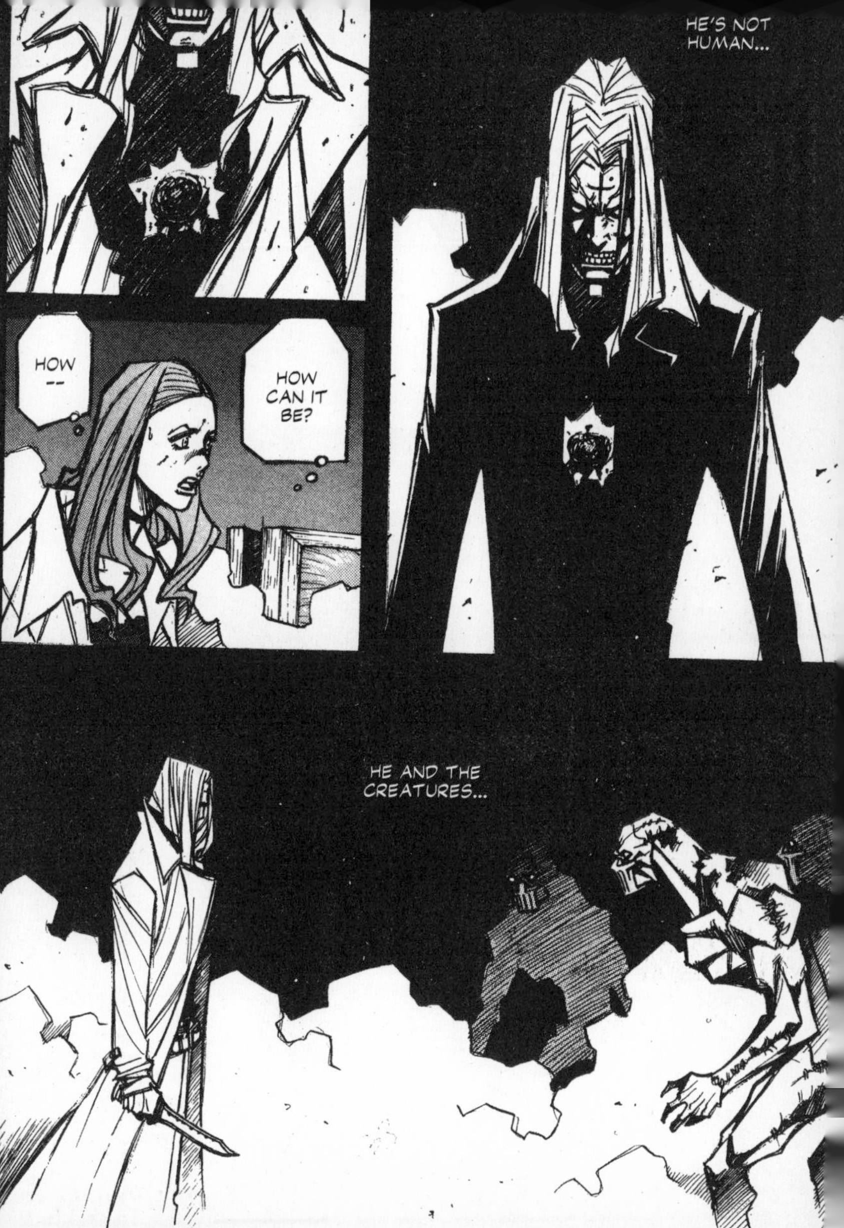
HOW --
HOW CAN IT BE?
HE'S NOT HUMAN...
HE AND THE CREATURES...

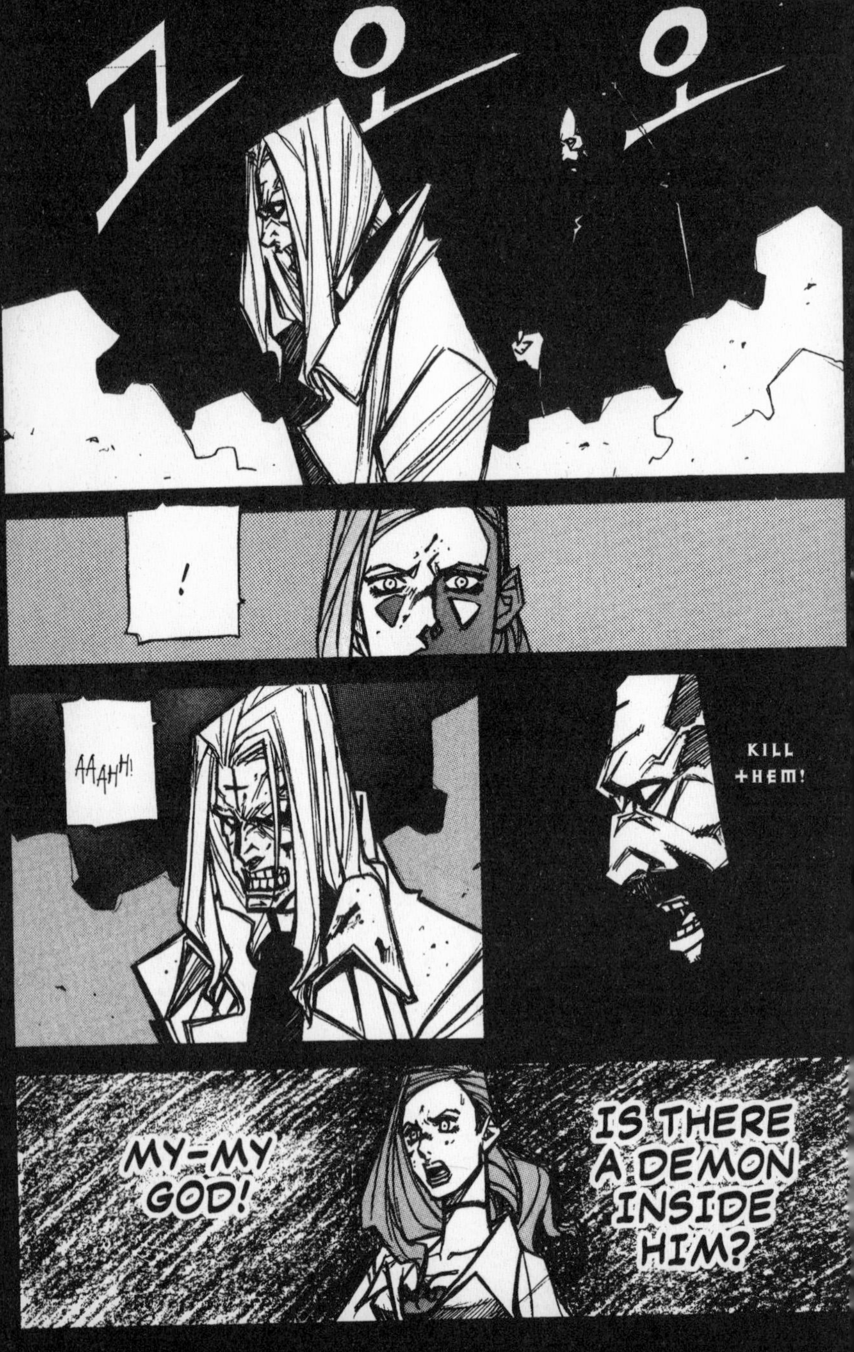
ZOO
!
AAAHH!
KILL THEM!
MY-MY GOD!
IS THERE A DEMON INSIDE HIM?

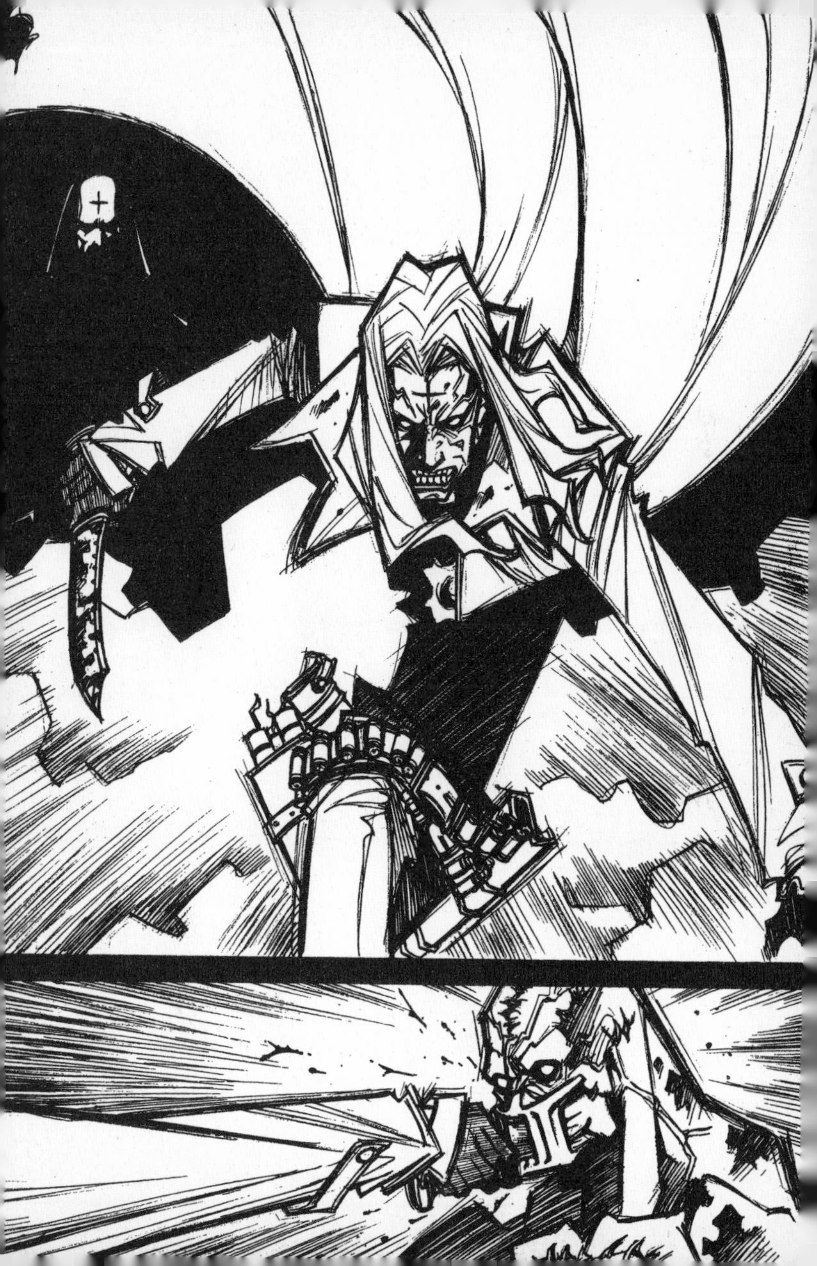

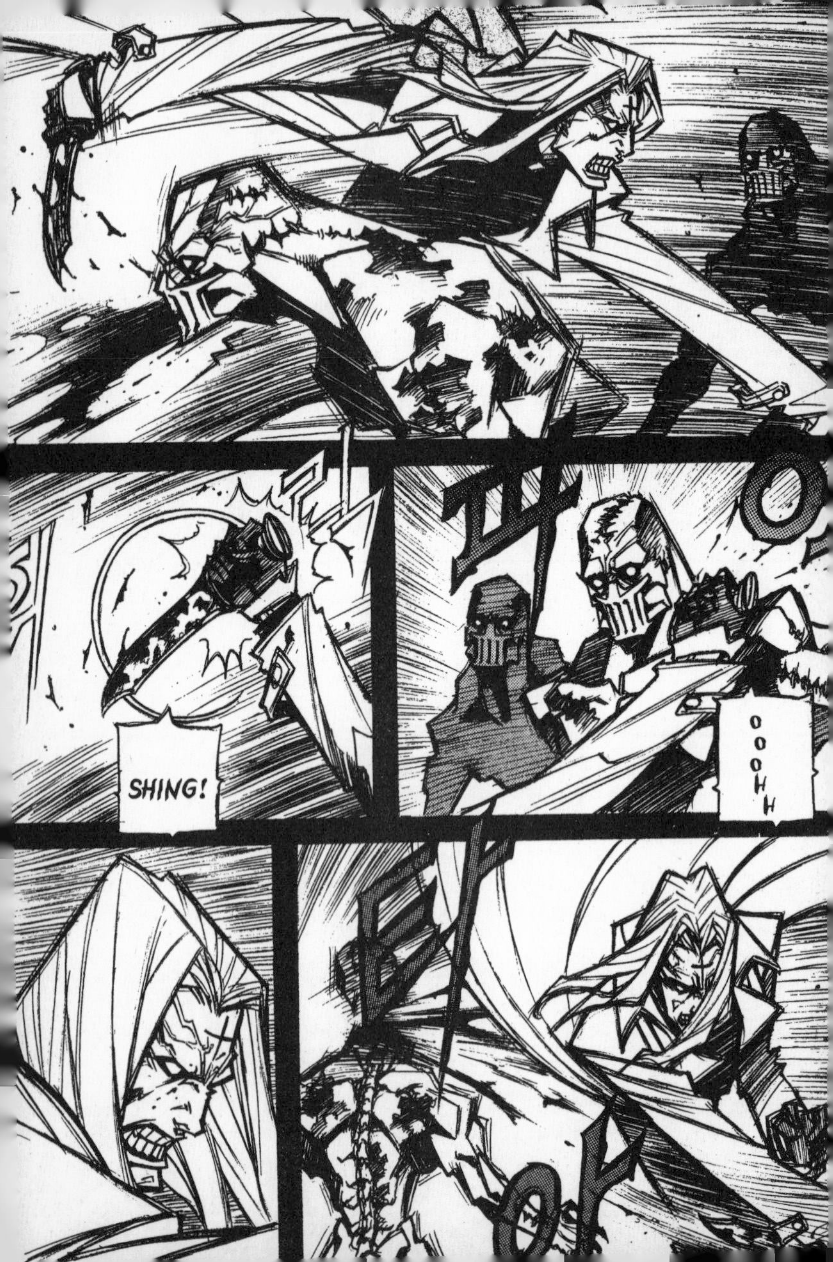
SHING!
OOOHH

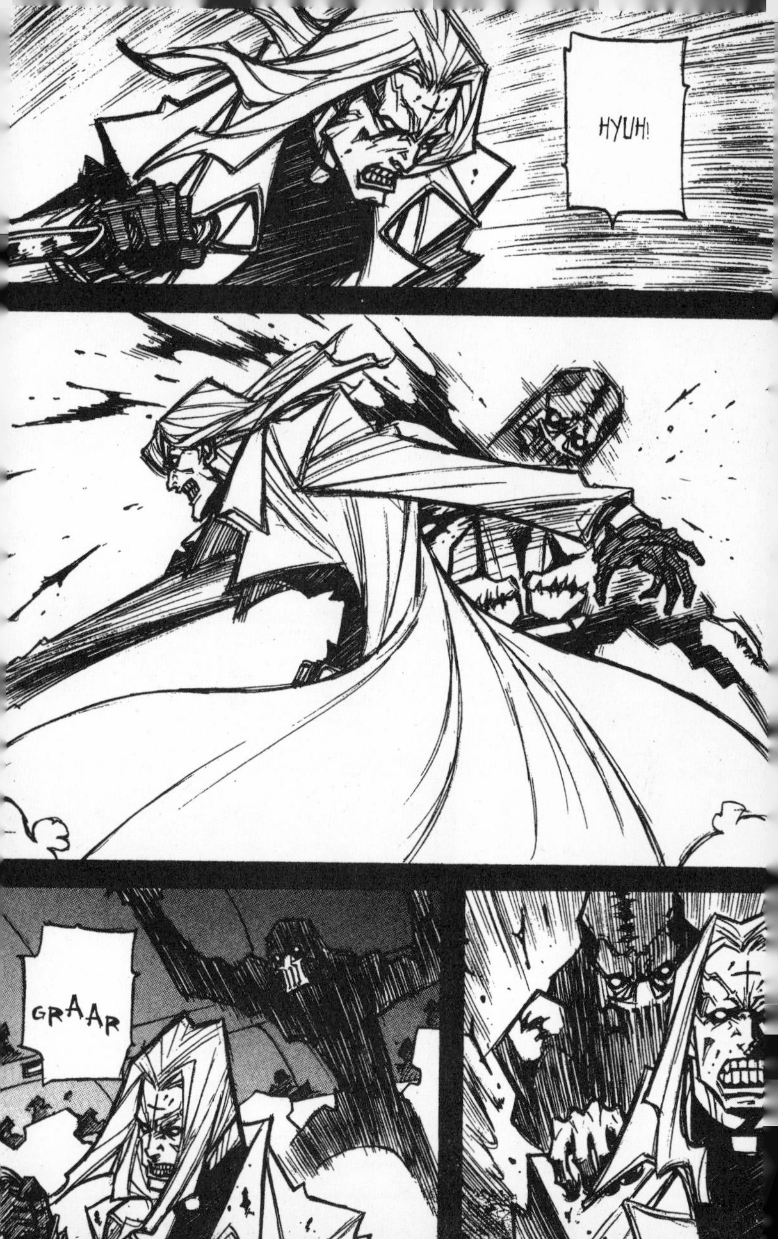
HYUH!
GRAAR

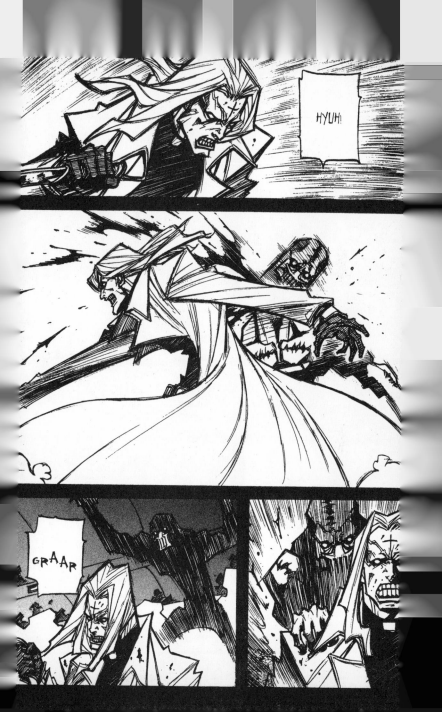

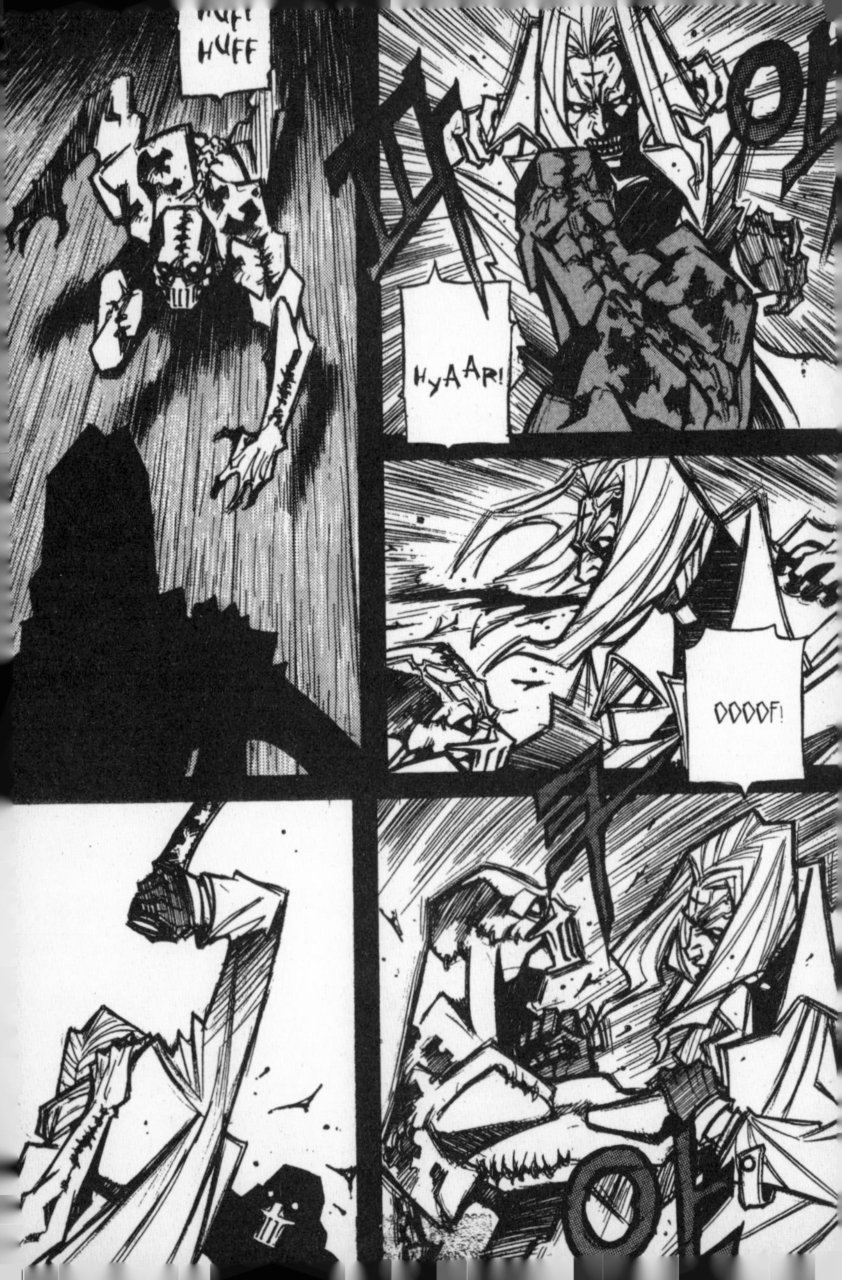
HUFF HUFF
HYAAR!
OOOOF!

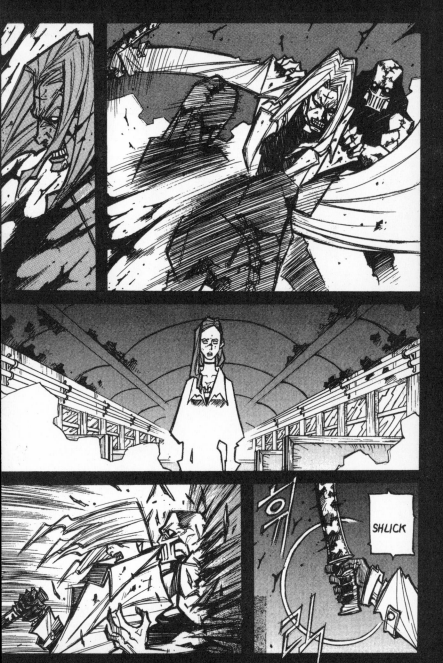

SHLICK

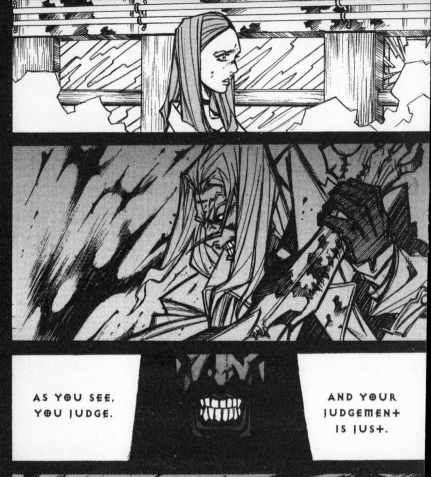

AS YOU SEE,
YOU JUDGE.

AND YOUR
JUDGEMENT
IS JUST.

FOR YOU
ARE MINE.

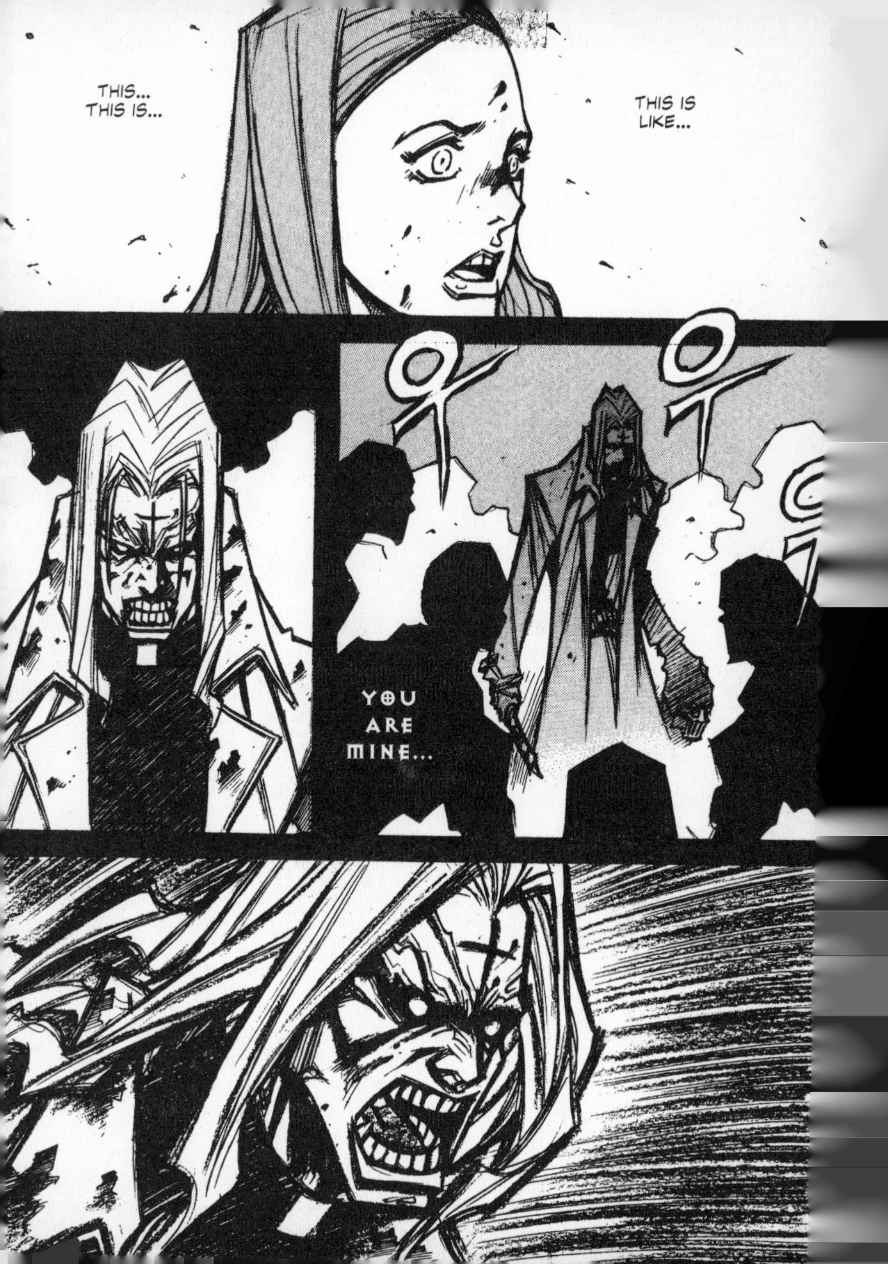
THIS...
THIS IS...
THIS IS
LIKE...
YOU
ARE
MINE...

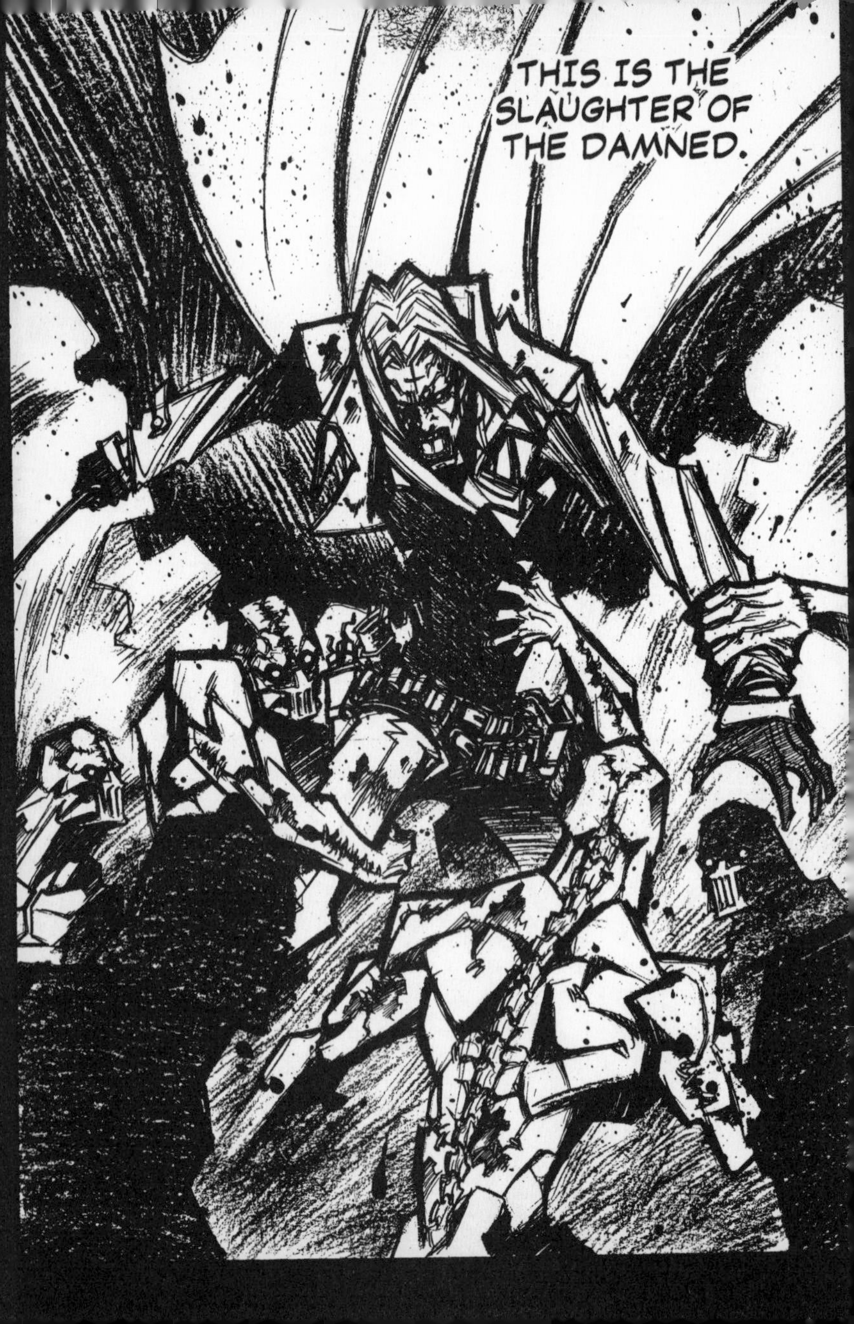
THIS IS THE SLAUGHTER OF THE DAMNED.

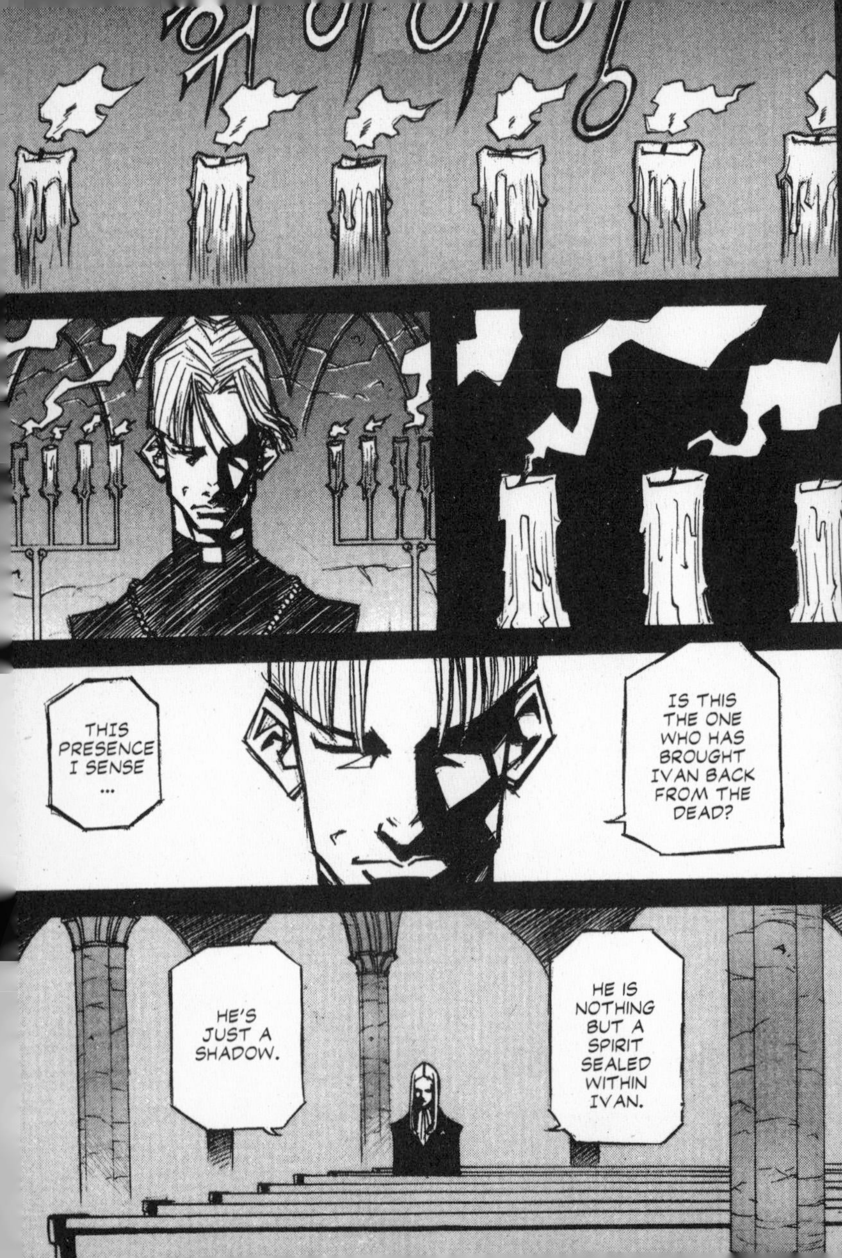
THIS PRESENCE I SENSE ...
IS THIS THE ONE WHO HAS BROUGHT IVAN BACK FROM THE DEAD?
HE'S JUST A SHADOW.
HE IS NOTHING BUT A SPIRIT SEALED WITHIN IVAN.

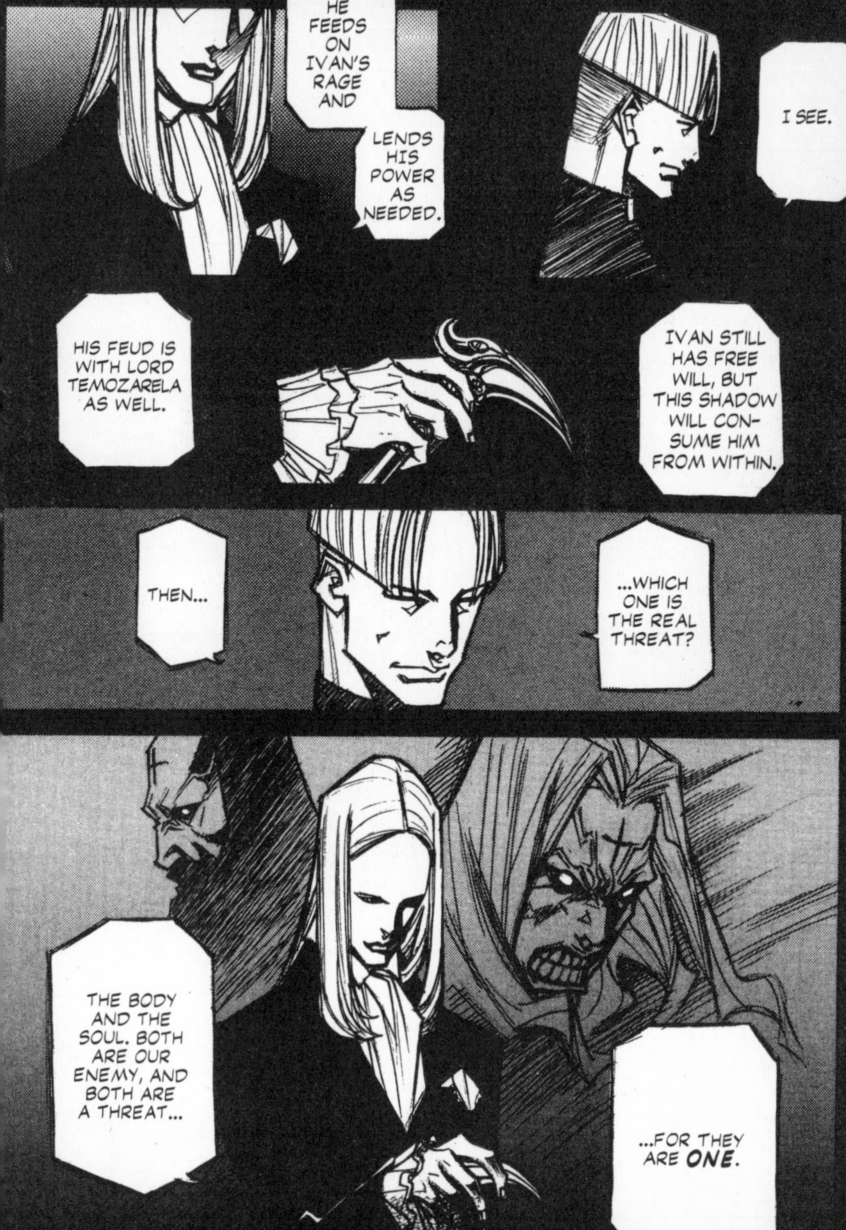
HE FEEDS ON IVAN'S RAGE AND
LENDS HIS POWER AS NEEDED.
I SEE.
HIS FEUD IS WITH LORD TEMOZARELA AS WELL.
IVAN STILL HAS FREE WILL, BUT THIS SHADOW WILL CON-SUME HIM FROM WITHIN.
THEN...
...WHICH ONE IS THE REAL THREAT?
THE BODY AND THE SOUL. BOTH ARE OUR ENEMY, AND BOTH ARE A THREAT...
...FOR THEY ARE **ONE**.

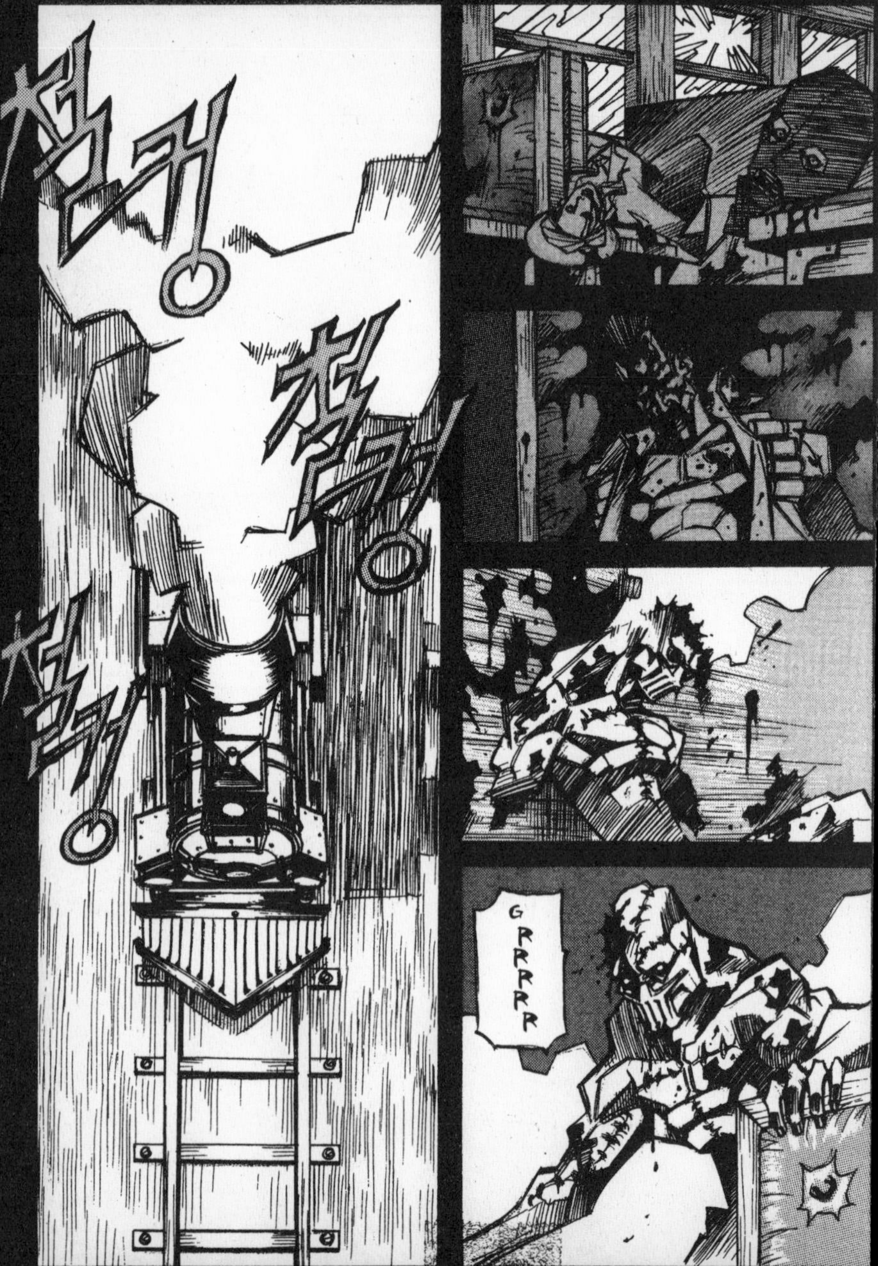
철컹
철컹
철컹
GRRRR

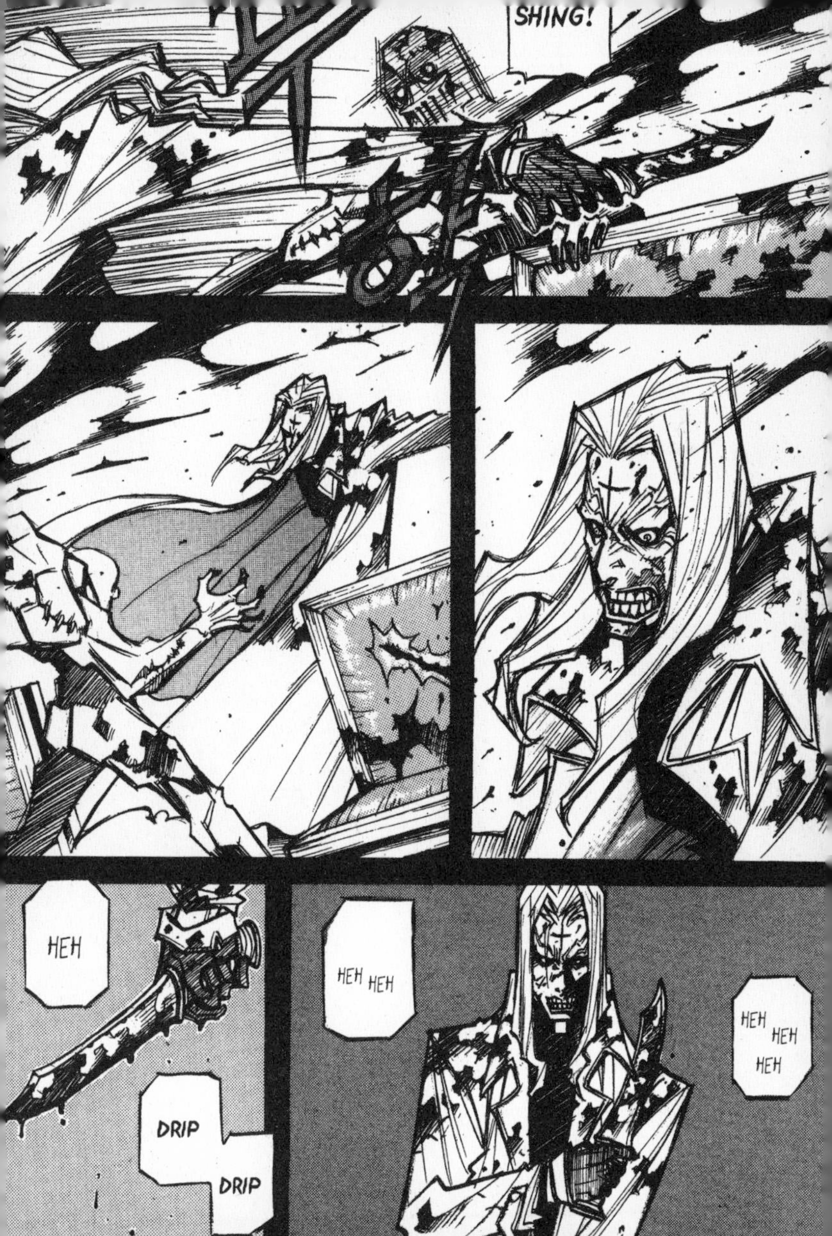
SHING!
HEH
DRIP
DRIP
HEH HEH
HEH
HEH
HEH

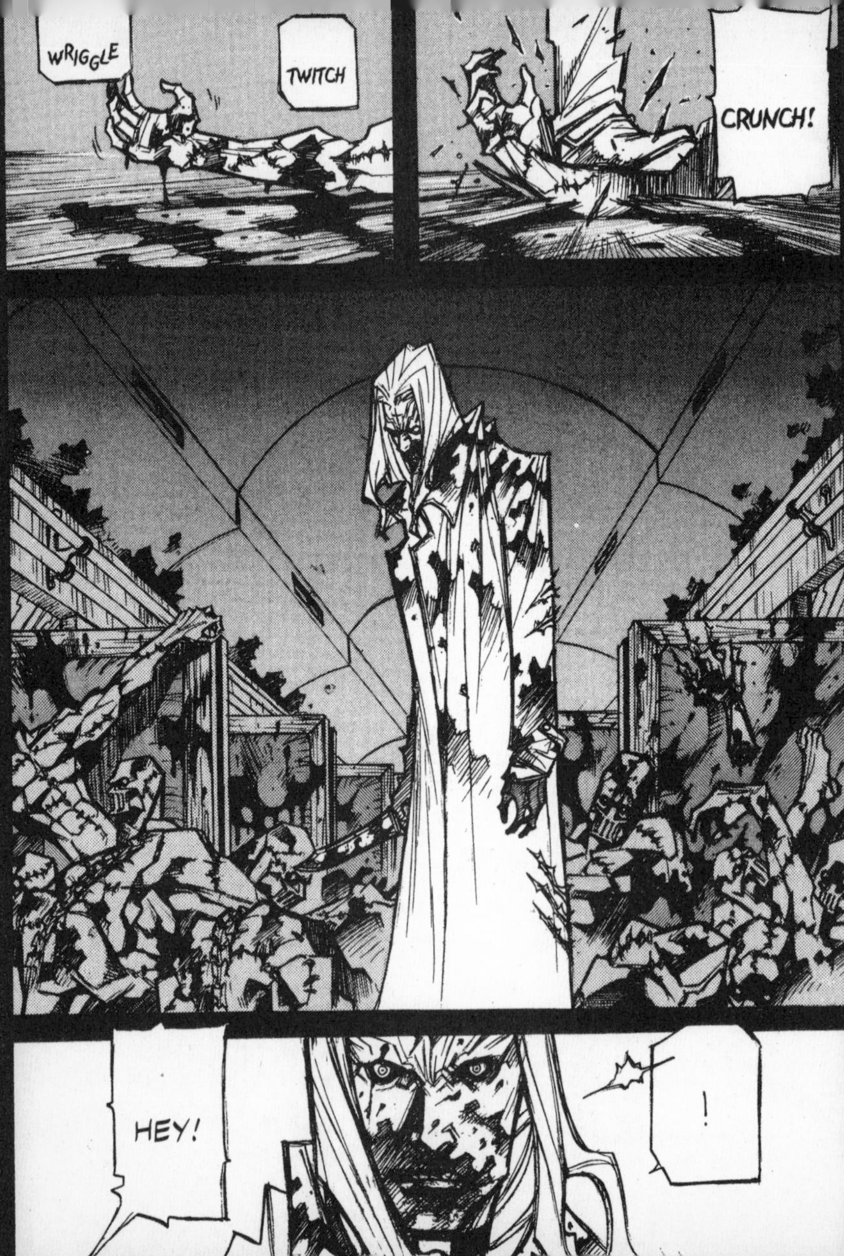
WRIGGLE
TWITCH
CRUNCH!
HEY!
!

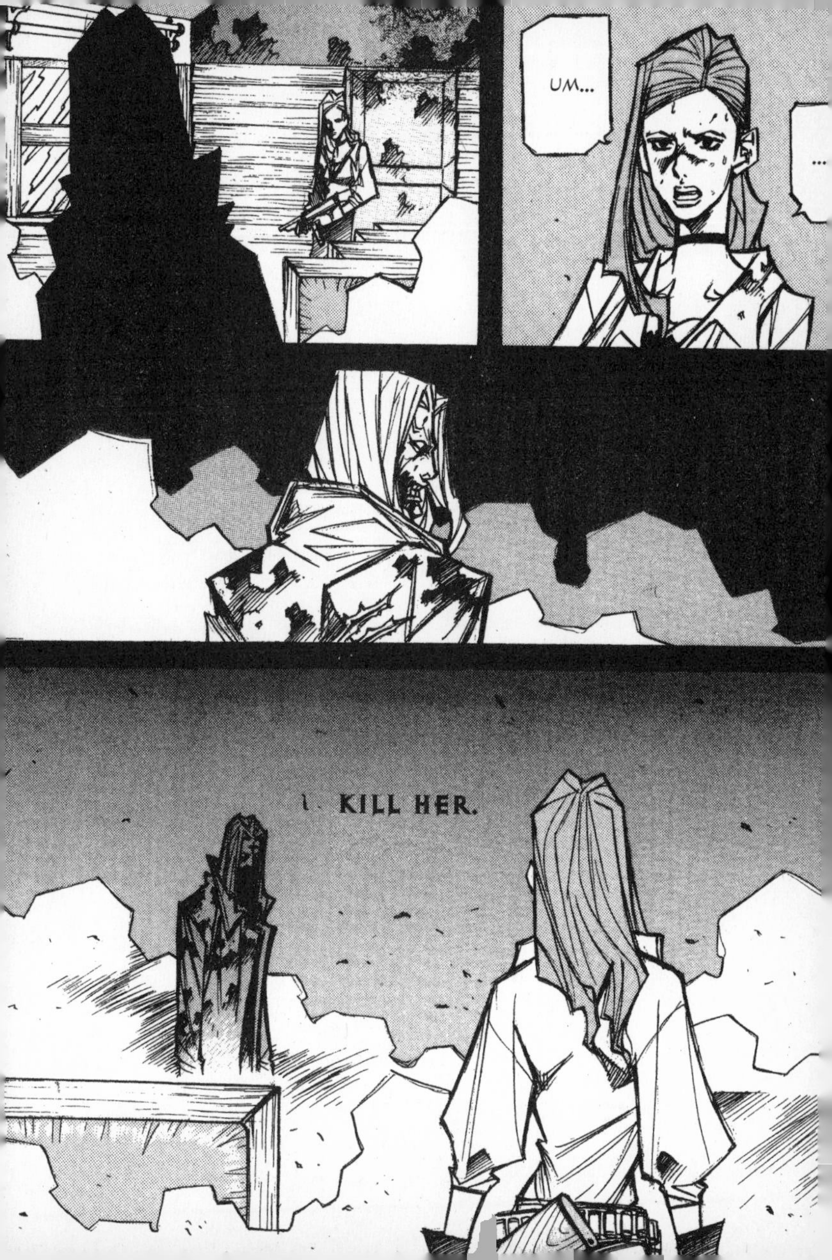
UM...
...
KILL HER.

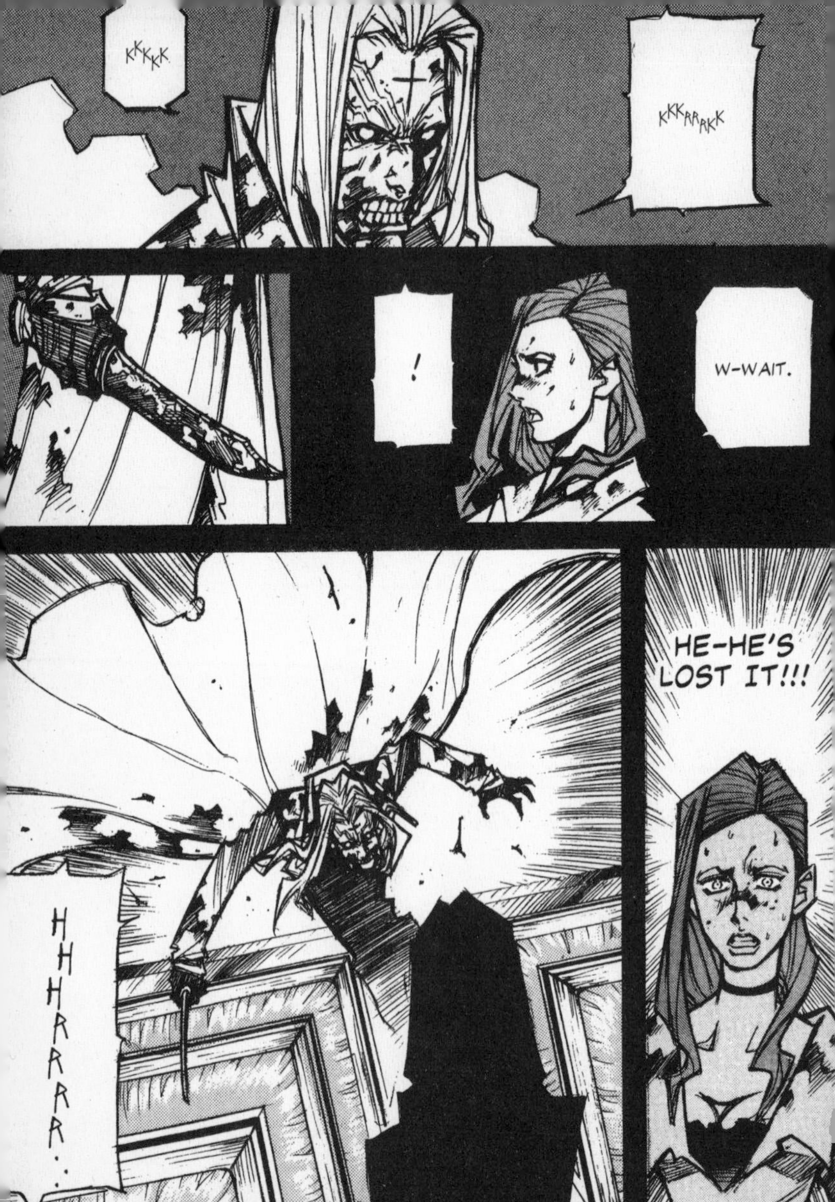
KKKKK.
KKKRRRKK
!
W-WAIT.
HHHRRRR..
HE-HE'S LOST IT!!!

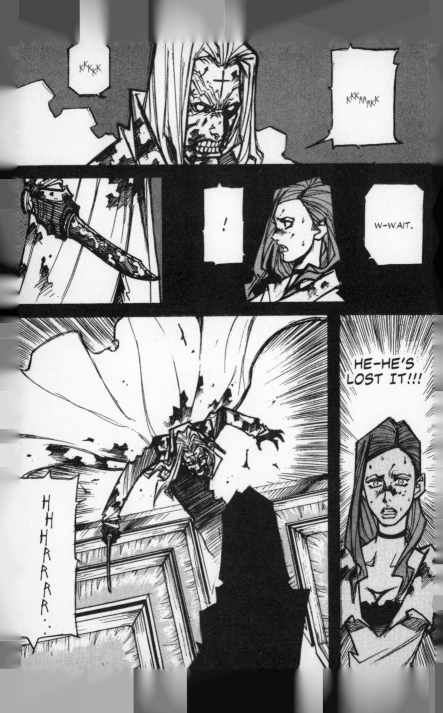

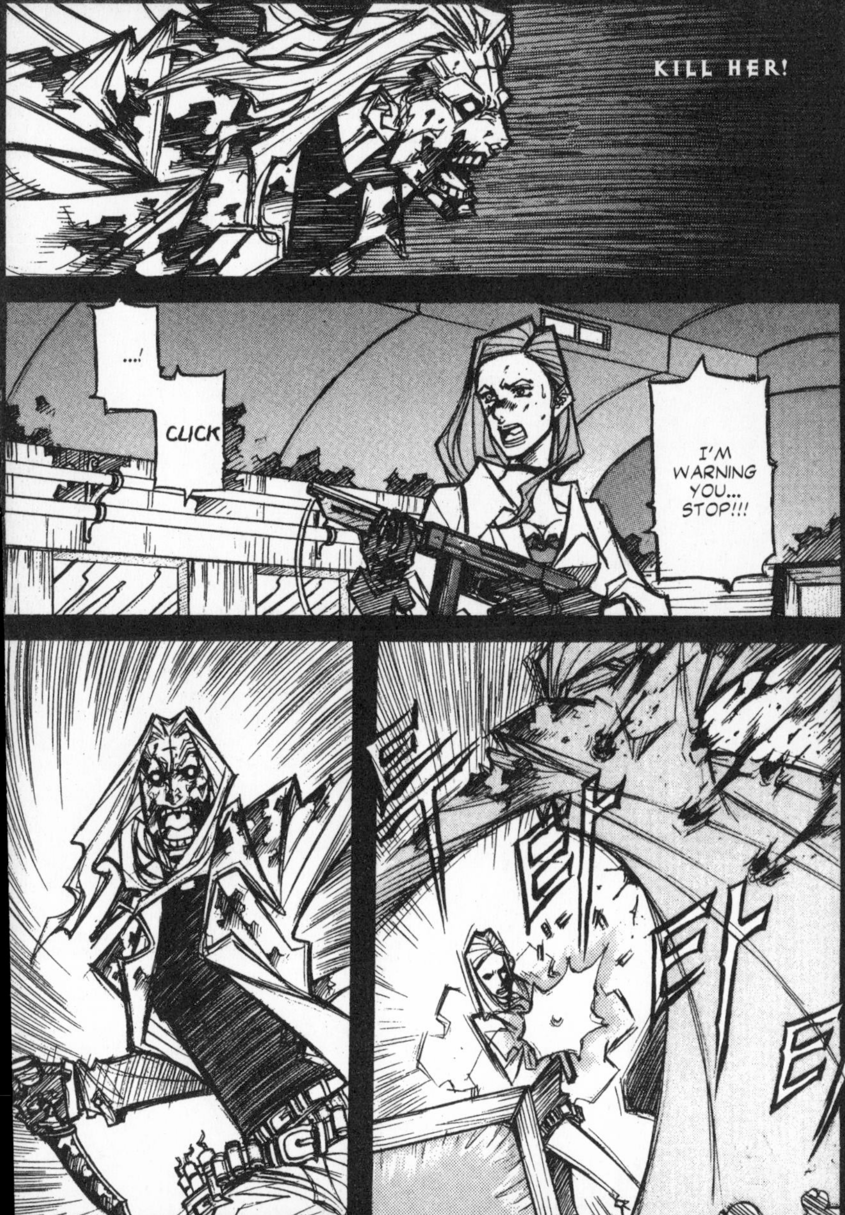
KILL HER!
...!
CLICK
I'M WARNING YOU... STOP!!!

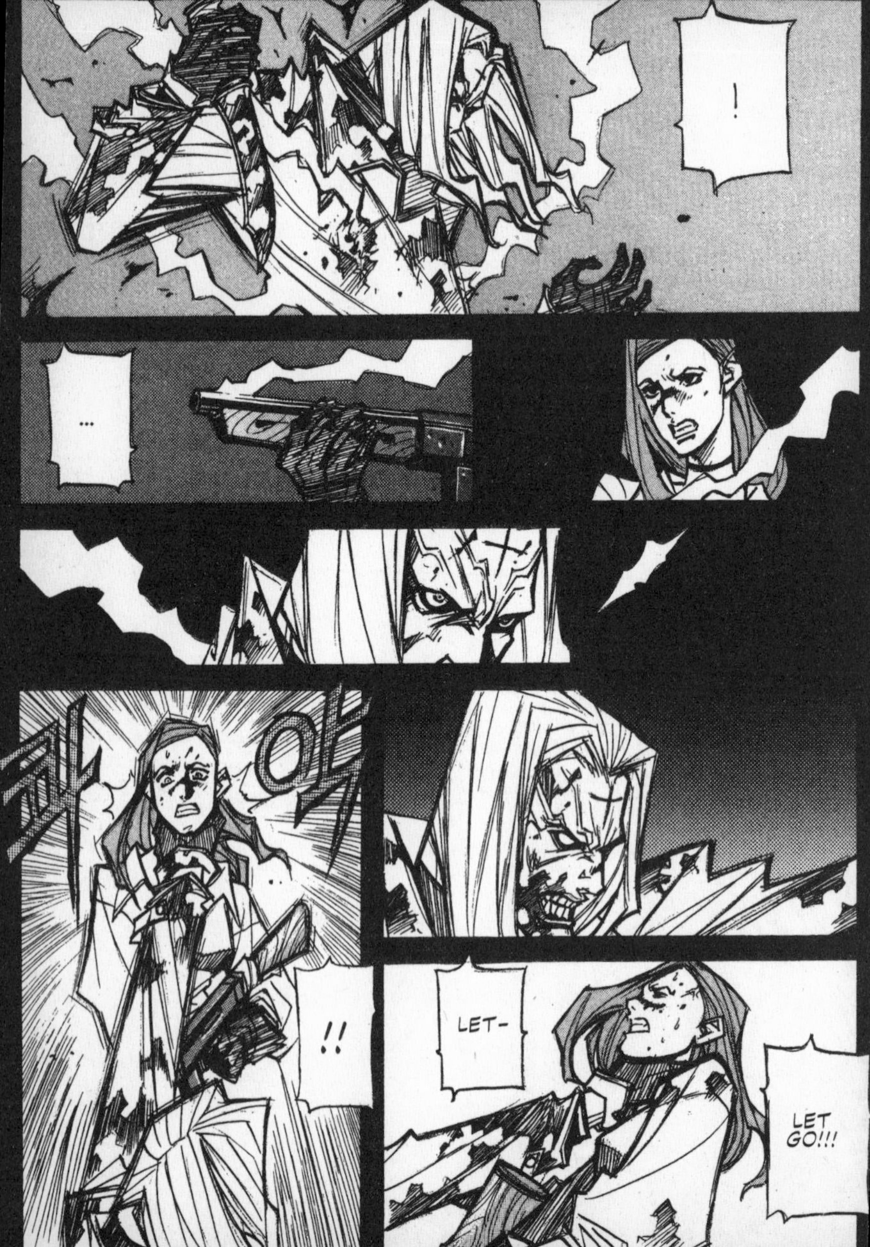
!
...
!!
LET-
LET GO!!!

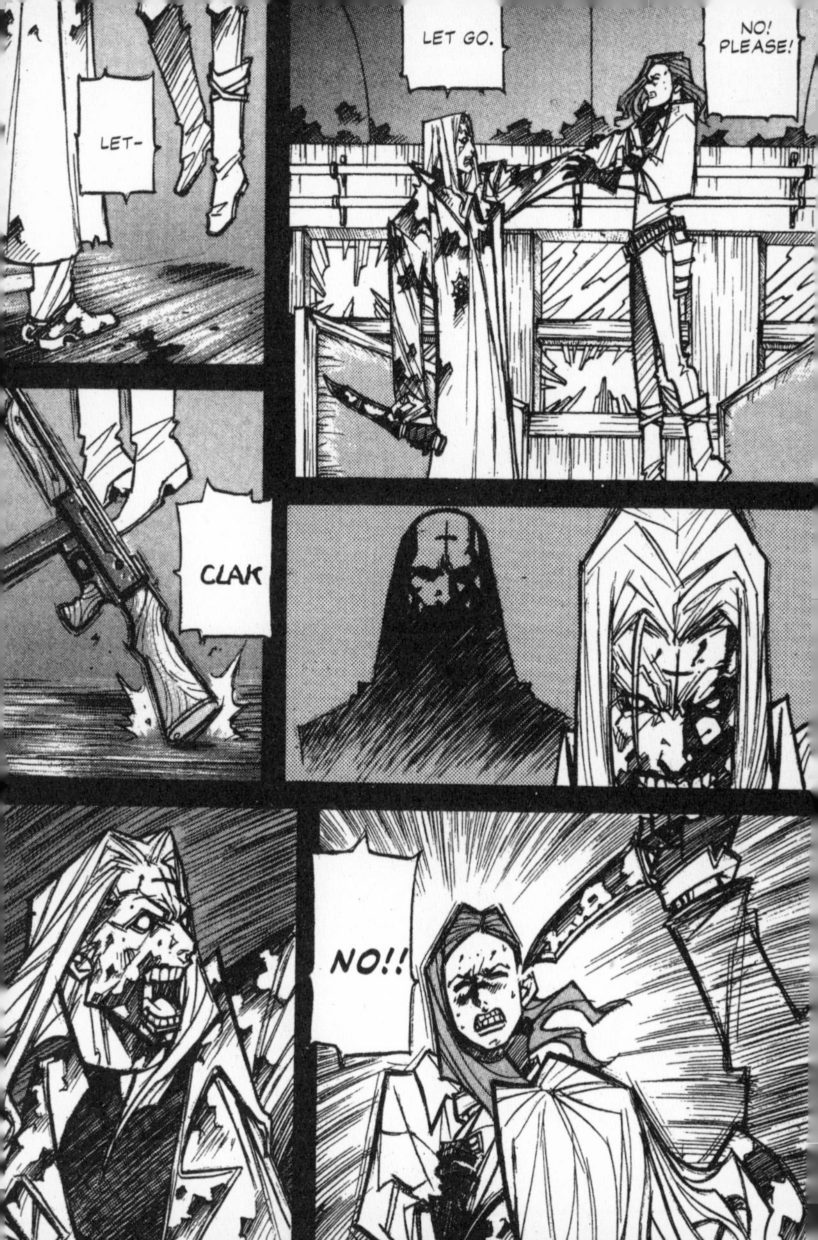
LET-
LET GO.
NO! PLEASE!
CLAK
NO!!

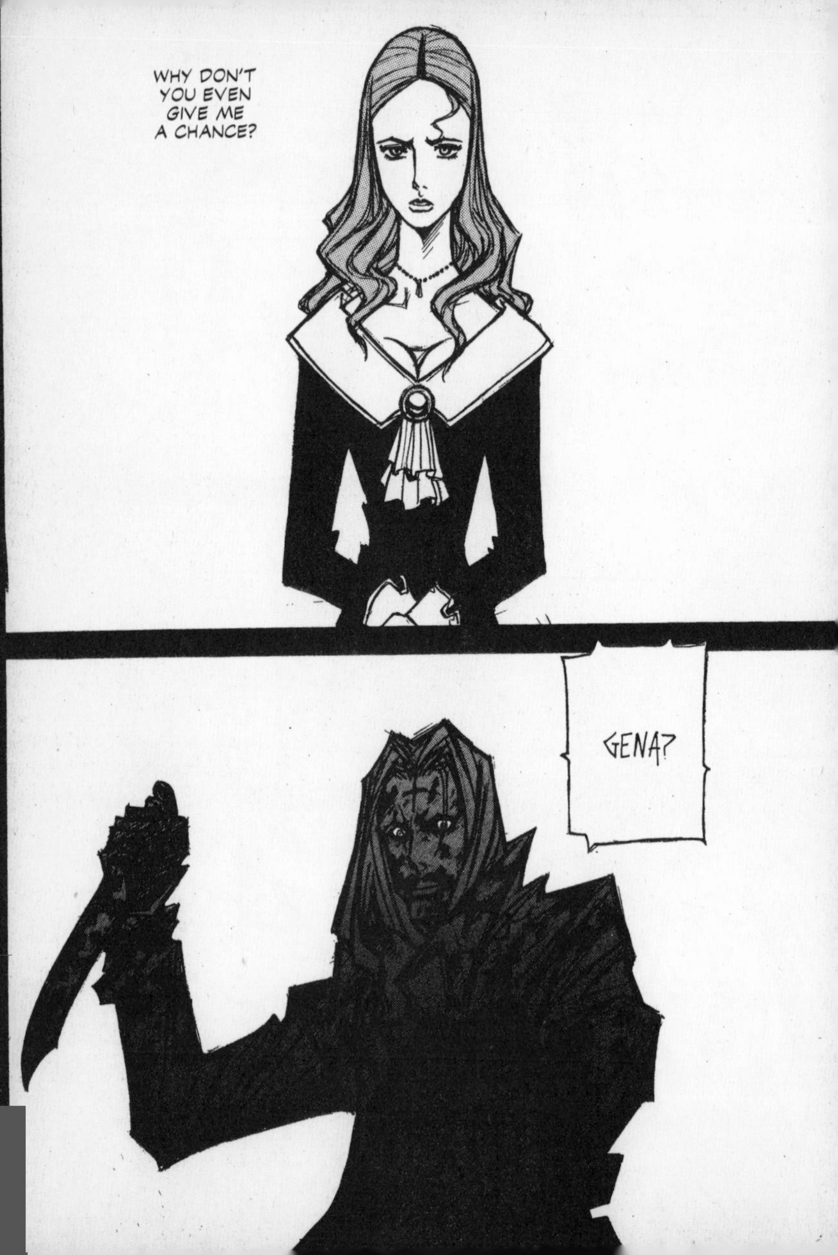
WHY DON'T YOU EVEN GIVE ME A CHANCE?
GENA?

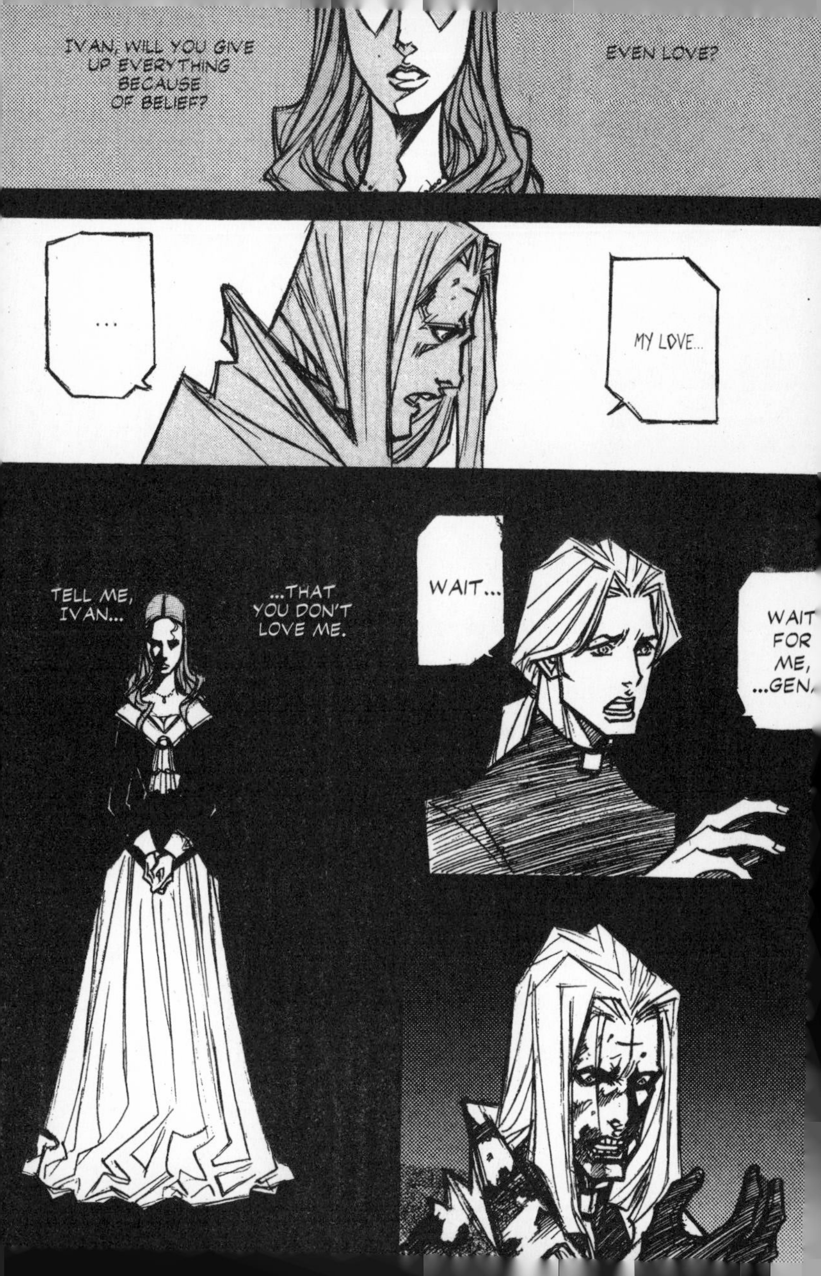
IVAN, WILL YOU GIVE UP EVERYTHING BECAUSE OF BELIEF?
EVEN LOVE?
...
MY LOVE...
TELL ME, IVAN...
...THAT YOU DON'T LOVE ME.
WAIT...
WAIT FOR ME, ...GEN

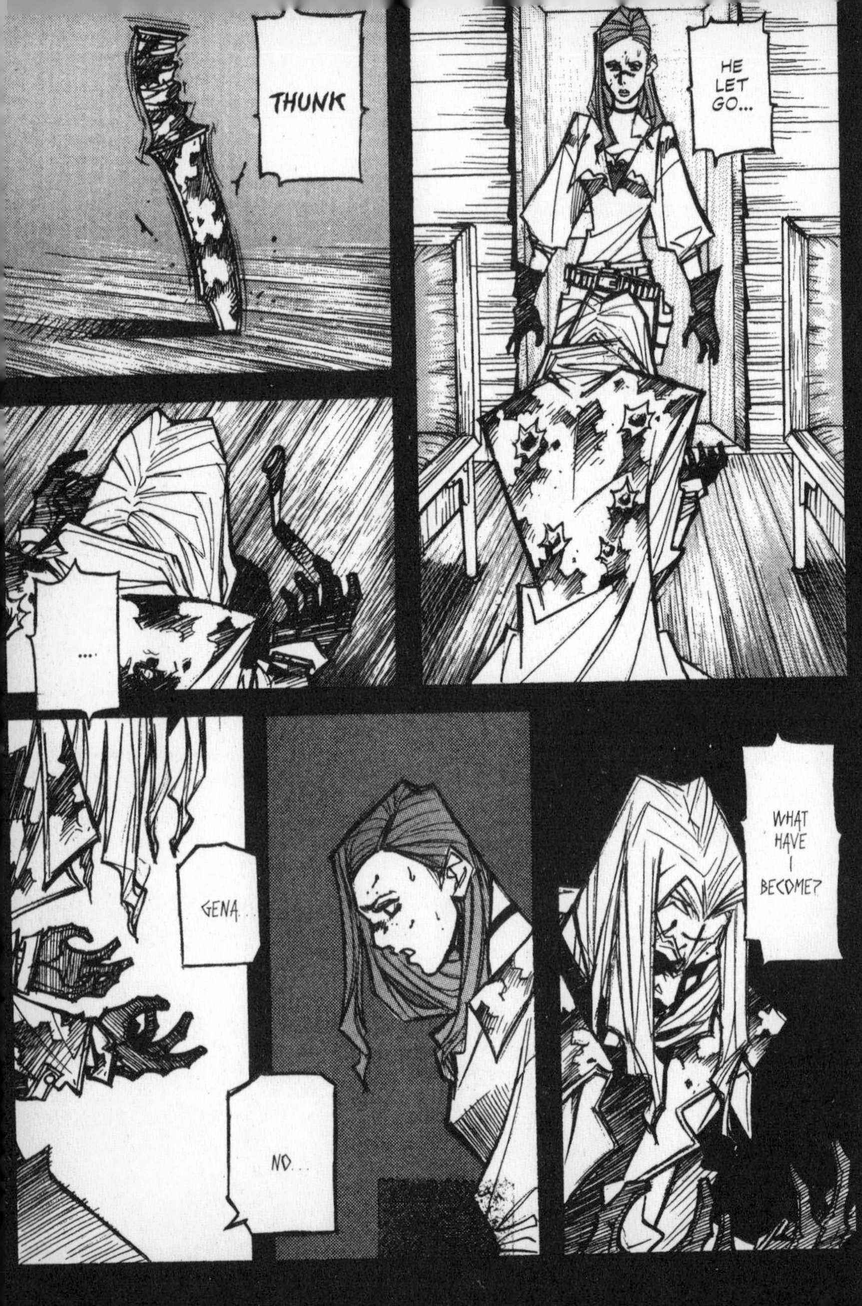
THUNK
HE LET GO...
....
GENA...
NO...
WHAT HAVE I BECOME?

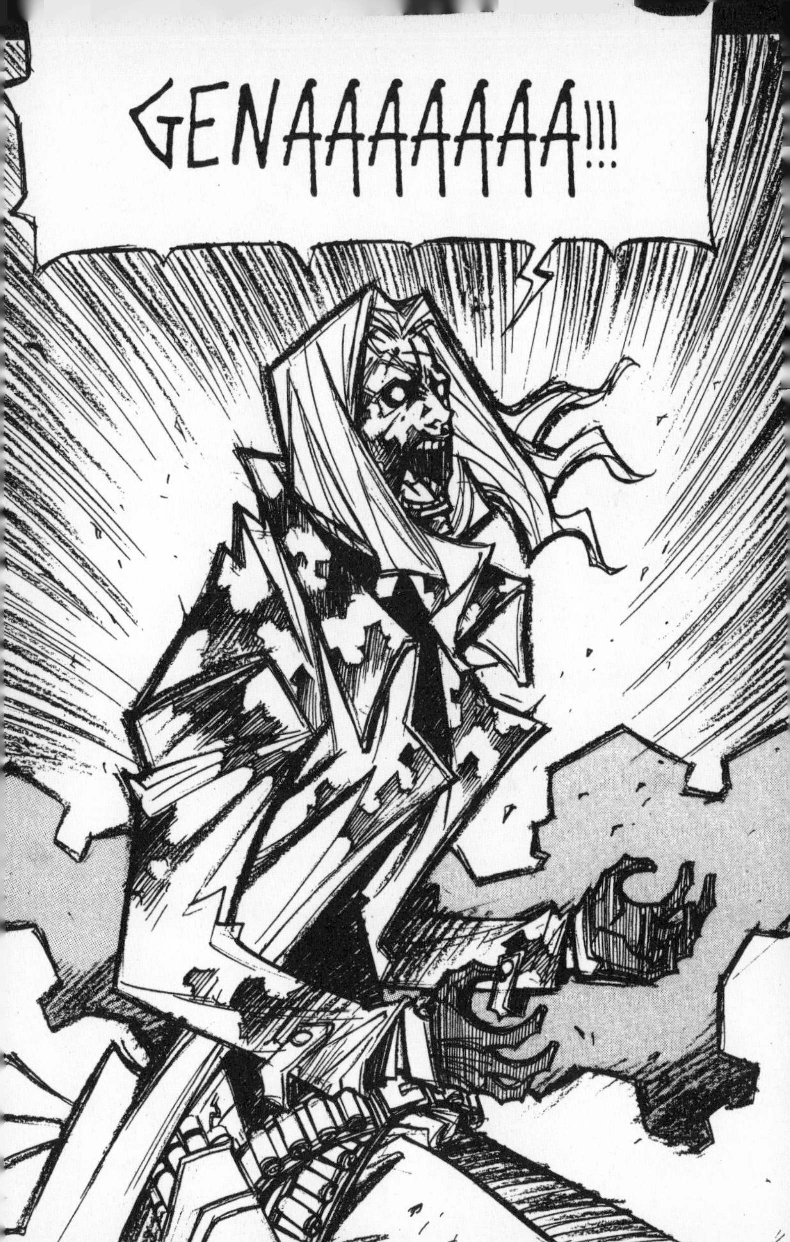
GENAAAAAAAA!!!

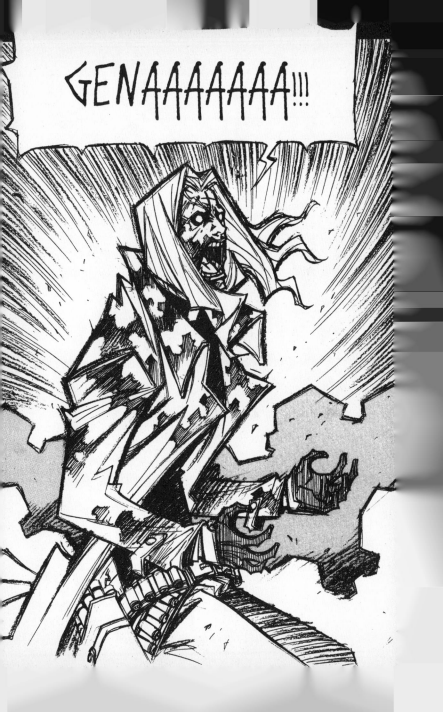

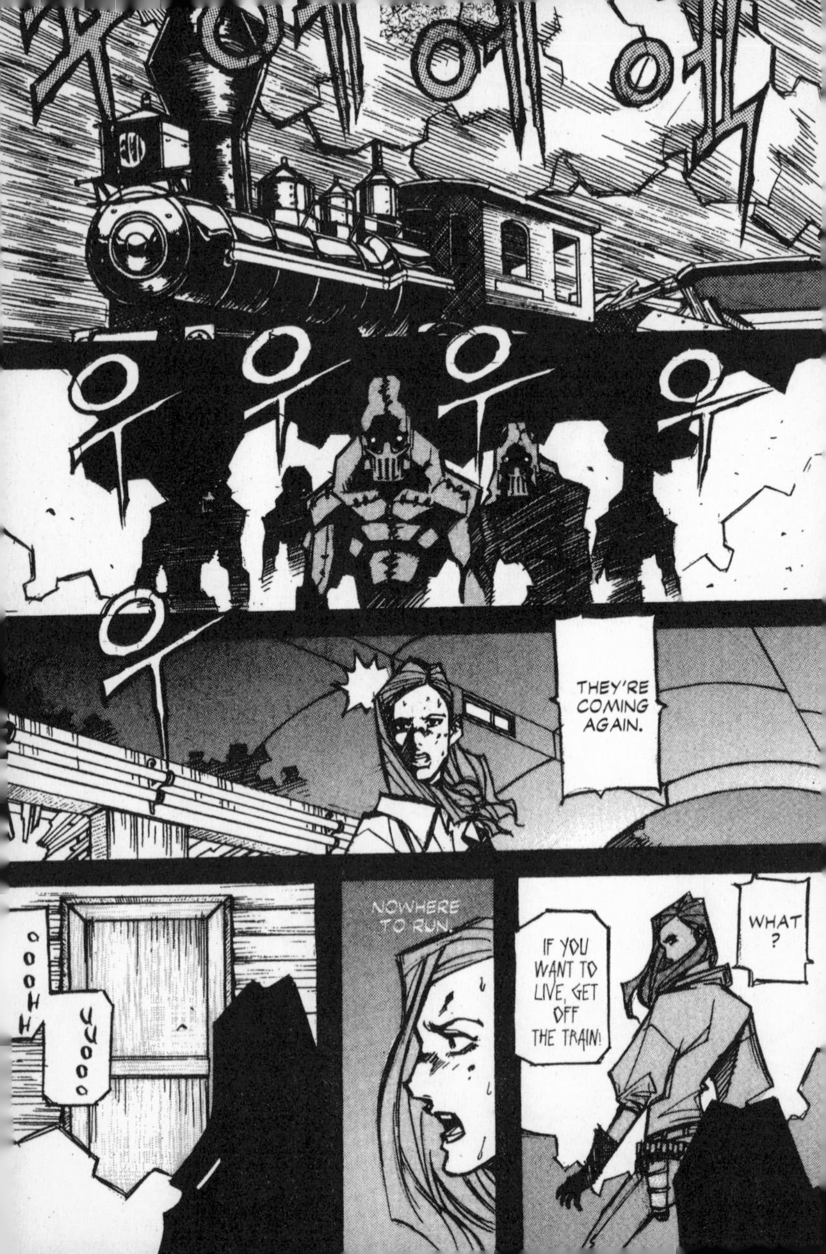
THEY'RE COMING AGAIN.
OOOHH
OOOO
NOWHERE TO RUN.
IF YOU WANT TO LIVE, GET OFF THE TRAIN!
WHAT?

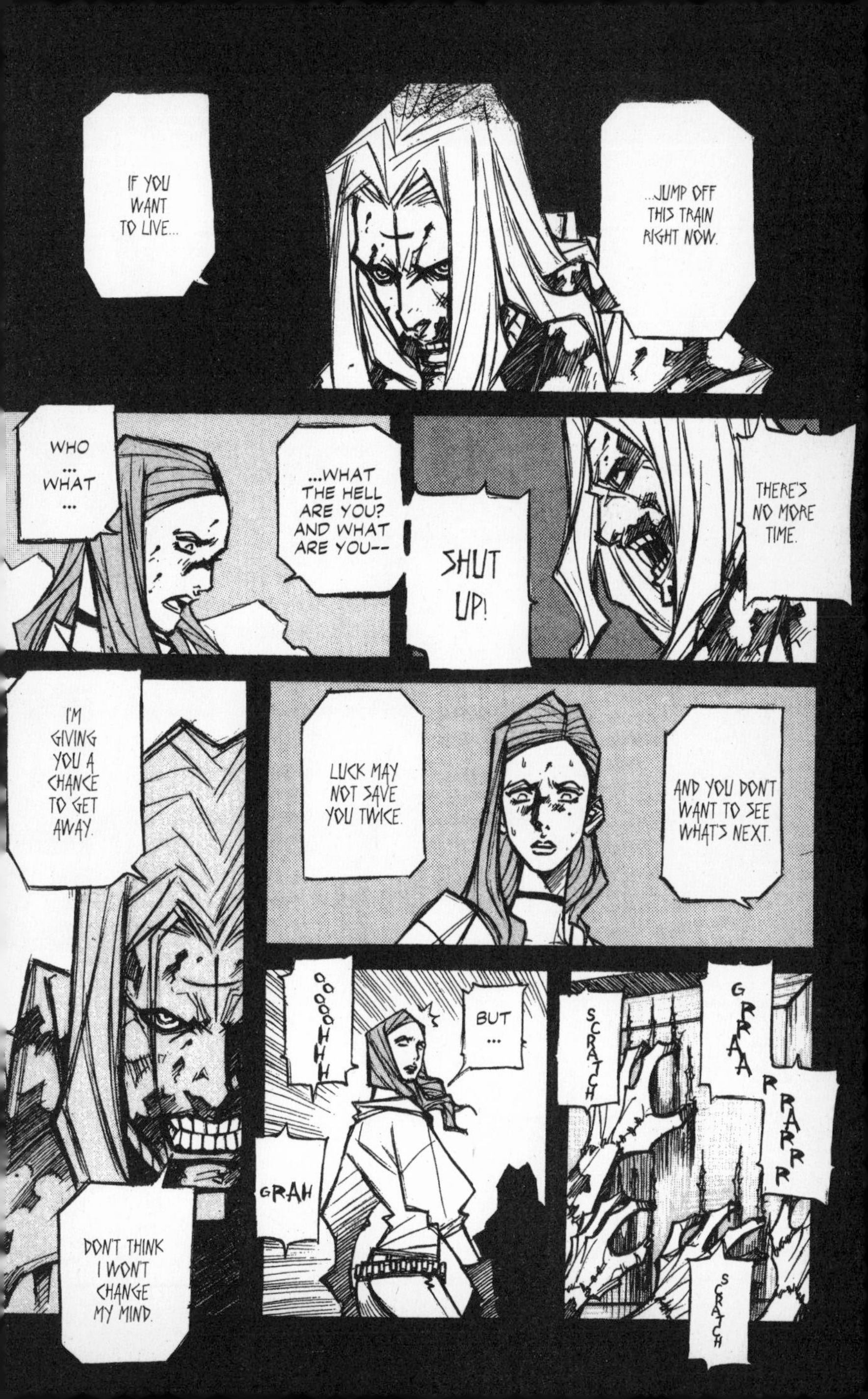
IF YOU WANT TO LIVE...
...JUMP OFF THIS TRAIN RIGHT NOW.
WHO ... WHAT ...
...WHAT THE HELL ARE YOU? AND WHAT ARE YOU--
SHUT UP!
THERE'S NO MORE TIME.
I'M GIVING YOU A CHANCE TO GET AWAY.
LUCK MAY NOT SAVE YOU TWICE.
AND YOU DON'T WANT TO SEE WHAT'S NEXT.
DON'T THINK I WON'T CHANGE MY MIND.
OOOOOHHH
BUT ...
GRAH
SCRATCH
GRRAAARRRARRR
SCRATCH

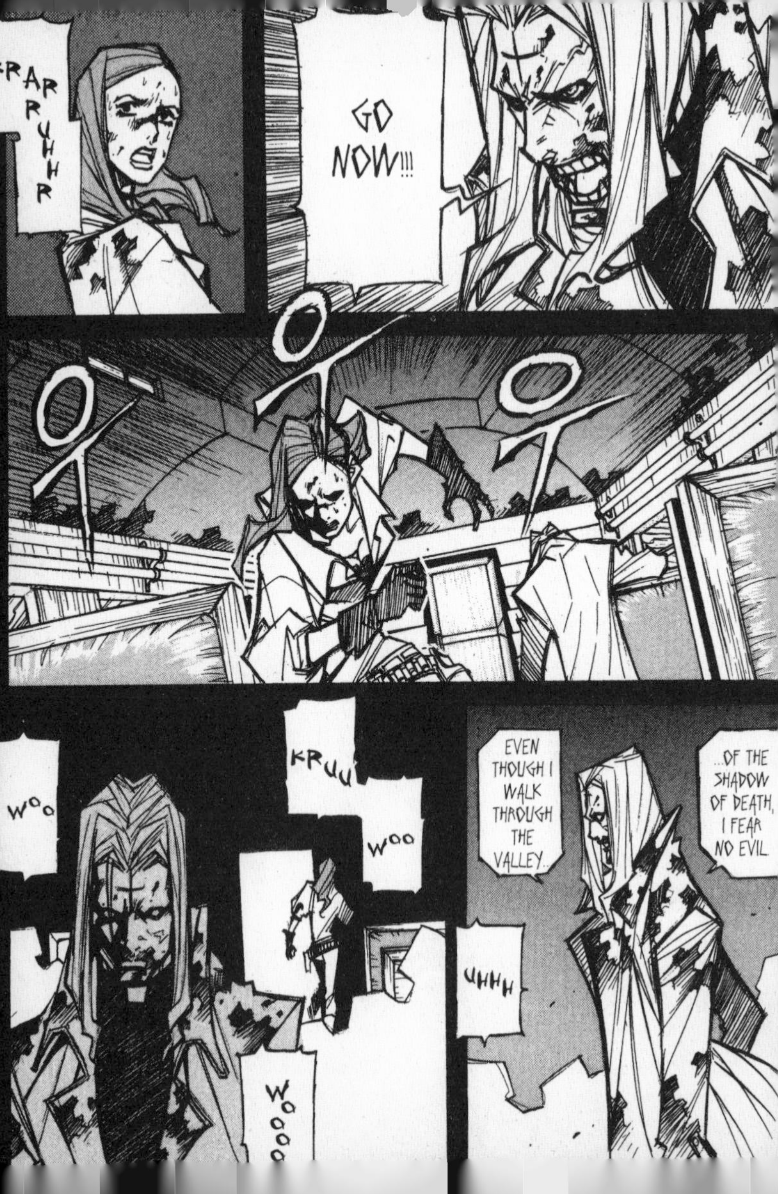

KRARRUHHR
GO NOW!!!
WOO
KRUU
WOO
WOOOO
EVEN THOUGH I WALK THROUGH THE VALLEY...
...OF THE SHADOW OF DEATH, I FEAR NO EVIL.
UHHH

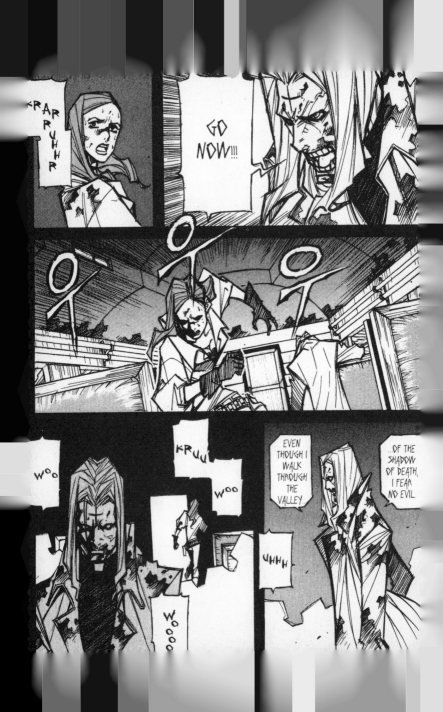

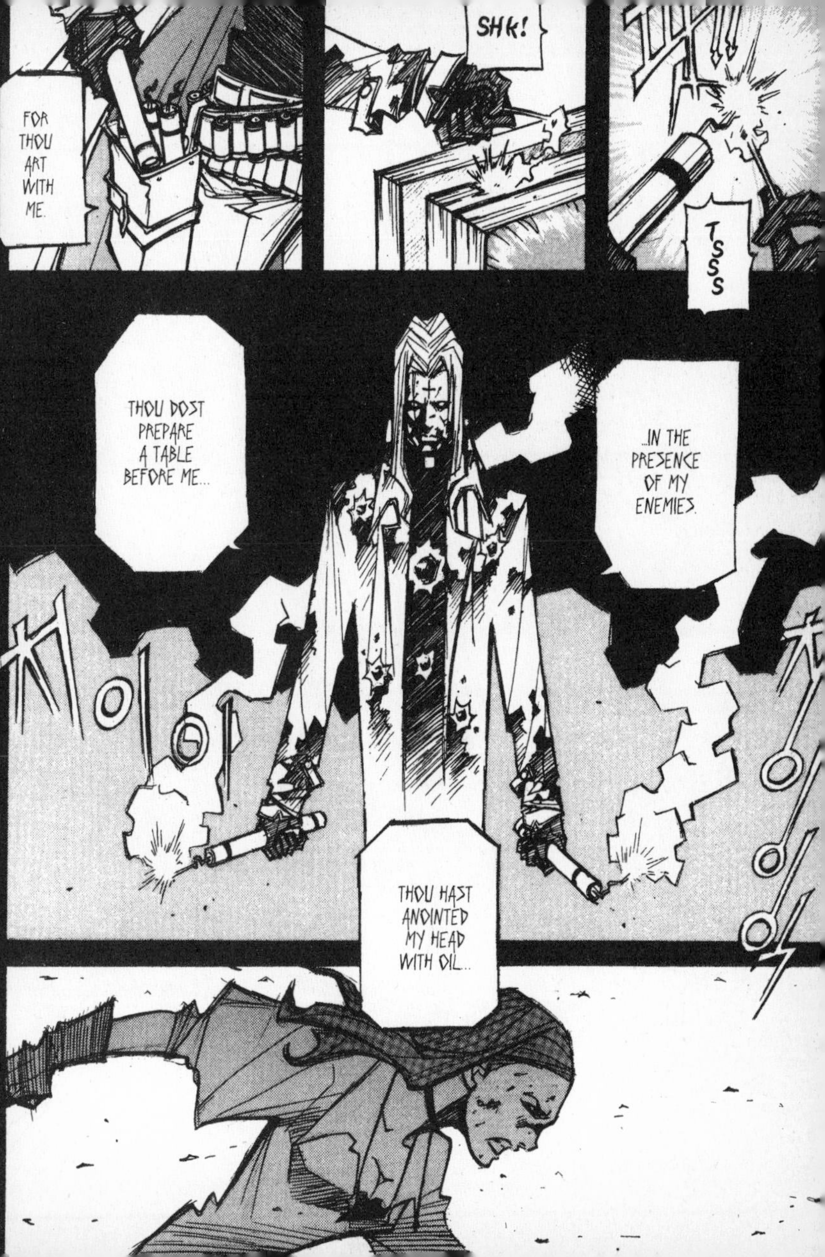
FOR THOU ART WITH ME.
SHK!
TSSS
THOU DOST PREPARE A TABLE BEFORE ME...
...IN THE PRESENCE OF MY ENEMIES.
THOU HAST ANOINTED MY HEAD WITH OIL...

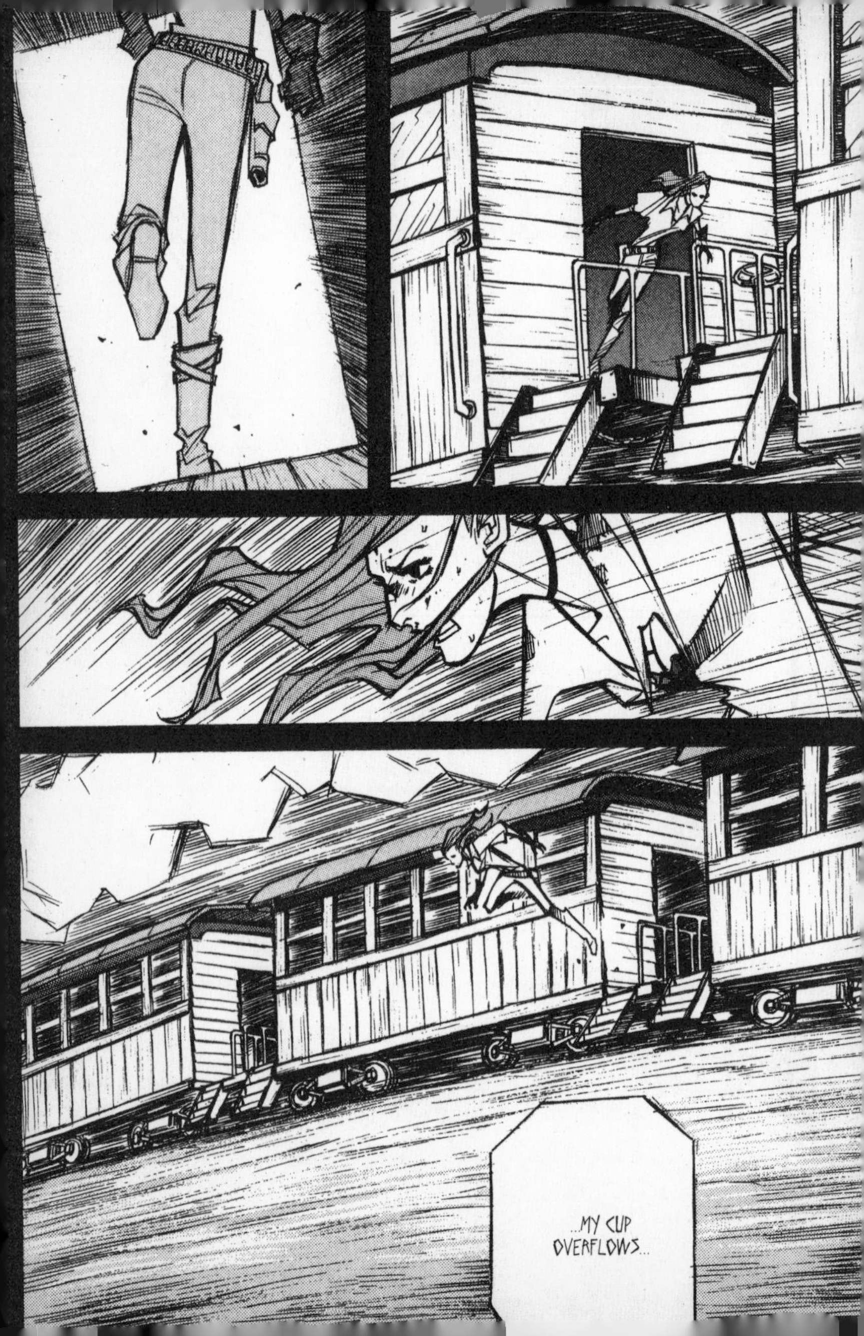
...MY CUP
OVERFLOWS...

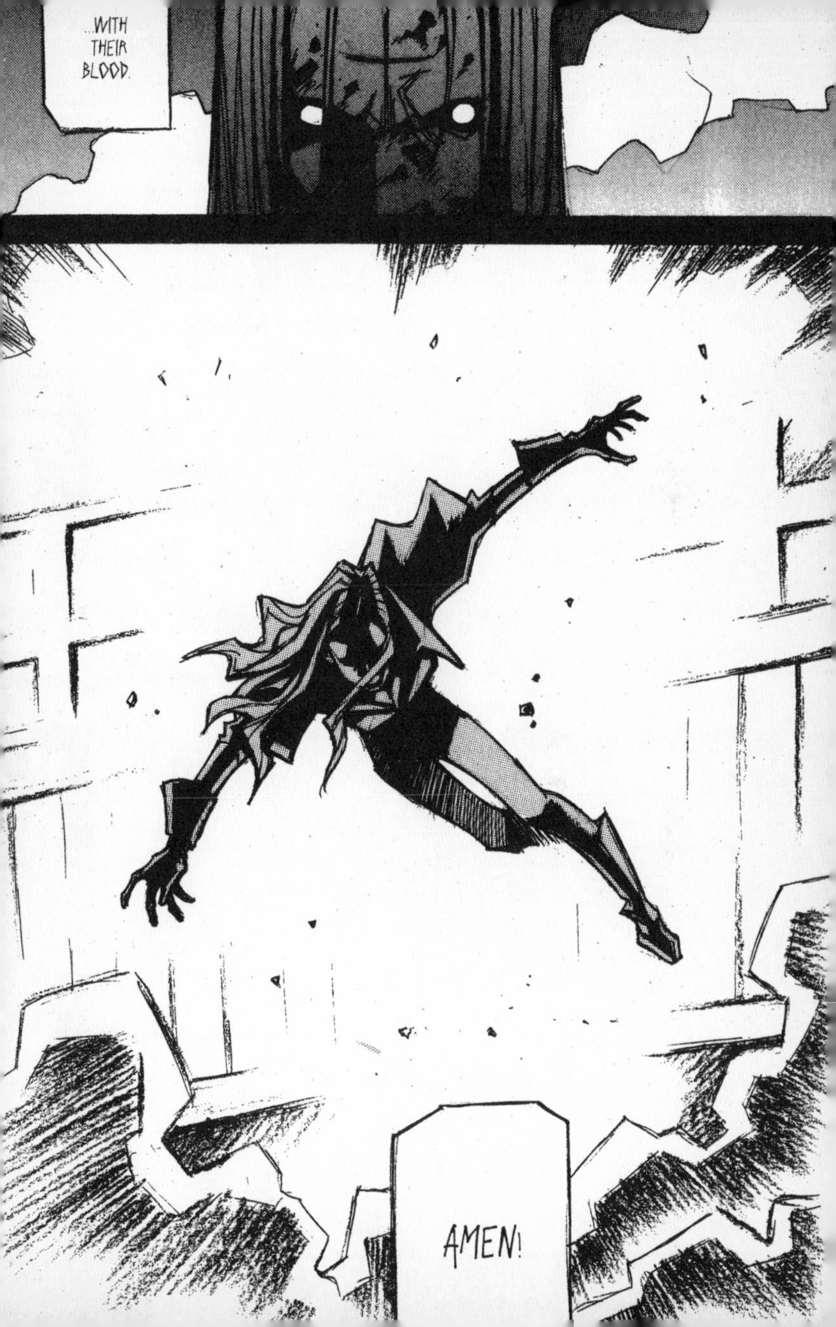
...WITH THEIR BLOOD.
AMEN!

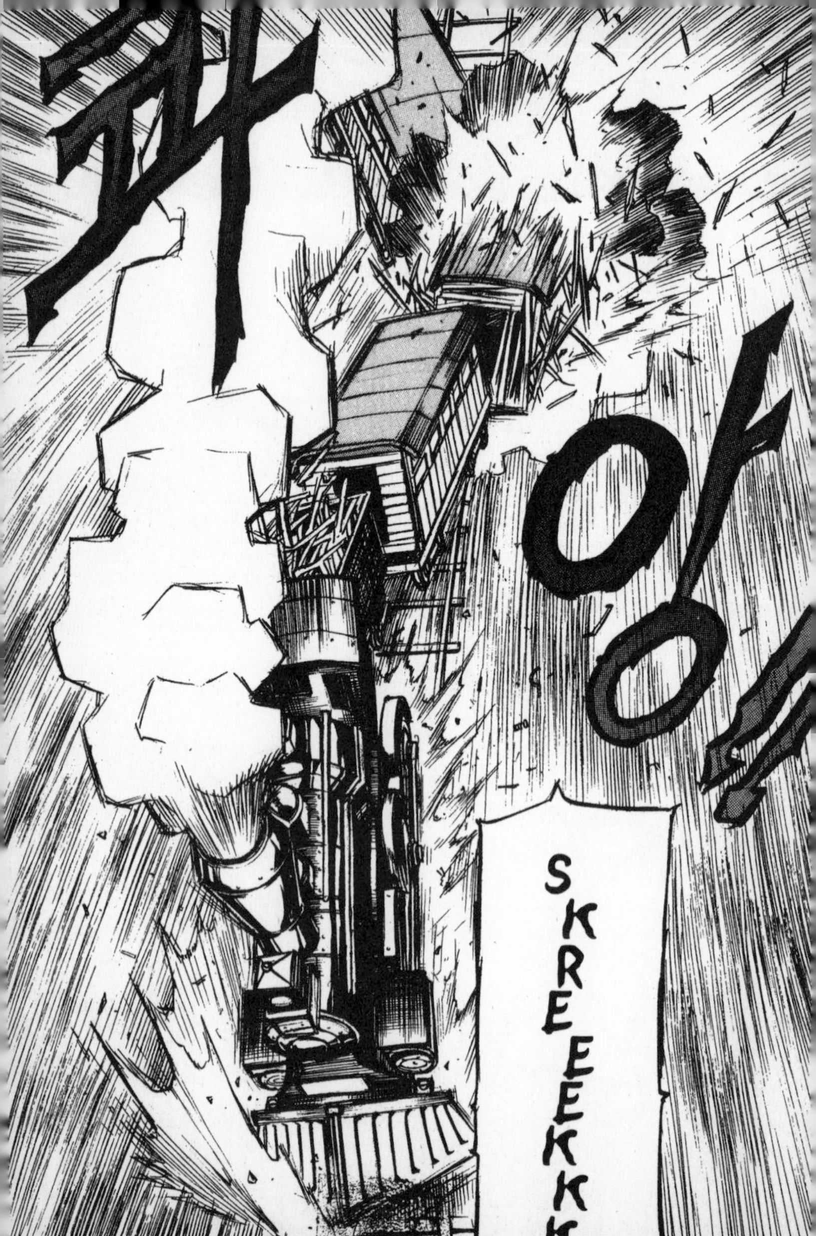
아!
SKREEEKKK

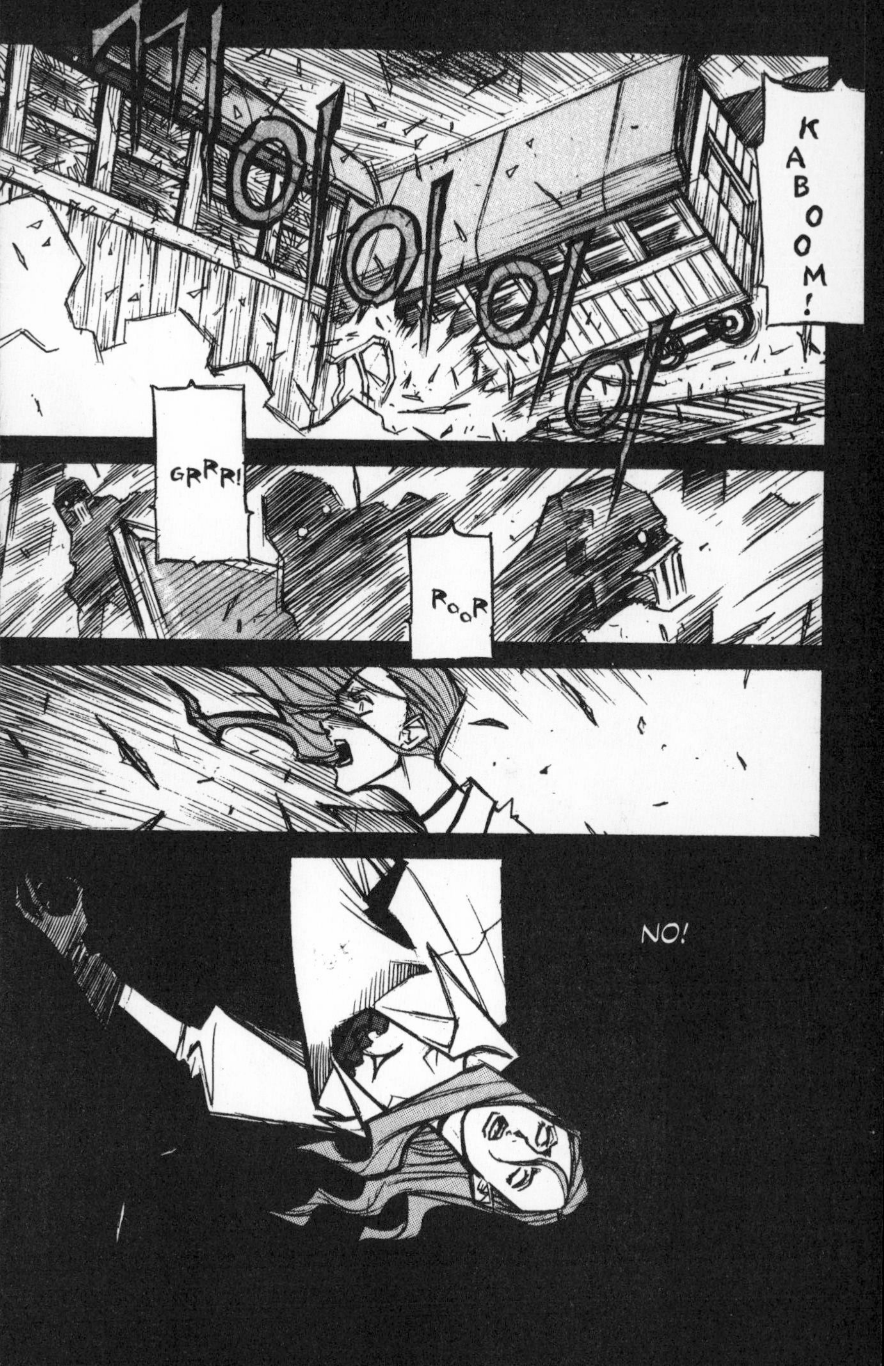
KABOOM!
GRRR!
ROOR
NO!

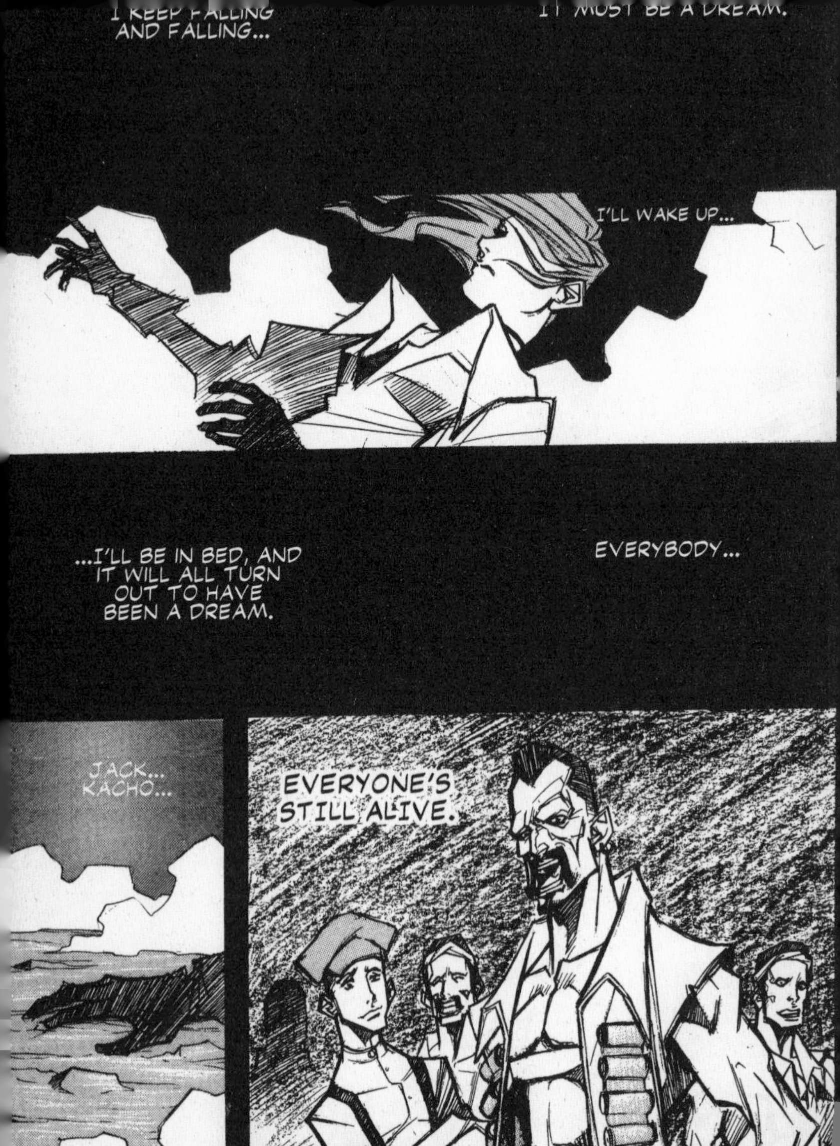
I KEEP FALLING
AND FALLING...
IT MUST BE A DREAM.
I'LL WAKE UP...
...I'LL BE IN BED, AND IT WILL ALL TURN OUT TO HAVE BEEN A DREAM.
EVERYBODY...
JACK... KACHO...
EVERYONE'S STILL ALIVE.

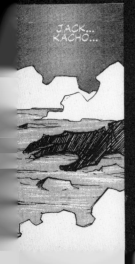

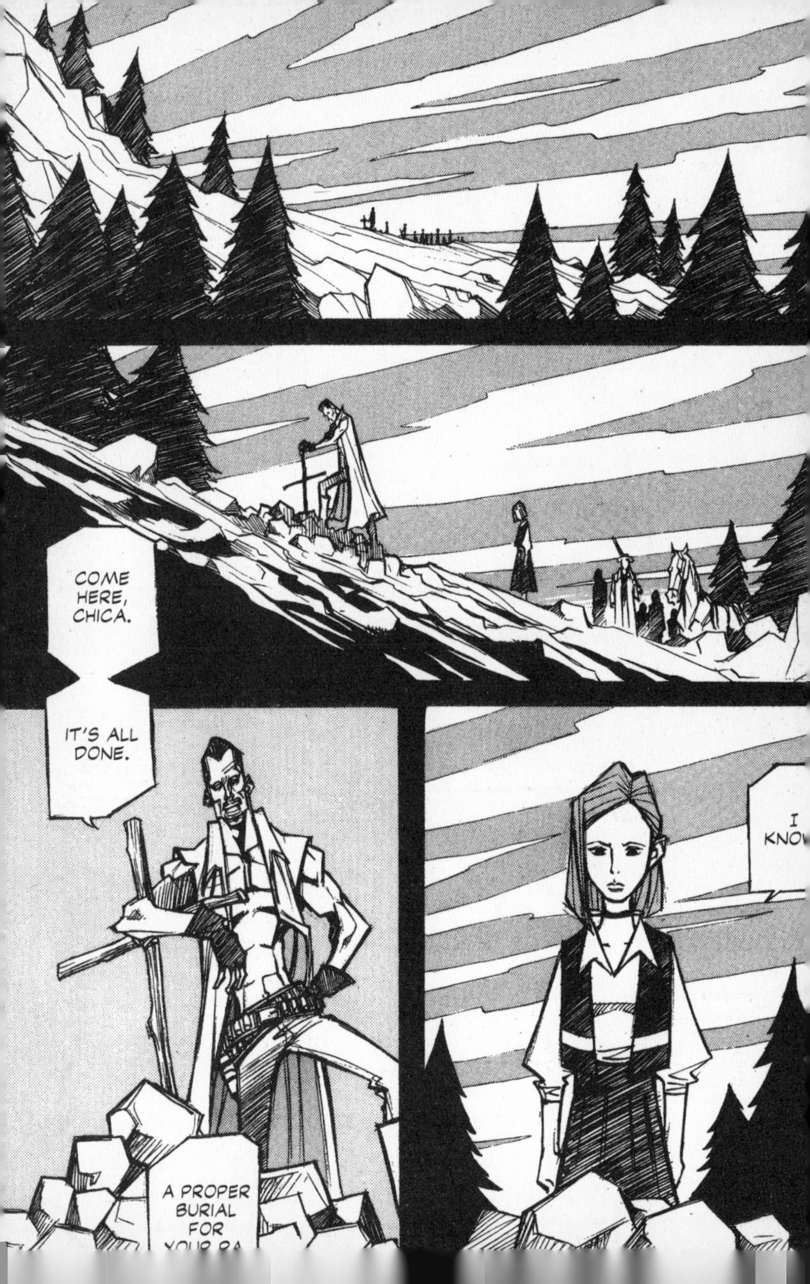
COME HERE, CHICA.
IT'S ALL DONE.
A PROPER BURIAL FOR
I

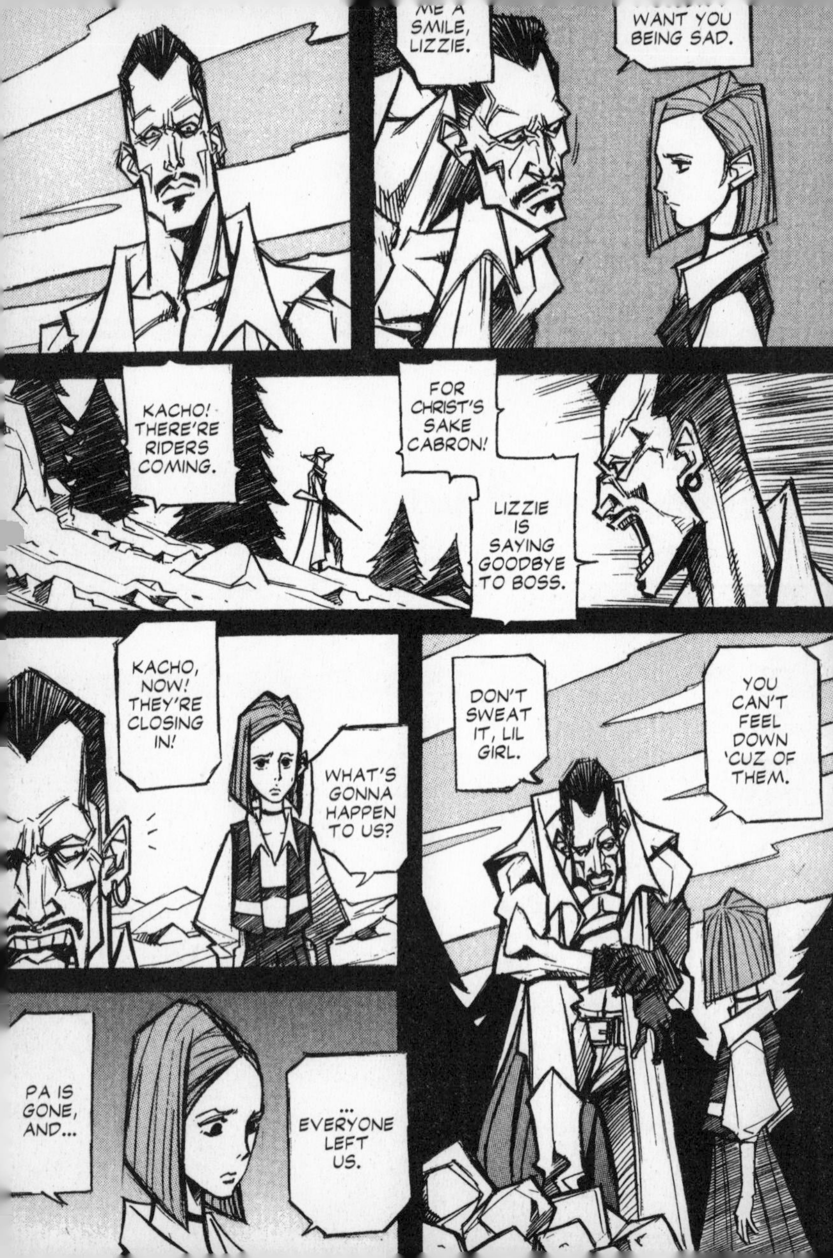
ME A SMILE, LIZZIE.
WANT YOU BEING SAD.
KACHO! THERE'RE RIDERS COMING.
FOR CHRIST'S SAKE CABRON!
LIZZIE IS SAYING GOODBYE TO BOSS.
KACHO, NOW! THEY'RE CLOSING IN!
WHAT'S GONNA HAPPEN TO US?
PA IS GONE, AND...
... EVERYONE LEFT US.
DON'T SWEAT IT, LIL GIRL.
YOU CAN'T FEEL DOWN 'CUZ OF THEM.

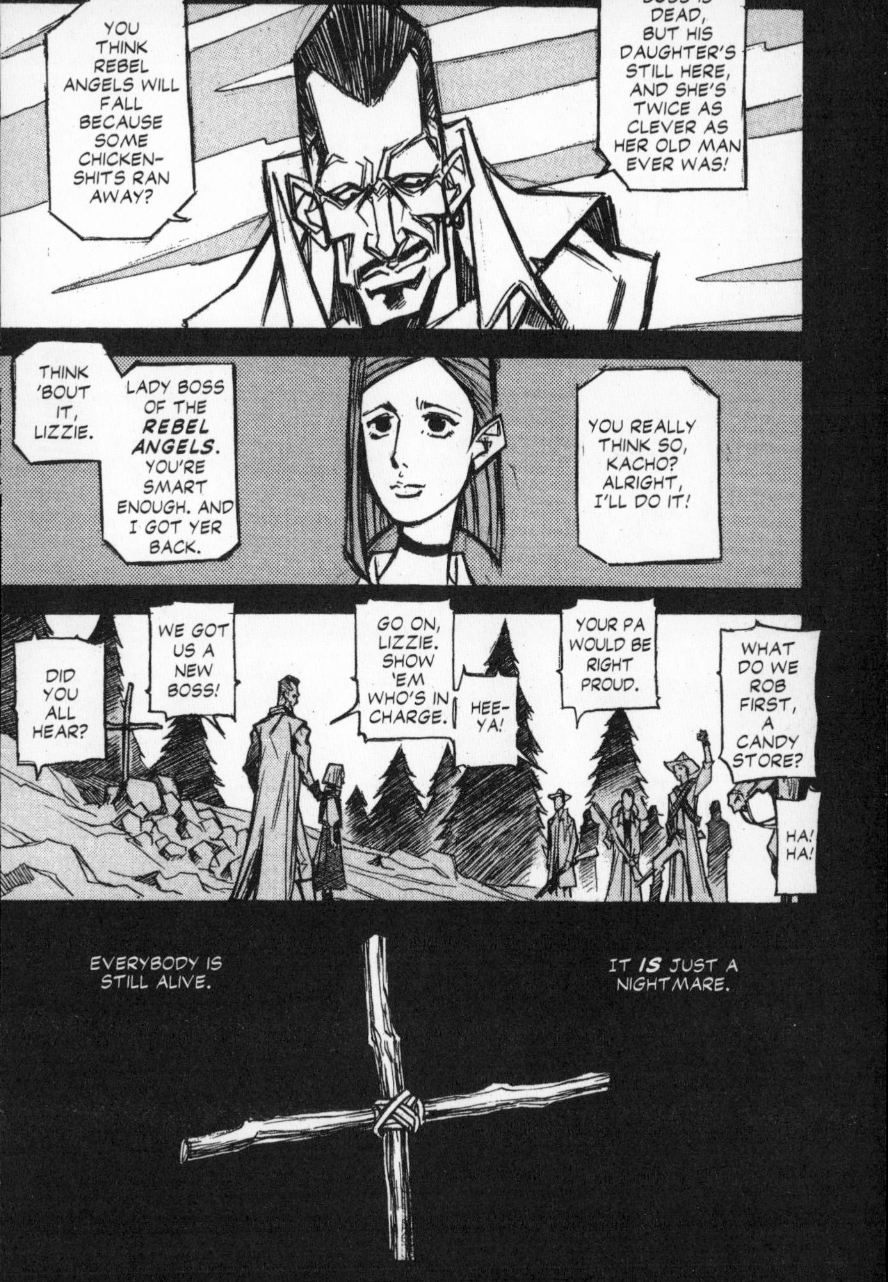
YOU THINK REBEL ANGELS WILL FALL BECAUSE SOME CHICKEN-SHITS RAN AWAY?
BOSS IS DEAD, BUT HIS DAUGHTER'S STILL HERE, AND SHE'S TWICE AS CLEVER AS HER OLD MAN EVER WAS!
THINK 'BOUT IT, LIZZIE.
LADY BOSS OF THE ***REBEL ANGELS***. YOU'RE SMART ENOUGH. AND I GOT YER BACK.
YOU REALLY THINK SO, KACHO? ALRIGHT, I'LL DO IT!
DID YOU ALL HEAR?
WE GOT US A NEW BOSS!
GO ON, LIZZIE. SHOW 'EM WHO'S IN CHARGE.
HEE-YA!
YOUR PA WOULD BE RIGHT PROUD.
WHAT DO WE ROB FIRST, A CANDY STORE?
HA! HA!
EVERYBODY IS STILL ALIVE.
IT ***IS*** JUST A NIGHTMARE.

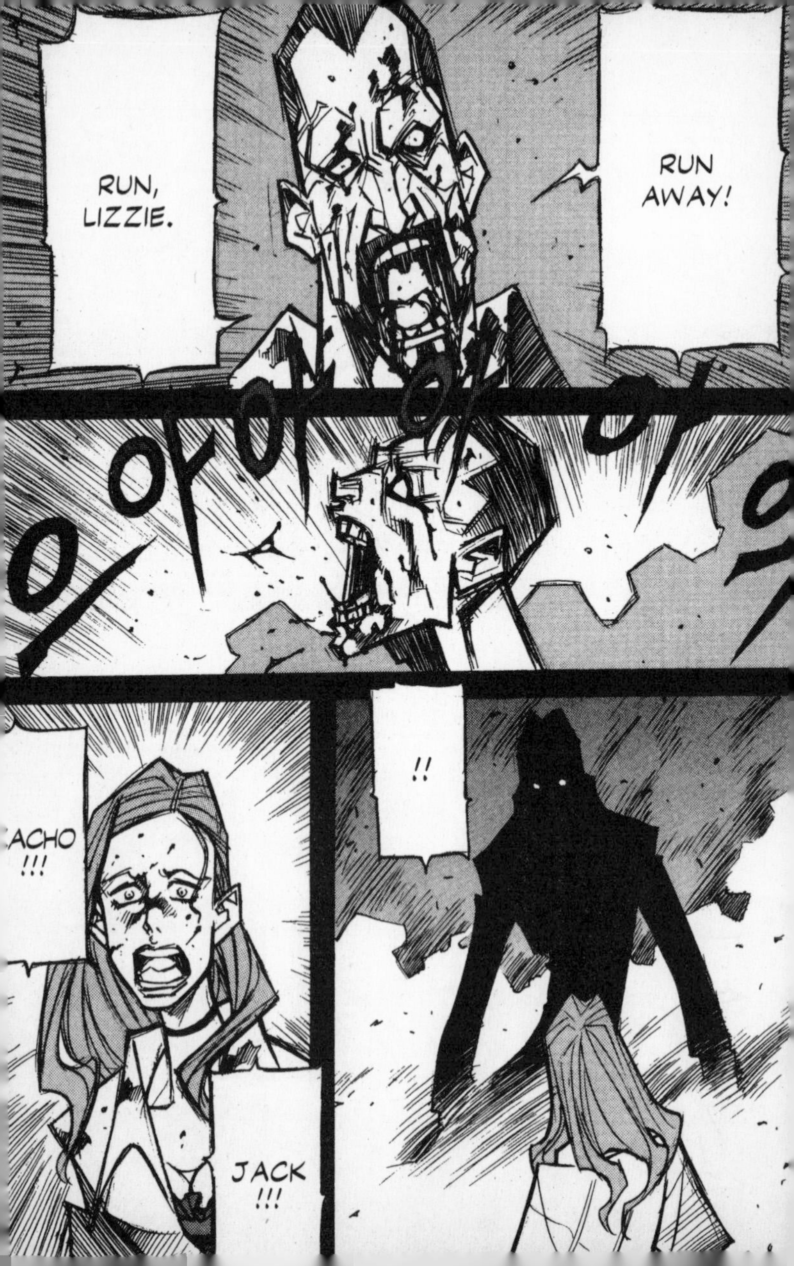
RUN, LIZZIE.
RUN AWAY!
ACHO!!!
JACK!!!
!!

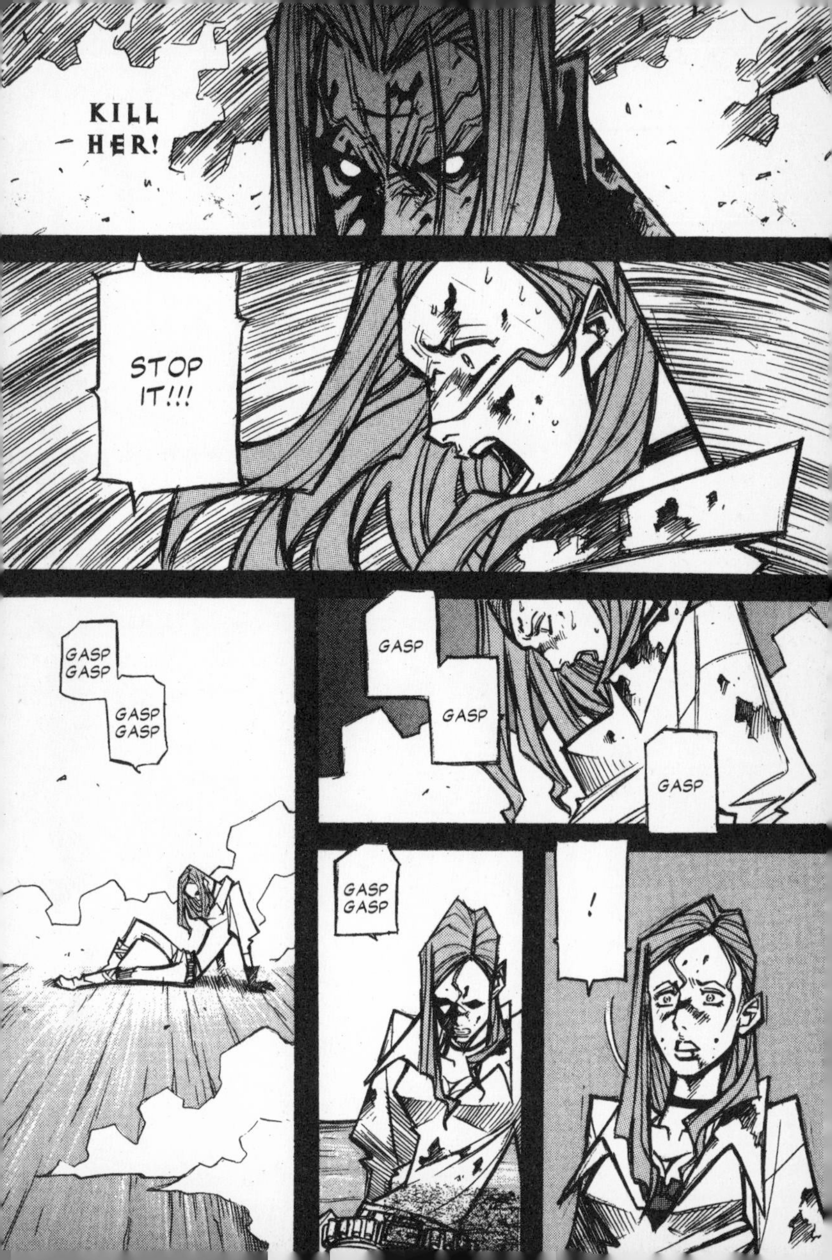
KILL HER!
STOP IT!!!
GASP GASP
GASP GASP
GASP
GASP
GASP
GASP GASP
!

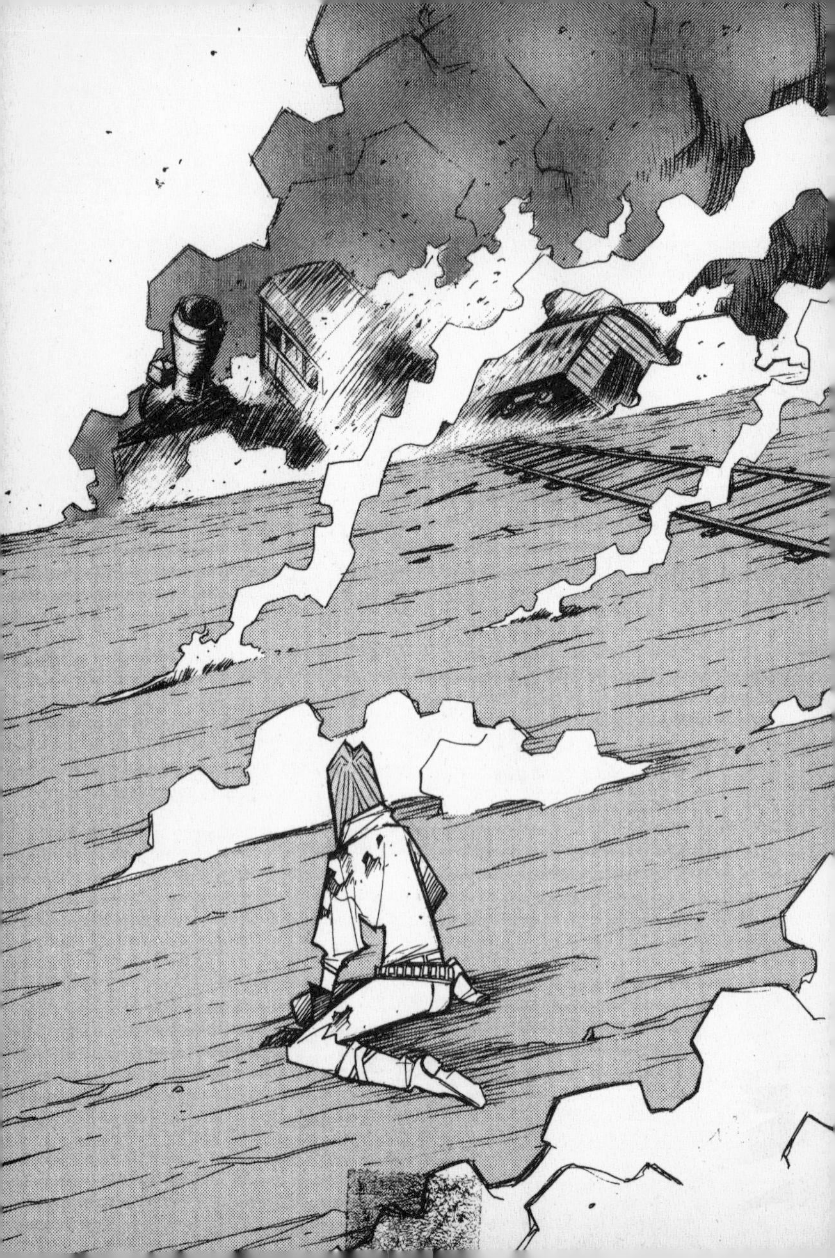

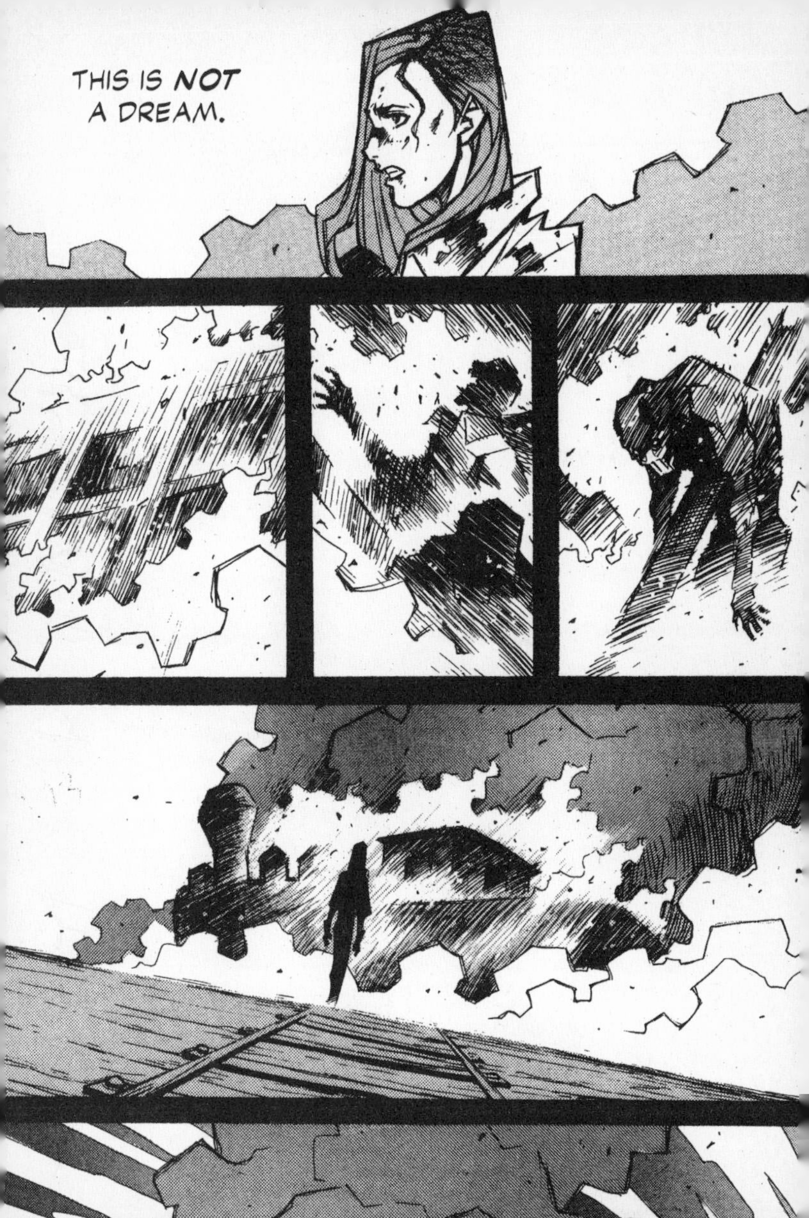
THIS IS NOT A DREAM.

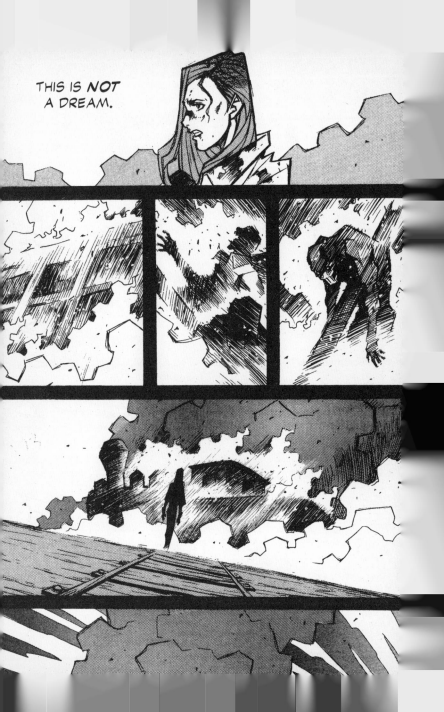

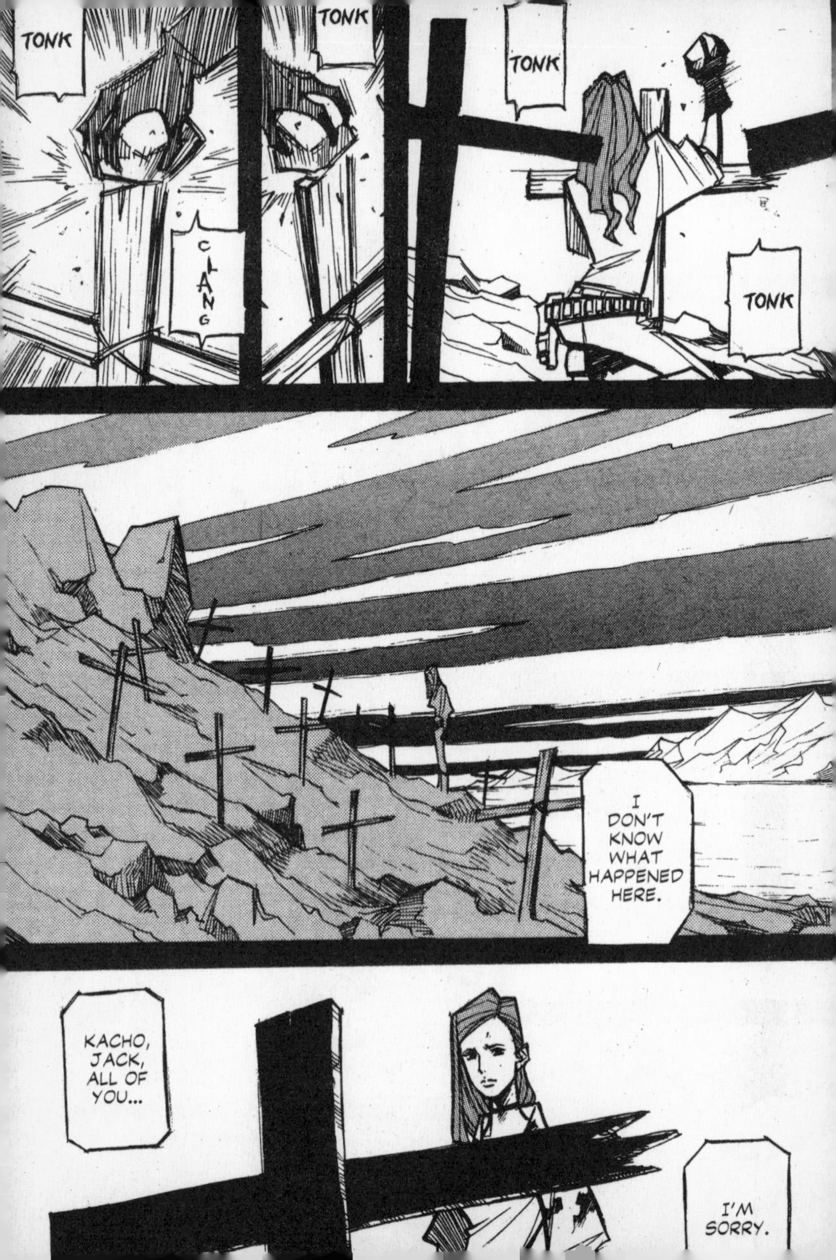
TONK
CLANG
TONK
TONK
TONK
I DON'T KNOW WHAT HAPPENED HERE.
KACHO, JACK, ALL OF YOU...
I'M SORRY.

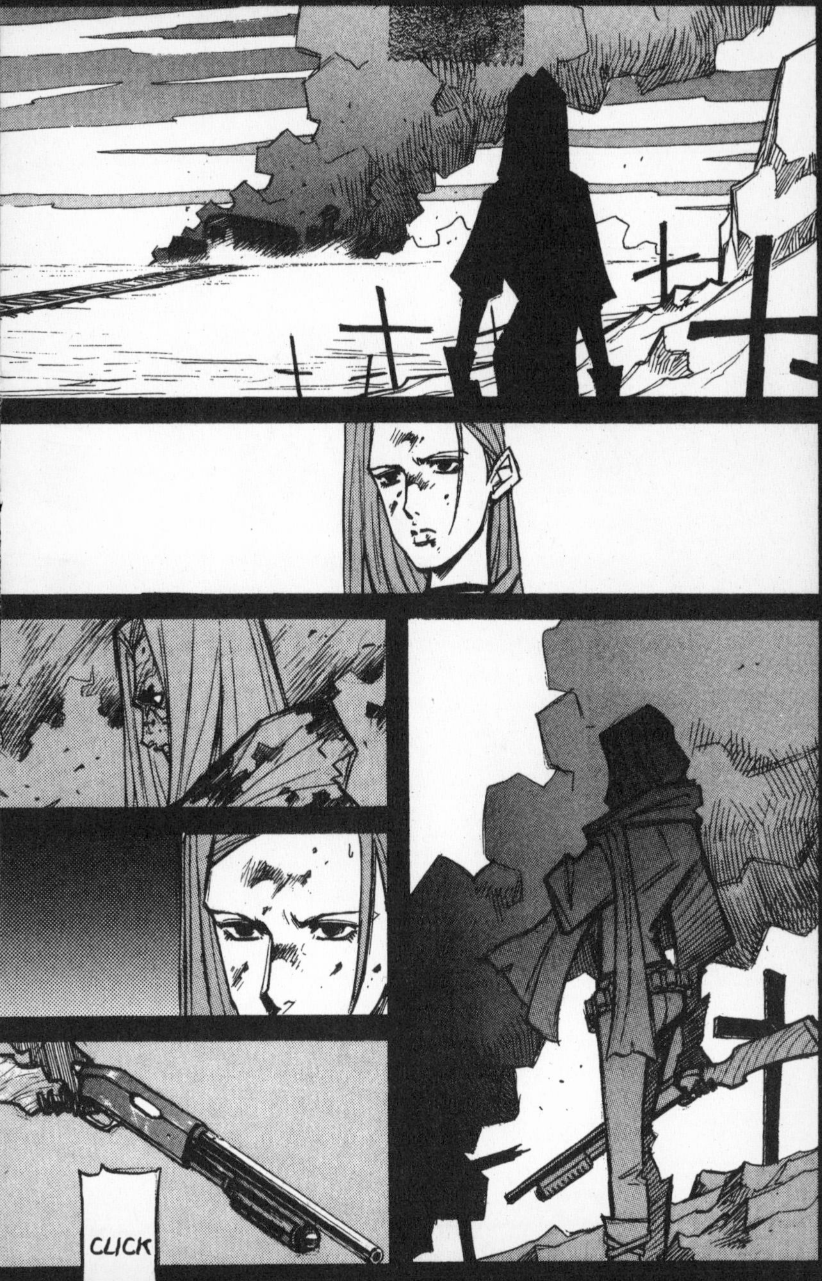
CLICK

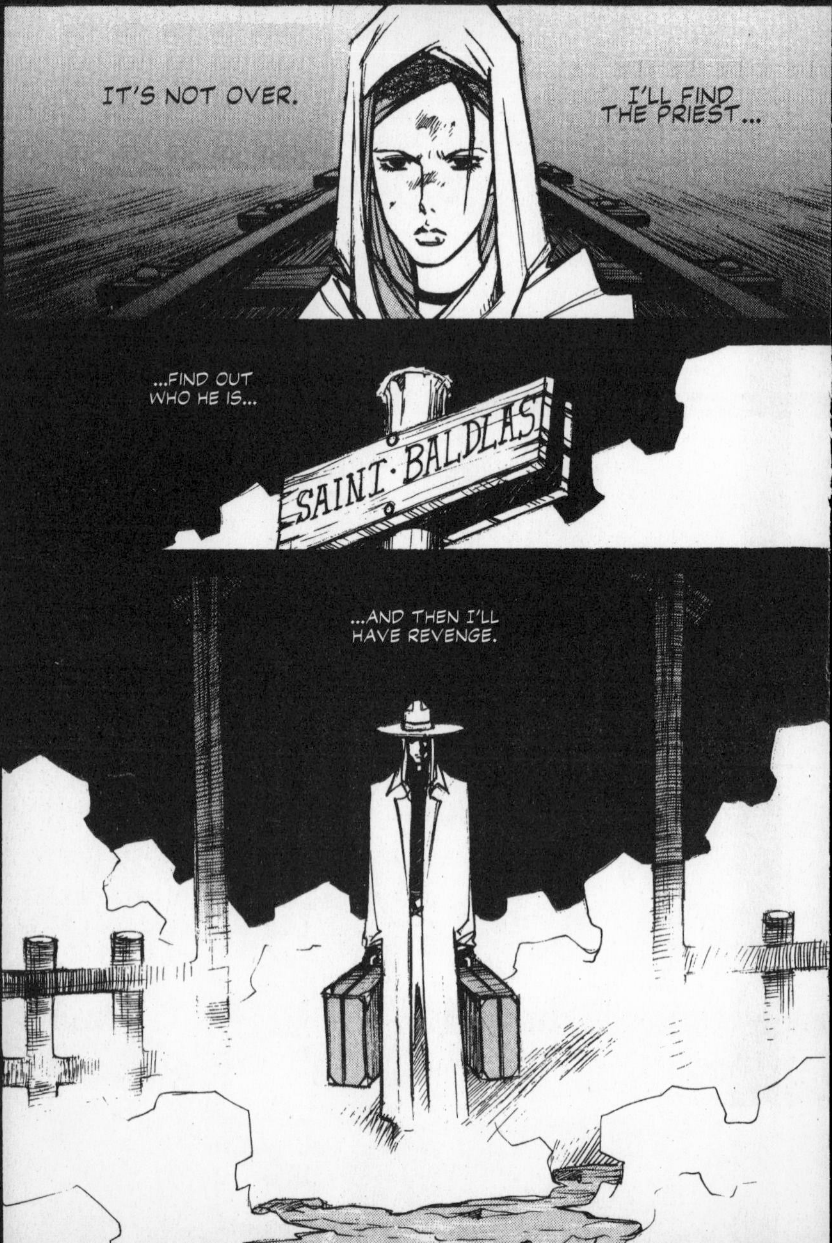
IT'S NOT OVER.
I'LL FIND THE PRIEST...
...FIND OUT WHO HE IS...
SAINT·BALDLAS
...AND THEN I'LL HAVE REVENGE.

TO BE CONTINUED...

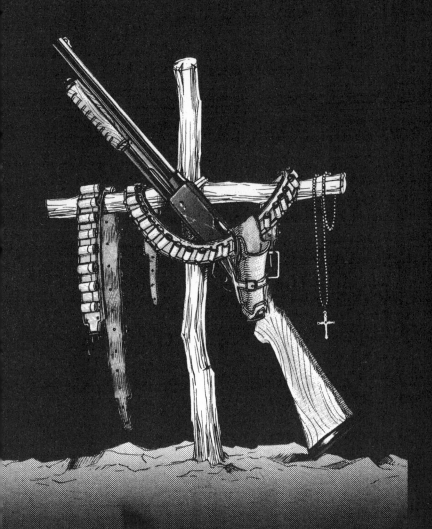

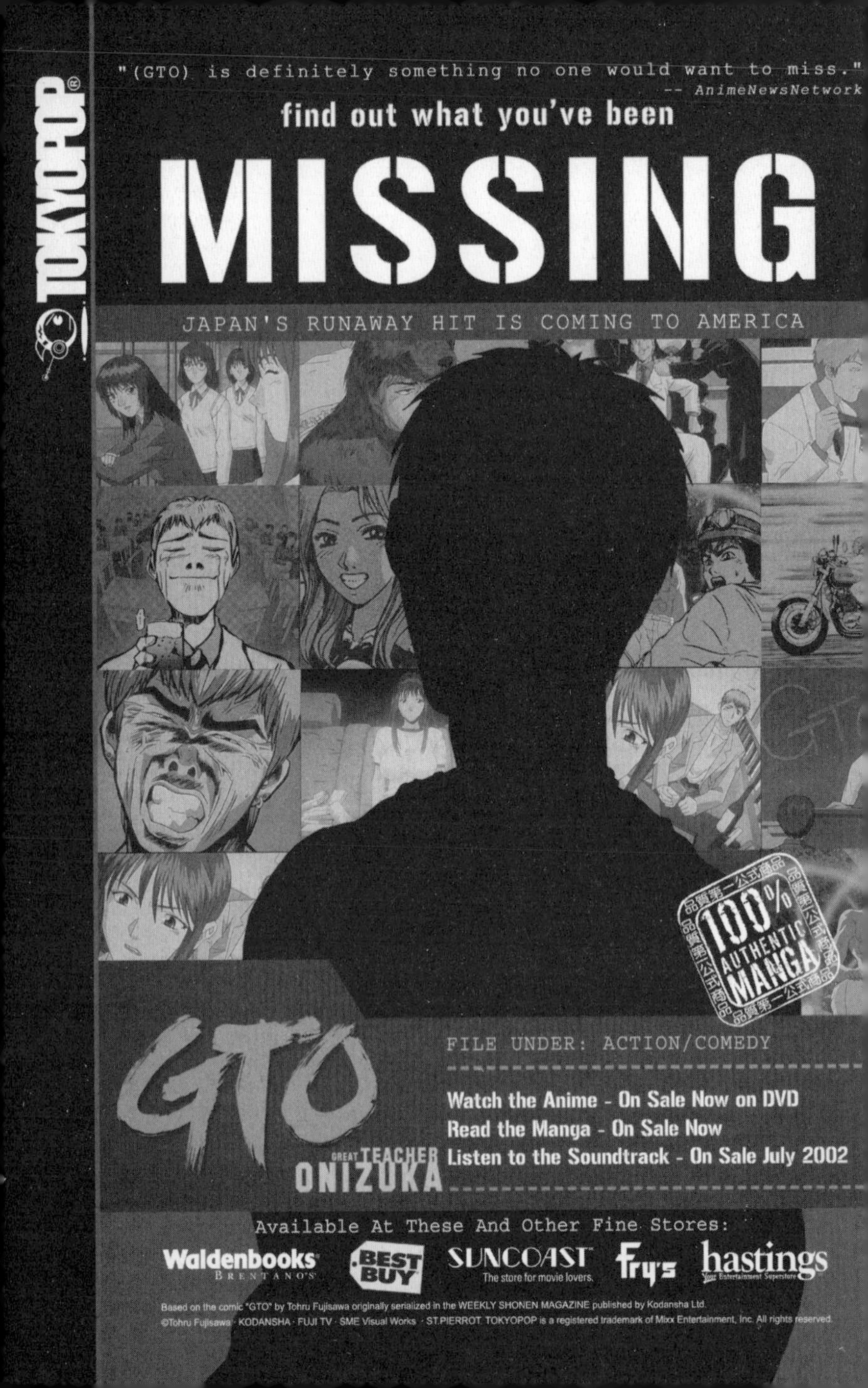

TOKYOPOP®
"(GTO) is definitely something no one would want to miss."
-- AnimeNewsNetwork
find out what you've been
MISSING
JAPAN'S RUNAWAY HIT IS COMING TO AMERICA
100% AUTHENTIC MANGA
GTO
GREAT TEACHER ONIZUKA
FILE UNDER: ACTION/COMEDY
Watch the Anime - On Sale Now on DVD
Read the Manga - On Sale Now
Listen to the Soundtrack - On Sale July 2002
Available At These And Other Fine Stores:
Waldenbooks BRENTANO'S
BEST BUY
SUNCOAST The store for movie lovers.
Fry's
hastings Your Entertainment Superstore
Based on the comic "GTO" by Tohru Fujisawa originally serialized in the WEEKLY SHONEN MAGAZINE published by Kodansha Ltd.
©Tohru Fujisawa · KODANSHA · FUJI TV · SME Visual Works · ST.PIERROT. TOKYOPOP is a registered trademark of Mixx Entertainment, Inc. All rights reserved.